Woman's "True" Profession

Voices from the History of Teaching

Table of Contents

Publisher's Acknowledgments

EARLY IN 1973, Mariam Chamberlain and Terry Saario of the Ford Foundation spent on day visiting The Feminist Press on the campus of the State University of New York, College at Old Westbury. They heard staff members describe the early history of The Feminist Press and its goal—to change the sexist education of girls and boys, women and men, through publishing and other projects. They also heard about those books and projects then in progress; they felt our sense of frustration about how little we were able to do directly for the classroom teacher. Advising us about funding, Terry Saario was provocative. "You need to think of yourselves," she said, "in the manner of language labs, testing and developing new texts for students and new instructional materials for teachers." Our "language" was feminism, our intent to provide alternatives to the sexist texts used in schools. The conception was, in fact, precisely the one on which the Press had been founded.

Out of that 1973 meeting came the idea for the *Women's Lives / Women's Work* project. This project, which would not officially begin for more than two years, has allowed us to extend the original concept of The Feminist Press to a broader audience.

We spent the years from 1973 to 1975 assessing the need for a publication project, writing a major funding proposal, steering it through two foundations, negotiating with the Webster Division of McGraw-Hill, our co-publisher. We could not have begun this process without the advice and encouragement of Marilyn Levy of the Rockefeller Family Fund, from which we received a planning grant in 1973. For one year, Phyllis Arlow, Marj Britt, Merle Froschl, and Florence Howe surveyed the needs of teachers for books about women, reviewed the sexist bias of widely used history and literature texts, and interviewed editorial staffs of major education publishers about their intentions to publish material on women. The research accumulated provided a strong case for the grant proposal first submitted to the Ford Foundation in the summer of 1974.

During the winter of 1974–1975, Merle Froschl, Florence Howe, Corrine Lucido, and attorney Janice Goodman (for the Feminist Press) negotiated a co-publishing contract with McGraw-Hill. We could not have proceeded without the strong interest of John Rothermich of McGraw-Hill's Webster Division. Our co-publishing agreement gives control over editorial content and design to The Feminist Press; McGraw-Hill is responsible for distribution of the series to the high school audience, while The Feminist Press is responsible for distribution to colleges, bookstores, libraries, and the general public.

In the summer of 1975, the final proposal—to produce for copublication a series of twelve supplementary books and their accompanying teaching guides—was funded by the Ford Foundation and the Carnegie Corporation. Project officers Terry Saario and Vivien Stewart were supportive and helpful throughout the life of the project. In 1978, The Feminist Press received funds from the National Endowment for the Humanities to help complete the project. Additional funds also were received from the Edward W. Hazen Foundation and from the Rockefeller Family Fund.

Once initial funding was obtained, The Feminist Press began its search for additional staff to work on the project. The small nucleus of existing staff working on the project was expanded as The Feminist Press hired new employees. The *Women's Lives / Women's Work* project staff ultimately included six people who remained for the duration of the project: Sue Davidson, Merle Froschl, Florence Howe, Elizabeth Phillips, Susan Trowbridge, Alexandra Weinbaum. Mary Mulrooney, a member of the project staff through 1979, thereafter continued her work as a free-lance production associate for the duration of the project. We also wish to acknowledge the contributions of Dora Janeway Odarenko and Michele Russell, who were on staff through 1977; and Shirley Frank, a Feminist Press staff member who was a member of the project staff through 1979. Helen Schrader, also a Feminist Press staff member, participated on the project during its first year and kept financial records and wrote financial reports throughout the duration of the project.

The *Women's Lives / Women's Work* project staff adopted the methods of work and the decision-making structure developed by The Feminist Press staff as a whole. As a Press "work committee," the project met weekly to make decisions, review progress, discuss problems. The project staff refined the editorial direction of the project, conceptualized and devised guidelines for the books and teaching guides, and identified prospective authors. When proposals came in, the project staff read and evaluated the submissions and made decisions regarding them. Similarly, when manuscripts arrived, the project staff read and commented on them. Project staff members took turns drafting memoranda, reports, and other documents. And the design of the series grew out of the discussions and the ideas generated at the project meetings. The books, teaching guides, and other informational materials had the advantage, at significant stages of development, of the committee's collective direction.

Throughout the life of the project, The Feminist Press itself continued to function and grow. Individuals on staff who were not part of the *Women's Lives / Women's Work* project provided support and advice to the project: Jeanne Bracken, Brenda Carter, Ranice Crosby, Shirley Frank, Brett Harvey, Frances Kelley, Carol Levin, Kam Murrin, Karen Raphael, Marilyn Rosenthal, Helen Schrader, Nancy Shea, Nivia Shearer, Anita Steinberg, Sharon Wigutoff, and Sophie Zimmerman.

The process of evaluation by teachers and students before final publication was as important as the process for developing ideas into books. To this end, we produced testing editions of the books. Field-testing networks were set up throughout the United States in a variety of schools—public, private, inner-city, small town, suburban, and rural—to reach as diverse a student population as possible. We field tested in the following cities, regions, and states: Boston, Massachusetts; Tampa, Florida; Greensboro, North Carolina; Tucson, Arizona; Los Angeles, California; Eugene, Oregon; Seattle, Washington; Shawnee Mission, Kansas; Martha's Vineyard, Massachusetts; New York City; Long Island; New Jersey; Rhode Island; Michigan; Minnesota. We also had an extensive network of educators—350 teachers across the country—who reviewed the books in the series, often using sections of books in classrooms. From teachers' comments, from students' questionnaires, and from tapes of teachers' discussions, we gained valuable information both for revising the books and for developing the teaching guides.

Three times during the life of the *Women's Lives / Women's Work* project, an Advisory Board composed of feminist educators and scholars met for a full day to discuss the books and teaching guides. The valuable criticisms and suggestions of the following people who participated in these meetings were essential to the project: Mildred Alpern, Rosalynn Baxandall, Peggy Brick, Ellen Cantarow, Elizabeth Ewen, Barbara Gates, Clarisse Gillcrist, Elaine Hedges, Nancy Hoffman, Susan Klaw, Alice Kessler-Harris, Roberta Kronberger, Merle Levine, Eleanore Newirth, Judith Oksner, Naomi Rosenthal, Judith Schwartz, Judy Scott, Carroll Smith-Rosenberg, Adria Steinberg, Barbara Sussman, Amy Swerdlow. We also want to express our gratitude to Shirley McCune and Nida Thomas, who acted in a general advisory capacity and made many useful suggestions; and to Kathryn Girard and Kathy Salisbury who helped to develop the teacher and student field-testing questionnaires.

Others whom we want to acknowledge for their work on *Woman's "True" Profession* are Jane Williamson, who prepared the index; Ruth Adam, who restored the historical photographs; Randi Book of McGraw-Hill, for administrative assistance; and Miriam Weintraub and Les Glass of Weinglas Typography Company, for the text composition.

The work of the many people mentioned in these acknowledgments has been invaluable to us. We would also like to thank all of you who read this book—because you helped to create the demand that made the *Women's Lives/Women's Work* project possible.

THE FEMINIST PRESS

Author's Acknowledgments

I RESEARCHED AND WROTE *Woman's "True" Profession* in isolation from universities and scholars. The project was a rich pastime, connected to my life, the lives of my friends, and my family's history. Those women friends who knew I was writing another book were not only unfailingly encouraging, they were possessive of the project. The told me innumerable "teacher" stories—most, about their mothers, grand-mothers, and aunts—and helped me puzzle out the appropriate perspective for a book that is neither history, nor literary criticism, nor sociology, and so seems to belong to us all: women who were taught by and are women teachers.

My mother, Malvina Hoffman, my aunt Alice Miller, and our friend Edith Kondell brought to life school experiences in the twenties and thirties, and Edith arranged my interview with the former principal Mary Agnes Dwyer—then ninety-three. Along with Barbara Lodor, unasked, these women sent me the obituaries and photographs needed to complete Miss Dwyer's story. My friend Sandy Kanter brought her economist's analysis and her stylist's pen to numerous troubling paragraphs, and Polly Kaufman, an historian whose work on women school board members I had read, tracked me down in Washington, and, with great generousity, offered me the use of selected letters and biographical notes from nineteenth-century teachers, a rare "find" of hers from the Connecticut Historical Society. She will tell their story in "A Wider Sphere of Usefulness: Teaching in the West."

Thorough substantive criticism came from women at The Feminist Press—first among them my editor, Sue Davidson. She not only tolerated the notes I sent her on the backs of diaper boxes and shopping lists, but assembled them into a coherent whole; she wrote enthusiastic-ally urging me on when I thought I would never find time for one more revision; and she helped me clarify numerous passages, often seeming to understand the point before I understood it myself. Florence Howe, Sandy Weinbaum, Merle Froschl, and others argued one long afternoon with me, and helped me understand some extremely sensitive issues of language and point of view. I am grateful to these women. I am especially grateful, too, to David Tyack, a feminist historian of education, who twice on short notice read the manuscript, and offered encouragement and corrections. Barbara Finkelstein, a second historian of education, also helped out.

This project could not have begun without the generous support of a Rockefeller Humanities Fellowship during 1975–1976. From research on adult literacy that year I gradually turned to the historical work which became *Woman's "True" Profession.*

NANCY HOFFMAN

Introduction

We hold the pointer to the words, the numbers, the alphabet.
Love for another generation.
Shelter of hope for another generation,
Life for our children.

—Tillie Olsen, "Utterance"[1]

WOMEN HAVE ALWAYS BEEN TEACHERS. Mother, sister, aunt, grandmother, woman friend—rare is the woman who has not instructed a child. Yet it is only in the last one hundred and fifty years that teaching has been a paid profession for women. *Woman's "True" Profession* explores some important phases in the development of teaching as paid work for women. The selections chosen to illuminate these phases are, with few exceptions, the autobiographical writing of women teachers—from Emma Hart Willard, a visionary in 1814 when she dreamed of a school for girls, to Grace Strachan, a union organizer who counted herself one among 14, 000 female elementary school teachers in New York City in 1907.

Early in the nineteenth century when this book begins, teaching was an activity largely embedded in family life, as it had been for most of human history. Schooling, particularly in rural areas, was still casual—reading, writing, and arithmetic for the brief month or two in a year when a teacher could be found. Most instruction occurred "naturally"; children were taught skills by an older person who needed their help with certain tasks, or, learning from observation, accomplished new tasks unaided. While this kind of teaching and learning, of course, survives today, during the course of the nineteenth century there rose to supplement, and even compete with family instruction a *system* of schooling where none had existed previously. Professional educators, concerned with the nation's future, saw that if citizens were to respond to economic forces "modernizing" American society, they would need increasingly complex knowledge. Aware that the pace of change no longer ensured continuity with past practices and beliefs, these educational leaders sought a philosophically coherent approach to education, one that attended not simply to rudimentary skills, but to the formation of character and conscience. At the beginning of the nineteenth century, before schooling gained this serious new kind of attention, one in ten teachers was a woman; by 1920, when this book ends, out of the greatly expanded force of 657,000 public school teachers, 86% were women, and almost all elementary school teachers were women. The story of "woman's 'true' profession" then is also the story of the development of the massive educational system we know today.

It would, of course, take many volumes to tell the full story of woman's profession as teacher, and that is not the intention of this book. This book has a more limited objective, yet one that breaks new ground. In assembling this anthology, I have attempted to reproduce the experience of teaching in the past from the *perspective of the teacher*, and at the same time, to highlight critical themes which defined teaching and characterized it as women's work. As often as possible, the book's sources were the voices of individual teachers, rather than documents from which one might constitute an "official" record of the past. And the question asked of each teacher's account was a modest but heretofore neglected one: given the choices available to a woman of her time, what had her choice of teaching meant to her?

The Perspective of the Teacher

In the vast literature on education, the teacher herself appears rarely as a subject of serious study. The work that describes her is of two genres: the biography, and the sociological study, although recent feminist history is beginning to change this picture.[2] The biographies can be generally characterized as hagiographies or "saints' lives"; they immortalize women of unvarying goodness. More significant are the sociological studies best represented by Willard Waller's *Sociology of Teaching* (1932)[3] and, more recently, Dan C. Lortie's *School Teacher* (1975). The best of their kind, these books make the teacher an *object* rather than a subject of study, and barely acknowledge the most significant fact in the teacher's identity—

her femaleness. There is due note taken of the date the profession was "feminized"—itself a derogatory term—and Lortie mentions that men enter teaching as a second choice career and intend to move up into administration, while women have "flat" career lines; their participation in teaching is a "function of the life cycle." Lortie also observes very perceptively that teaching is "special but shadowed"; the public rhetoric of respect the profession elicits is made suspect by private ridicule. But he fails to see that teaching is in part relegated to second place because it is women's work.[4]

In 1938, Frances Donovan published her thorough sociological study, *The Schooma'am*. The experience and psychology of the woman teacher are at the center of this book. Donovan examined the variety of teachers, the impact of being unmarried, the motivation for teaching ("many [teachers] prefer to work with women rather than with men"), the teacher's economic position, her private life, her place in the community, and so on. She questioned as well the stereotypic portrait of the teacher as a "tall, thin, slab-sided female," the "old maid" who tortured "the kingdom of helpless childhood." Donovan went on, however, to "average" the lives of individuals, to create composite case studies, and to classify "types."[5] Thus, although she saw teaching as a *woman's* experience, the vivacity, individuality, and viewpoint of the teacher herself rarely penetrate the study.

Unlike past studies, *Woman's "True" Profession* is an attempt to study the profession through the eyes of insiders. While there are limitations to this approach—the autobiographer's reliability as a reporter and the selectivity of the reporting are conventional puzzles of the genre—the method has the advantage of revealing the thoughts and feelings of the women who have been teachers. To supplement the autobiographical material, I searched for imaginative literature similarly capable of rendering the texture of the teacher's experience; thus, each section includes one short story, and section 3 includes a student account by an acute observer. These selections focus on subjects of importance to teachers themselves, as evidenced in the autobiographical writings. In letters, diaries, and essays, teachers write about classroom experiences, about ill health and other hardships, about pleasure in their power. They write of personal life—

relationships with family, loneliness, and friendship. One gets a sense of daily events, cares, triumphs, and disappointments seldom captured by the sociologist or the historian. The selections in *Woman's "True" Profession*, then, add a new and living dimension to our view of teachers. The selections also allow us to test the teacher's perspective against prevailing views. In some areas, that perspective conflicts provocatively with popular wisdom.

The woman teacher's description of her motivation in seeking a teaching job in the nineteenth century, for example, is at odds with ideas then generally accepted. In the 1840s, fifties, and sixties, theorists argued that women were better suited than men "to begin the first work in the Temple of education," in Horace Mann's quaint phrase.[6] They claimed that teaching unlocked woman's instinct for mothering and prepared her for marriage. Women, they believed, took teaching jobs primarily because they loved children. Conversely, they assumed that women who remained in teaching had had no offers of marriage. The issue was further complicated by the code of behavior enforced by educators and school committee members. When a woman took a teaching job, in most states well into the twentieth century, she knew that she was legally required to resign when she married. Many school committees forbade such activities as riding in a carriage with a man, frequenting confectionary shops, and being out after 8 P.M.[7] While these regulations revealed a preoccupation with woman's marital status on the part of the regulators, writing by teachers does not reveal a corresponding preoccupation; neither their love of children nor their attitude toward marriage dominates their comments. In general, their comments indicate that they entered teaching because they needed work. Women had only a few choices of occupation; and compared with most—laundering, sewing, cleaning, or working in a factory—teaching offered numerous attractions. It was genteel, paid reasonably well, and required little special skill or equipment. In the second half of the century and beyond, it also allowed a woman to travel, to live independently or in the company of other women, and to attain economic security and a modest social status. The issue of marriage, so charged with significance among male educators, emerges in stories of schoolmarms pressured reluctantly into marriage by family fearful of having an "old maid" on their hands, rather than in teachers accounts of their own eagerness or anxiety about marriage. There are also explicit statements, in these accounts, of teachers *choosing* work and independence over a married life that appeared, to them, to signify domestic servitude or social uselessness. Finally, the accounts of some women tell us that they chose teaching not because they wanted to teach children conventional right from wrong, but in order to foster social, political, or spiritual change: they wanted to persuade the young, move them to collective action for temperance, for racial equality, for conversion to Christianity. What these writings tell us, then, is that from the woman teacher's perspective, the continuity between mothering and teaching was far less significant than a paycheck and the challenge and satisfaction of work.

Critical Themes of the Woman Teacher's Experience

Each of the essays which introduce the three sections of this book identifies significant themes in the development of women's work as teachers. The writings included in the sections follow from these themes, grouped under the section titles, 1, "Seminary for Social Power: The Classroom Becomes Woman's Sphere"; 2, "A Noble Work Done Earnestly: Yankee Schoolmarms in the Civil War South"; 3, "Teaching in the Big City: Women Staff the Education Factories." The summaries that follow here are an overview of the material in the book; they also briefly suggest the ways in which these themes continue to be issues, both in women's work today, and in education.

"Seminary for Social Power" describes the transformation of teaching from a temporary *job,* usually held by a man, to a *profession* for women. It describes as well a transformation of popular thinking in the course of fifty years, so that by 1880 one would ordinarily assume that a teacher was a person of the female sex. The rapid industrialization and urbanization of the East Coast opened jobs more lucrative than teaching to men, just as the number of children seeking schooling was rising rapidly on account of massive immigration. Educators—notable, here, Catherine Beecher—seized the moment to suggest that women were natural teachers, and school committees hired women rapidly—at salaries a half to a third of a man's. Women were seen as self-sacrificing—Beecher envisioned training women teachers who would work "not for money, nor for influence, nor for honour, nor for ease, but with the simple, single purpose of doing good..."[8]

While teaching exploited women as workers, the profession nevertheless considerably altered the life chances of studious young women. With normal schools and classes to give specialized training, and schools seeking teachers throughout the country, women entered the profession in great numbers. By the end of the century, although teaching was salvation to individual women otherwise destined for the factory, domestic work, or marriage, it had not attained the status and respect of men's work. Men had become administrators in the graded schools and theorists of education. Section 1 thus describes a poignant and familiar pattern in women's history. While women had attained a profession of their own, they were able neither to control it, nor "make it equal."

"A Noble Work Done Earnestly" tells a happier, and even an inspiring story, the story of teaching as a nineteenth-century social movement. In the years during and after the Civil War, some 7,000 teachers went South to teach blacks newly freed from slavery how to read, write, calculate—and how to claim their place in society. Abolitionist or evangelical Christian in belief, with the support of a network of aid committees at home, the Yankee teachers set out to discover blacks' true intellectual capacity, and to form "the people who are to influence very largely the country's future, for better or for worse."[9] Usually in the company of female companions, the schoolmarms lived in the black community not only as teachers, but as preachers, doctors, domestic advisors, and politicians.

The many teachers who stayed on in the South through the 1870s and 1880s escaped the rapid and degrading bureaucratization of the schools taking place in the Northern cities, and became powers in their own right. They also set an example of interracial cooperation previously unknown. By their chosen work—teaching blacks—they made a public, political statement that thrust them into the heart of a passionate national controversy, and removed them from their proper domestic circle. Teaching in that social movement, as well as in the civil rights and women's movements of contemporary times, illuminates a second critical theme of the profession: as an activity to sharpen critical judgment, to test morality, and to encourage action on the basis of one's beliefs, teaching, like preaching, can be seen as an effective strategy to foster change.

The final section, "Teaching in the Big City," is perhaps best summed up by the theme of simultaneous power and powerlessness. In the big city schools at the turn of the century, the teacher faced immigrant children profoundly dependent on her for their introduction into American language and culture—but she faced, as well, increasingly professional and elite administrators who dared to think of her as if she were a factory hand. To the children "below" her, she was all things; to the men above her, she was to be drilled into conformity, molded to fit the machinery of the growing bureaucracy. Industrialization and the need for a literate work force were in part responsible for the regulation of teachers, but this regulation occurred simultaneously with the massive influx of non-Anglo Saxon immigrants. Native-born teachers and the newly "Americanized" daughters of immigrants, alike, came to recognize that the elite administrators did not trust them to control their classrooms and impart acceptable values that would ensure the future homogenity of American society. In Chicago, and then in New York and elsewhere, women teachers began to organize on their own behalf, and achieved, however briefly, a degree of domination over their own profession.

Biases and Problems

Woman's "True" Profession is a preliminary study. In the next few years historians of women will find in private collections and in archives the letters, diaries, and other writing that will fill out our knowledge about teachers. Scholars will correct, for example, the geographical bias of this book. While the transformation of teaching from a temporary job for a man to a profession for a woman began on the East Coast, where industrialization first emerged, by the late nineteenth century, women were working in schools throughout the country. The three sections of this book, however, are based on East Coast materials, most readily available to the author.

More significant than geographical bias are the silences of this book, the omissions that further research can only partially restore. This book is a social history—a history of the ordinary, the daily, written largely by the women whose work it records. Unfortunately, the accounts are almost uniformly those of white women. Because the lives of women of color have been virtually unrecognized, there are few public records of their work, and few private writings have come to light. Nevertheless, women of all races have taught. Like the black woman referred to in Tillie Olsen's "Utterance," above, they taught at home "to shelter love for another generation/Only to shelter hope." They also taught outside the home, not only in the segregated southern system. Although the census did not count non-white teachers until 1930, they had made their way into the schools before that time. A case in point is the black teacher Sarah J. Smith Thompson Garnet (1831–1911), born in a farm family on Long Island. At age fourteen, she began to teach in an African Free School in Brooklyn, and after completing normal school became the first black principal in a New York City public school.[10] How many others were there like her? It will be some time before we know. Only the names of women of color who distinguished themselves in extraordinary ways occur. Charlotte Forten, Ida Wells Barnett, Mary Church Terrell, Mary McCleod Bethune—all were teachers for a least a part of their careers.[11]

Has Teaching Served Women Well?

Is teaching a good profession for women? This book will probably leave the reader undecided. When women had few choices, the answer was undoubtedly yes. Even then, they labored under terrible hardships—forty, fifty, sometimes sixty children in a classroom, and pay so meager as to have led one woman to testify in a National Education Association hearing, "I am so worn out from teaching sixty pupils that most of my money goes for medicine and trips for my health...How few [of us] live to enjoy the pension."[12] There was an incredible petty tyranny to endure, no promise of status or power in the future, and a system which encouraged conformity. Charging in 1904 that no school in the United States submitted "questions of methods, discipline and teaching...to those actually engaged in the work of teaching," Margaret Haley, a teacher-organizer, quoted educator John Dewey: "How can the child learn to be a free and responsible citizen if the teacher is bound?"[13]

In the bureaucratized urban schools at the turn of the century, and on into the present, women were not treated very differently from young children by patriarchal school administrators and school boards. Rather than helping women to break away from the traditional behavior of daughter, sister, mother, or wife in becoming members of the work force, teaching tended to institutionalize this behavior. Women found the pattern all too familiar; many found it secure and acceptable. They saw male teachers at work in the high schools, and in administration. The structure of the school reinforced the notion that women were capable of teaching the ABC's and the virtues of cleanliness, obedience, and respect, while men taught about ideas, and organized the profession. This division of labor has changed only slightly in recent years.

On the other hand, many women love their pupils, and some genuinely feel themselves engaged in a socially significant activity. A white Boston teacher, fired in 1968 for walking out of her ghetto school with protesting black pupils and their parents, told me that she sees education as a key for shifting some power from the rich and privileged to the disenfranchised poor.[14] Her belief that teaching is part of a movement for social change is shared by some other women teachers. And finally, there are the old advantages of teaching—convenient hours for a mother, job security (the means by which my mother, for example kept our family solvent through the Depression), and, since the union movement of the 1950s, collective bargaining, which has improved working conditions and wages substantially.

Marion Moultrie, a black woman teaching in a "run-of-the-mill" school in Philadelphia in the early seventies, presents the advantages of her job in typical fashion: "When I finished college, I went right to the social workers school. Then I did social work for about three years. I came into teaching after I started raising a family. It gave me more time with my own children. I got out at two-thirty and had my summers off." Besides permitting her to integrate work and home life, teaching opens up social relationships with children. In her case, delinquent girls become "friend[s] for life." But most important, she makes sure a student can fill out a job application, manage basic skills and concepts, and imagine "the type of environment he wants all his life, and what he can do about it." She separates herself from "missionary" teachers who only teach "black is beautiful," and may neglect "moral and 'just living' issues of today." She is helping the young to "find something to hold onto...", and she is happy in her work.[15]

Woman's "True" Profession

Voices from the History of Teaching

For Mark, in hope of a feminist manhood

"Vast numbers of American women have spent
at least part of their lives in front
of a classroom. We learned our basic skills from
these women, and although they knew us,
we know almost nothing about them."

—*Margaret Nelson, Middlebury College, Vermont*

ONE: Seminary for Social Power

The Classroom Becomes Woman's Sphere

EARLY IN THE 1840s, educator Catherine Beecher addressed a gathering of her countrywomen to arouse support for her favorite scheme—to send an army of "Christian female teachers" to start schools "at the West." The scheme had dual purposes: to

save untutored children from ignorance, and to create an honored profession for women who had not yet married, or who were to remain single. About the first purpose, there was no argument, but Beecher had to convince her audience of the second. "Our sex" is depressed, Beecher claimed, because there is no road to "competence, influence, and honor" but marriage, no antidote to the "suffering that results from the *inactivity of cultivated intellect and feeling....* This is not so because providence has not provided an ample place for...a profession for woman, but because custom or prejudice or a low estimate of its honorable character, prevents her from entering it. *The*

educating of children, that is the true and noble profession
of a woman—*that* is what is worthy the noblest powers and
affections of the noblest minds."[1]

Some forty years later, Minerva Leland, a recent graduate of
Colby College in Maine, and a teacher in Brandon, Vermont,
received a letter from her brother Sam back home in Massachusetts. As if he had taken to heart Catherine Beecher's plea that
women needed intellectually challenging work before, or
instead of, marriage, he wrote,

Dear Sister, we did enjoy your last letter very much. I am positively
delighted that you are so enthusiastic about your school work. There is
no doubt that a new life has opened before you. Not that I am desirous
that you be obliged to earn your own living and remain single, but I
know that life can mean more if you are actively engaged in it than
it can mean to you shut up at home.

When June came, Minerva sent a letter and a check for her
savings account home to her father. To him, she wrote proudly,
"I've earned a good, comfortable living for myself, and I'm truly
thankful for that."[2]

In just a few decades, Catherine Beecher's dream of a profession
for women had been fulfilled. Between 1840 and 1880, the
number of female teachers tripled to make up 80% of the
elementary school teaching force. In the 1880s, women were
routinely trained as teachers in colleges, in special post-
secondary schools and classes, and actively recruited for jobs in
the new graded schools in cities and large towns. Like a
multitude of young women of her generation, Minerva Leland
had chosen work honored by her family, and she could be
confident of her economic independence. The "custom" and
"prejudice" which had once prevented woman from entering the
profession, now held her to be more suited than man to the
"sacred office."

This section tells the story of the transformation of common
school teaching from its pre-1840 status as stop-gap or last
choice work for men to a profession for normal, well-educated
women. It tells another less happy story as well, typical in the
history of women's work: a woman's profession suffers because it

is not attractive to men. This story emerges as well in Minerva Leland's correspondence.

In the same year that Minerva Leland was feeling so pleased with herself, she received a letter from a *male* college friend who had left New England for a teaching job in Mississippi. "When I arrived there," wrote the young man, "I found a community unappreciative of the fact that there are teachers and teachers.... There was another teacher there to underbid for the work, an old wreck of a man...so that, not being desirous of the school anyway, I ceased effort for it."[3] Minerva's friend added that he was now studying law. If "the old wreck of a man" represents Beecher's generation, Minerva's male friend represents the new. Common* or public school teaching never became a first choice *career for a man*—men prepared for administration, or wrote on the subject of education. Without male prestige, teaching held only momentarily the nobility Catherine Beecher had claimed for it. By the 1880's, "custom" and "prejudice" had become forces that assigned women to an undervalued and sometimes restrictive profession.

Teaching Before It Became Woman's Profession

"Civil society must be built on the four cornerstones of the church, the school-house, the militia, and the town-meeting," said John Adams, the second President of the United States.[4] Adams' word "cornerstone" suggests the simple, but fundamental, task of the school in pre-Civil War America. The red or white frame schoolhouse on the village green did its part to support civil society by making sure that young children were literate. In the typical twelve or fourteen weeks each winter that school "kept," boys and some girls, released from farm work, learned to read, to write, and to cipher by the method of rote recitation. Among agricultural people, parents assumed that generation

---

*The term "common school," used in the nineteenth century for schools held "in common" or "owned" by all citizens, designated what are today called public schools.

would follow generation on the land. To want education for its own sake would have been thought odd, and certainly few would have approved schools which taught children more than their fathers knew. As for values, there was a commonplace morality—obedience, respect, truthfulness, thrift—which appeared in the few current school books.

The teacher of the village school was usually a man. A student of the ministry or at college to learn a profession, he taught not for love, but to earn money during his long winter vacation. Farther from the city, the teacher was often a college drop-out or a fellow with some handicap that ill-suited him for farm life. Said one forthright commentator in 1890, teaching is "a half-way house for those bound for the learned professions, and a hospital for the weak-minded of those who have already entered them."[5] Unpredictable in qualifications and frequently committed to no more than a single winter in a school, the teacher accurately reflected the low priority given to education in agricultural society. Carpenters, blacksmiths, carters and other artisans critical to rural survival earned more money and respect.

Adult women and young girls also taught, though in small numbers, and rarely in winter school when travel was treacherous, at least in the North. The older women, often widows in need of income, kept private "dame schools." For a small sum, a cord of wood, or a supply of eggs or milk, the dame would have three or four young children in her home to learn the abc's and ciphering. Her instruction insured that the child could later participate in village religious life, and keep track of simple financial transactions. These Dame Schools also apparently reflected the priorities of the village. There were numerous jokes at the expense of the dame, and stories of her cruelty. "These apologies for schools," wrote an anonymous author in *Harper's* in 1878, speaking of an earlier time, "are often kept by some Miss Hepzibah Pyncheon, who has a little shop with gingerbread and tape for sale; and in the window, by the side of these tempting wares, a sign is displayed announcing that 'a school is kept here'. . . . Young America, so scornful of all relics of the past, has forgotten that he . . . was pinned to an old woman's apron while he said his letters."[6]

The rare young girl who kept school, like the widow, also wanted to earn money, but she often saw teaching as an escape from farm work; and her family was less likely to frown on her love of books than if she had been a boy. In accounts like those of Emma Hart Willard, Lucia Downing, and Mary Pratt included in this section, the young women seemed to be taken with the idea of teaching in an instant. All three had revelled in surpassing the achievements of their classmates and siblings in school, and teaching offered one of the rare chances for a young woman to earn further public recognition for excellence. Although Lucia Downing described herself deprecatingly as unable to sing and unskilled at drawing, at age fourteen, by her own account, she taught her four scholars "the entire realm of knowledge" by means of "instructive Questions and Answers" that she had composed herself, and was pleased to be given a school of fifteen children the following year. Sixteen year old Emma Hart, destined to become a pioneer educator of women, made her school a show place, "the admiration of the neighborhood." Unlike men who taught, both young women sought further schooling with the firm idea that teaching would be their life's work, their calling. In the informal, rural school, each had discovered the pleasure of exerting her intellect and her will.

The Teacher "Becomes" a Woman

While informal rural schools supported directly by parents survived in America late into the nineteenth century, the 1840s and fifties marked the first attempts to create a state-supported system of common schools and to redefine the mission of schooling.* One might characterize the extremes of the old schooling and the new as follows. Until the first decades of the

*It is worthwhile to remind the reader here of the "unevenness" of historical change. This chapter focuses on New England; much of the country lagged behind both in the spread of common schools and the employment of high percentages of women. The employment of women seems especially linked to the development of an urban market for teachers. (See the final pages of this section and section 3, and my acknowledgment of debt to Myra Strober and David Tyack, p. 305, n 10.)

nineteenth century, schools had taught a few relatively insignificant skills to farm children. The crucial lessons—how to plant, to weave, to can, to milk, to sew—were learned "naturally" in the family, but now schools were to supplant or at least compete with the family as teacher. While in the past, the village doctor or minister had examined, hired, and supervised teachers according to a local standard of his own, now from their offices in state government, educated "schoolmen" were to enforce *their* ideas of education. Where once the teacher had been the butt of humor—a laughable, absent-minded weakling; a crotchety old maid—now the teacher was popularly portrayed as an exalted figure, a custodian of American character whose mission it was to discipline and inspire the young. The teacher was also portrayed as a woman.

Three intertwined, massive social changes gave woman her new profession and education its new respect: industrialization, immigration, and urbanization. As abstractions, these terms obscure a human drama which altered daily experience for most Americans in the course of three or four decades. But set as the changing landscape for an individual life, these abstractions have more immediate significance. Because Catherine Beecher might be called the genius of woman's "true" profession, and because she came to adulthood just as the massive changes began, her life offers an illuminating example of the complex intersecting of the individual actor and the historical moment. In 1800, when Beecher was born, the United States was largely a society of small farmers. In Southern New England, to which she moved with her family in 1810, two-thirds of the population lived in villages smaller than 3,000 inhabitants. As the oldest daughter in the busy household of the sought-after minister Lyman Beecher, Catherine made or supervised the making of all daily necessities. These included the weaving of cloth and the sewing of garments, done by women in the household. By 1823, when Catherine and her sister Mary opened a girls' school in Hartford, Connecticut, other young women of their age were leaving their families also. The landscape of New England had begun to change. Factories where cloth was woven by machine hired, housed, and paid decent wages to Yankee mill girls. "Daughters are now emphatically a blessing to the farmer," wrote an observer in 1831.[7] Wages sent home gave woman economic value. They also gave her the taste for independence.

During the 1830's, Catherine Beecher moved to Cincinnati with her father. There she began her campaign to train teachers for Western children growing up beyond the reach of schools. As she traveled between the Western cities, Beecher saw in the stream of westward migrants, the results of overcrowding and competition for jobs in New England. Thousand upon thousand of immigrants, seven out of ten escaping persecution and famine in Ireland, were pouring into Boston, drawn by tales of lucrative factory jobs. The population of Beecher's Connecticut increased 31% in the ten years between 1840 and 1850, then an astonishing 42% between 1850 and 1860.[8]

As Beecher penned her popular *Treatise on Domestic Economy* (1841), its sequel *The Domestic Receipt Book* (1846), and *The Evils Suffered by American Women and American Children* (1846), excerpted in this section, the housewife to whom she wrote needed all manner of advice. The young Yankee husband who was not inclined to farm now had an alternative to ministering and teaching. Leaving his wife to guard the hearth of their home near the city, the Yankee farmer's son responded to the lure of the business world. There were money, status, and excitement in trading cotton futures at the stock market, planning railroads, managing factories, and working out legal agreements, as Minerva Leland's friend planned to do. Man spends his life "in the collisions of the world," wrote Beecher, and desires "notoriety and the praise of men."[9] At the end of the Civil War in 1865 and thirteen years before Beecher's death, these "collisions" had resulted in a society dominated by industrial and business interests, a society more similar to that of the 1980's than to the world of Beecher's birth.

This radical transformation of society had its impact on education. First, there were simply more children, many in the city or nearby. In the industrial world, they had to know much more than their fathers had learned. And, second, thousands of teachers were needed just at the moment when the expanding economy provided unprecedented choices for men. Teachers were needed as well at a moment when cities were designing schools and school *systems* that paralleled the hierarchical organization of factories and business enterprises. Educators seized the moment—mid-nineteenth century—to declare that women, the "natural" teachers, should staff the graded schools. Accustomed to a subordinate economic position, women would be grateful to work, despite the fact that they received a third to a half of a man's pay.[10]

Catherine Beecher, the early and eloquent spokesperson for woman's profession, was a harbinger of the shift of public opinion. Since the founding of Hartford Female Seminary, she had been a tireless proselytizer for women's education. In her twenties she had already defined and exalted woman's work as teacher within the family circle. Women were more suited than men to the work of human development, she argued, because they were more "benevolent," more willing to "make sacrifices of personal enjoyment." Beecher thought that the mother's "curriculum" should consist of healthful habits, graceful manners, and above all, the formation of conscience. By 1830, Beecher had identified a second arena for woman's power. "To enlighten the understanding and to gain the affections," she wrote to a friend, is "a teacher's business." For this work, woman is "best fitted." Always a proponent of separate "spheres" of influence for male and female, Beecher distinguished teaching from improper intrusions of females into the male world of paid work: the school was an extension of or substitute for the domestic culture of the home. In her public addresses on the subject, Beecher reassured her audience that the female teacher remained truly feminine; she had no desire for notoriety, but like the ideal mother, worked "not for money, not for influence, nor for honour, nor for ease, but with the simple, single purpose of doing good."[11]

Beecher had a second purpose in promoting women as teachers: women needed "a high and honorable profession to engage their time." Troubled by woman's economic vulnerability, Beecher identified its cause in woman's limited choices of work. In the densely populated eastern states, Beecher saw women engaged in dangerous work "at prices that will not keep body and soul together." The clothing manufacturers "grow rich on the hard labors of our sex. Tales there are to be told of the sufferings of American women in our eastern cities so shocking that they would scarcely be credited, and yet they are true beyond all dispute." Beecher also recognized that teaching, with its missionary ideology and its image as an extension of mothering, could be accepted as a *chosen* alternative to marriage for a woman of the educated classes. Marriage was, of course, the first choice, but, Beecher asserted, "Woman ought never to be led to married life except under the promptings of pure affection. To marry for an establishment, for a position, or for something to do is a deplorable wrong. But how many women, for want of a high and honorable profession are led to this melancholy course." Only the teacher could "discern before her the road to honorable independence and extensive usefulness" where she need not outstep the prescribed boundaries of feminine modesty. Like Beecher herself, a teacher could travel, live in the company of other women, spend money as she chose, and still remain a true woman.

Beecher's first two arguments were buttressed by a third which, in a sense, contradicted the image of the self-sacrificing woman, and recognized in an extraordinarily modern way that idle, educated, and unmarried, women grew sick from the absence of serious work. Such women often became parlor ornaments, forced into rounds of superficial social obligations. Teaching, Beecher believed, no doubt from her own experience as an unmarried woman with a career, would end this debilitating and enforced idleness, end the "consequent diseases of the mind and body that afflict females of the higher classes."[12]

There were, of course, many idea-makers who, along with Beecher, caused Americans to shift their image of "teacher" from second rate young man to exemplary woman. Most of these, however, were more interested in shaping the minds and moral values of untutored children than they were in developing education programs for women which would lead to paying work. Cyrus Peirce, Horace Mann, Henry Barnard,* and other

*Horace Mann, (1796–1859), leader among the pre-Civil War schoolmen, served for over a decade as secretary to the first Massachusetts Board of Education. His controversial annual reports spell out the philosophy and vision of the common school movement. Henry Barnard (1811–1900) was the first secretary of the Connecticut Board of Education. A theorist and scholar of American and European education, Barnard wrote and lectured on education throughout his life and founded the *American Journal of Education*. For Cyrus Pierce, see below, pages 64–74.

New England schoolmen represented educational reform so sweeping that they believed it would transform society. A common school system would be the "great equalizer"; it would create wealth; it would "perfect" the new Republic. Most importantly, it would form character. Like Beecher, the schoolmen feared not only for the newly arrived immigrant child, but for the child of the new industrialist—indulged, undisciplined, and soft.

The schoolmen were not alone in their fears. While the writings of the period are filled with testimonies to the thriving American economy, to American inventiveness, practicality, and "admirable material progress," they are filled as well with earnest cautions. Urban industrial society, most old New Englanders believed, had a devastating effect on character. The "outward show" of the city destroyed inward strength, and, furthermore, it encouraged envy and emulation (or competition). To get rich quickly now seemed more a matter of luck than of hard work, self-discipline, and conservatism. The school was to save the middle class child from "the race for wealth, luxury, ambition and pride," and the immigrant child from "the inherited stupidity of centuries of ignorant ancestors."[13] Clearly, such an enterprise required more than instruction in the three r's, and the reinforcement of the communal values of the pre-industrial village.

The schoolmen began with the teacher. If the common schools were to form character, the untrained, temporary male teacher was inadequate. Indeed, he was symbolic of the low status and lack of respect for the common school. And many established teachers were resistant to change. Needed were institutions to train a new teaching force to carry out the schoolmen's mission. Who would be the new teachers? Young women who loved books, were self-sacrificing, had an instinct for mothering, and sought dignified work. Designed on the model of the European *école normale*, the first American normal school or teacher's college was soon on the drawing board. Approved and funded, in part privately, in part by the state legislature, Lexington Academy, the first of three state normal schools or teachers' colleges in Massachusetts, opened in 1839 with Cyrus Peirce as its principal. Here twenty-five young women began to study the "common branches" or academic disciplines, a philosophy of forming character, and a pedagogy for succeeding at both. Here a profession for women was born.*

By Example and Precept: Normal School Education

On the morning of August 1, 1839, seventeen year old Mary Swift took her place in the Lexington Academy lecture hall for the first day at the first state normal school in America. In her new Journal, purchased "agreeably to the wishes of our teacher," she began to record all that transpired in the creation of the new profession: its theory and practice; the themes of lectures given by a procession of distinguished visitors; the behavior of the young lady students. For her and her teachers, as the Journal entries reprinted below make evident, the venture had great seriousness. Here young women were being educated as they had never been before—not to teach in private seminaries for the educated classes, not to go as Christian missionaries among "the heathens," but to take part in a public venture financed by the state on behalf of the populace. They were to be workers who would transform the inadequate rural schools and staff the new city institutions that would shape urban society. As Cyrus Peirce anxiously reminded them, all "friends of education" awaited their success.[14]

The themes of seriousness and professionalism were reinforced daily. On that first day, a visiting professor compared the young women to medical students, and suggested that they take lecture notes as future doctors did. In addition, he urged the future teachers to "think seriously upon the subject of [elevating

---

*The establishment of normal schools symbolized the elevation of teaching to a profession thought to require special training; however, normal schools prepared only a small number of teachers, on into the twentieth century. Other teachers attended summer institutes held on college campuses; some took a year's training in high school; but most simply met the requirement to have completed a year of school beyond the grade they wished to teach.

the moral standards of the schools]." They would influence the pupils "both by example and precept." Two weeks later, in "Father Peirce's" weekly lecture, he explicitly attacked the current image of teachers as "qualified for nothing else." This image, he declared, was historically inaccurate—the ancients employed only their wisest men as teachers. As if to encourage his teenage students to their best efforts, he also stressed the teacher's significance to society. "Inadequacy in the common trades," he told the young women, "is felt only by the person himself, but in the teacher, its consequences are felt by the pupils, and their influence does not only extend to this moment or year, but is felt by succeeding generations.... It is better to make one thousand machines go wrong, than to train up a child as he should not go."[15]

Despite the fact that most students attended only for a year or at most two, the first normal schools were a gift to studious girls who wanted to work and had not their brothers' option of enrolling in college. Like a college, Lexington Academy required its students to study science, math, and philosophy. In addition, the first American theorists of education tried out radical, new ideas on the young women. Against all current practice, they argued that rote recitations—the chant of the abc's, and the times tables—should be exchanged for a pedagogy that engaged children's cooperation in learning to solve problems and seek information for themselves. Peirce compared the old and the new in the story of two boys, "both eager to see all they can." One was carried to the summit of a hill by his parents, the second ascended alone, "by the use of much dexterity." At the next hill, the first child was again carried, but the second ascended alone, and more easily. The parable illustrated that teaching a scholar to assist herself is better than assisting her in every difficulty.[16]

No narrow taskmaster, Peirce set an example of the new education for his students by fostering such a degree of speculation and critical inquiry that visitors remarked on it. Nor did he require conformity. In his own journal, he wrote, "We have no block or mold by which all are cast, so that there may be uniformity of character in the Prepared Teacher." To illustrate the new mode of teaching and learning, Peirce established a

Model School for village children. Here the young women began an apprenticeship in their new profession. Usually taciturn about herself, according to the style of early nineteenth century journal writers, Mary Swift was sufficiently inspired by the experience of teaching to write regretfully, "This day a new class of instructors go into the Model school, and I resign my place.... My attachment to the school is much greater than I could have anticipated from so short a connection with it."[17]

Woman's "True" Profession: "Special, but Shadowed"

By 1860, young women trained like Mary Swift had a profession of their own. The "sacred office" gave them public status, the claim to a decent income, freedom to marry only for "pure affection," and their own institutions of higher education. But like many victories for women, this one was contradictory and qualified, tinged with the inescapable marks of sexism. During the middle decades of the nineteenth century, women entered the profession in such great numbers that the common image of teaching as "women's work" resulted in its demotion to a second-rate profession. Because women themselves were viewed as subordinate to men, women's profession could not equal law, medicine, theology, or even the management of education. And by the final decades of the century, the normal school, that gift to studious girls, could not compete with traditional colleges. Under the direction of an uninspired, "second generation" of schoolmen who prepared teachers for the growing urban schools—with their graded classrooms, prescribed curricula, and heavy-handed control from male administrators and school-boards—the normal schools became pedestrian, restrictive, and "domesticated," educating not for inquisitiveness and moral fortitude, but for obedience and conformity.[18] The profession of teaching now moved into a position that it would hold for the rest of the century, and on into modern times: less than equal in status to male professions, *and* a source of satisfaction and power for women. Teaching was still "special," but it had also become "shadowed."[19]

A short story which appeared in 1865 in *Harper's New Monthly* demonstrates how the lofty calling defined by Beecher, Peirce, Mann, and others began to be viewed in the popular imagination as a burden assumed by women. Here, then, was the shadow. The key phrases in the following excerpt from the story ("Tom's Education") link "true woman" with "self-sacrifice," and oppose both to "stalwart man." Note that the woman as well as the man disparage teaching. In the story, Tom has returned home after flunking out of college; his sister Milly, a teacher, urges him to "hear little Frank St. Clair's lessons," in order to "have something laid up against the fall." The following dialogue ensues:

"Now, Milly, that's a little too much," answered Tom, with quite an injured air. "Do you think I'm adapted to teaching stupid little brats? Do you think I could spend my time hammering ideas into a wooden-headed youngster? No, I thank you. I would rather measure ribbons, if you please; it is far more entertaining and easy."

"And yet, Tom," I answered, with a throb of pain at my heart, "I have this to do. I have to retrace all the dusty and dry paths of elementary knowledge that you think so terrible."

"Ah, yes!" answered Tom, conceitedly; "but you are a woman, and women somehow adapt themselves so easily to circumstances. Now I have not the least adaptation to such things. I'd rather hang myself than be a schoolteacher."

I was silent. I knew a better name than adaptation to apply to that readiness with which a true woman assumes burdens that a stalwart man would find intolerable. It was self-sacrifice."[20]

In the short story "The Schoolmarm," reproduced in section 1, we see another side to the meaning of teaching for a woman, and one equally valid in the nineteenth century. For the story's central character, Mary William Pratt, teaching in a village common school in the 1860s was not just an escape from household drudgery, but the beginning of an independent, self-confident womanhood. Against her grandmother's warnings that she would end up an old maid, Mary took a job for $350 a year in the village school as an assistant.

She had never been so happy in her life as she was the day on which she stepped upon the platform at school and assumed the responsibilities of "schoolmarm." Mary William loved to teach, and she loved to rule—an art she understood to perfection. There were some pretty black sheep among her flock, but before she had had them a month they had learned a lesson in wholesome discipline.... By Christmas time Miss Pratt's name was mentioned in connection with a $500 vacancy in the high school. Meanwhile Mary revelled in her independence; and if she thought of matrimony in connection with herself, it was as a state of bondage to be avoided at any cost.[21]

Acknowledging the shadow over teaching, its ambiguous status, a writer in *The National Teacher* (1872) still argued that teaching was the only way for a woman to become mature, realistic, and competent in the late nineteenth century. Much of his practical analysis might describe the impact of teaching on the teacher at least to the turn of the century, and on into the 1950s in small towns. First, the writer recognized that a well-educated young woman had really only two choices: to stay at home, or to teach. About the first choice, he agreed with Catherine Beecher—women waste their power, they languish without the purposefulness demanded by a career, and a niche in public life. He criticized young women who left school "unable to lead their fellow beings, with no idea of responsibility to anybody for anything.... What an insecure position this is for any human being they sooner or later find out."

The writer had as well an unsentimental grasp of the virtues of the classroom as a school for the female teacher. The teacher might "shape the soul and mould the character" of the young— the aspect of the job earlier, more romantic writers had emphasized—but she would only be successful if she learned the rules of work in the public world—"the homely virtues of punctuality, persistence, conformity to the imperative facts of daily life, regard for others, business accuracy, precision." She would mature as a leader under the discipline of "the pitiless frame-work of iron school law."[22] He called the classroom a "seminary for social power," and urged women not to worry about society's prejudices against the woman who worked, but to teach. It was the best choice a nineteenth century woman could make.

Pioneering the Education of Young Women

Emma Hart Willard

From *Educational Biographies, Memoirs of Teachers, Educators, and Promoters and Benefactors of Education, Literature, and Science, Part I: Teachers and Educators,* 2nd ed. (New York: F.C. Brownell, 1861).

Excerpted from an autobiographical sketch, the selection below by Emma Hart Willard (1787–1870) describes her first experiences as a teacher at age seventeen. Willard's account exemplifies the challenge a young woman could set for herself in the village school before teaching became a woman's profession. The teachers a village might attract, however, varied widely in quality, as no training was required and there were no mandated school taxes. Emma Willard flourished in her schoolroom unconstrained by a tradition of serious education for women—there was none. First at Middlebury, Vermont, then at Troy Female Seminary, which she founded in 1821, Willard taught young girls subjects previously believed beyond their ken. Science courses, for instance, were more rigorous than those at many men's colleges. Persistent in her mission to improve the education of females, she also challenged tradition by addressing a treatise to the New York state legislature, advocating public support of female academies—a campaign that was ultimately successful.

In 1838, Willard relinquished Troy Seminary to her daughter-in-law and son, and spent the rest of her years advocating woman's right to intellectual equality. She was also briefly superintendent of schools in Hartford, Connecticut, under Henry Barnard.

In my childhood I attended the district school, but mostly from causes already related, none of my teachers so understood me as to awaken my powers or gain much influence over me. My father, happily for his children, left to his own family, used to teach us of evenings, and read aloud to us; and in this way I became interested in books and a voracious reader. A village library supplied me with such books as Plutarch's Lives, Rollins' Ancient History, Gibbon's Rome, many books of travels, and the most celebrated of the British poets and essayists.

Near the close of my fifteenth year, a new academy was opened about three-quarters of a mile from my father's house, of which Thomas Miner, a graduate, and once a tutor of Yale College, was the Principal, afterwards well known as an eminent physician president of the State Medical Society, and one of the most learned men of our country. Before the opening of the Academy, my mother's children had each received a small dividend from the estate of a deceased brother. My sister Nancy determined, as our parents approved, to spend this in being taught at the new school; but having at that time a special desire to make a visit among my married brothers and sisters in Kensington, (whose children were of my own age), I stood one evening, candle in hand, and made to my parents, who had retired for the night, what they considered a most sensible oration, on the folly of people's seeking to be educated above their means and prescribed duties in life. So Nancy went to school, and I to Kensington. A fortnight after, one Friday evening, I returned. Nancy showed me her books and told me of her lessons. "Mother," said I, "I am going to school to-morrow." "Why, I thought you had made up your mind not to be educated, and besides, your clothes are not in order, and it will appear odd for you to enter school Saturday." But Saturday morning I went, and received my lessons in Webster's Grammar and Morse's Geography. Mr. Miner was to hear me recite by myself until I overtook the class, in which were a dozen fine girls, including my elder sister. Monday, Mr. Miner called on me to recite. He began with Webster's Grammar, went on and on, and still as he questioned received from me a ready answer, until he said, "I will hear the remainder of your lesson tomorrow." The same thing occurred with the Geography lesson. I was pleased, and thought, "you never shall get to the end of my lesson." That hard chapter on the planets, with their diameters, distances, and periodic revolutions, was among the first of Morse's Geography. The evening I wished to learn it, my sister Lydia had a party. The house was full of bustle, and above all rose the song-singing, which always fascinated me. The moon was at the full, and snow was on the ground. I wrapt my cloak around me, and out of doors of a cold winter evening, seated on a horseblock, I learned that lesson. Lessons so learnt are not easily forgotten. The third day Mr. Miner admitted me to my sister's class. He used to require daily compositions. I never failed, the only one of my class who did not; but I also improved the opportunities which these afforded, to pay him off for any criticism by which he had (intentionally though indirectly) hit me,—with some parody or rhyme, at which, though sometimes pointed enough, Mr. Miner would heartily laugh—never forgetting, however, at some time or other, to retort with interest. Thus my mind was stimulated, and my progress rapid. For two successive years, 1802–3, I enjoyed the advantages of Dr. Miner's school, and I believe that no better instruction was given to girls in any school, at that time, in our country.

My life at this time was much influenced by an attachment I formed with Mrs. Peck, a lady of forty, although I was only fifteen. When we were first thrown together, it was for several days, and she treated me not as a child, but an equal—confiding to me much of that secret history which every heart sacredly cherishes; and I, on my part, opened to her my whole inner life, my secret feelings, anxieties and aspirations. Early in the spring of 1804 when I had just passed seventeen, Mrs. Peck proposed that a children's school in the village should be put into my hands.

The school-house was situated in Worthington street, on the great Hartford and New Haven turnpike; and was surrounded on the other three sides by a mulberry grove, towards which the windows were in summer kept open.

At nine o'clock, on that first morning, I seated myself among the children to begin a profession which I little thought was to last with slight interruption for forty years. That morning was the longest of my life. I began my work by trying to discover the several capacities and degrees of advancement of the children, so as to arrange them in classes; but they having been, under my predecessor, accustomed to the greatest license, would, at their option, go to the street door to look at a passing carriage, or stepping on to a bench in the rear, dash out of a window, and take a lively turn in the mulberry grove. Talking did no good. Reasoning and pathetic appeals were alike unavailing. Thus the morning slowly wore away. At noon I explained this first great perplexity of my teacher-life to my friend Mrs. Peck, who decidedly advised sound and summary chastisement. "I cannot," I replied; "I never struck a child in my life." "It is," she said, "the only way, and you must." I left her for the afternoon school with a heavy heart, still hoping I might find some way of avoiding what I could not deliberately resolve to do. I found the school a scene of uproar and confusion, which I vainly endeavored to quell. Just then, Jesse Peck, my friend's little son, entered with a bundle of five nice rods. As he laid them on the table before me, my courage rose; and, in the temporary silence which ensued, I laid down a few laws, the breaking of which would be followed with immediate chastisement. For a few moments the children were silent; but they had been used to threatening, and soon a boy rose from his seat, and as he was stepping to the door, I took one of the sticks and gave him a moderate flogging; then with a grip upon his arm which made him feel that I was in earnest, put him into his seat. Hoping to make this chastisement answer for the whole school, I then told them in the most endearing manner I could command, that I was there to do them good—to make them such fine boys and girls that their parents and friends would be delighted with them, and they be growing up happy and useful; but in order to [do] this I must and would have their obedience. If I had occasion to punish again it would be more and more severely, until they yielded, and were trying to be good. But the children still lacked faith in my words, and if my recollection serves me, I spent most of the afternoon in alternate whippings and exhortations, the former always increasing in intensity, until at last, finding the difference between capricious anger and steadfast determination, they submitted. This was the first and last of corporeal punishment in that school. The next morning, and ever after, I had docile and orderly scholars. I was careful duly to send them out for recreation, to make their studies pleasant and interesting, and to praise them when they did well, and mention to their parents their good behavior.

Our school was soon the admiration of the neighborhood. Some of the literati of the region heard of the marvelous progress the children made, and of classes formed and instruction given in higher branches; and coming to visit us, they encouraged me in my school, and gave me valuable commendation.

At the close of this summer school, I determined to seek abroad advantages, especially in drawing and painting, with reference to future teaching. The two only remaining sons of my mother had become merchants in Petersburg, Virgina, and were able and willing to furnish assistance to their younger sisters, and also to relieve our parents from the dread of indebtedness, which at one time their utmost exertions could scarcely keep from crossing the domestic threshold.

After several years of alternate teaching and studying, Emma Hart joined her old teacher Dr. Miner as an assistant. Then at age twenty-one she took over a female seminary in Middlebury, Vermont, and two years later married John Willard, a doctor there.

When I began my boarding school in Middlebury, in 1814, my leading motive was to relieve my husband from financial difficulties. I had also the further object of keeping a better school than those about me; but it was not until a year or two after, that I formed the design of effecting an important change in education, by the introduction of a grade of schools for women, higher than any heretofore known. My neighborhood to Middlebury College, made me bitterly feel the disparity in educational facilities between the two sexes; and I hoped that if the matter was once set before the men as legislators, they would be ready to correct the error. The idea that such a thing might possibly be effected by my means, seemed so presumptuous that I hesitated to entertain it, and for a short time concealed it even from my husband, although I knew that he sympathized in my general views. I began to write (because I could thus best arrange my ideas) "an address to the——Legislature, proposing a plan for improving Female Education." It was not till two years after that I filled up the blank. No one knew of my writing it, except my husband, until a year after it was completed (1816), for I knew that I should be regarded as visionary, almost to insanity, should I utter the expectations which I secretly entertained in connection with it. But it was not merely on the strength of my arguments that I relied. I determined to inform myself, and increase my personal influence and fame as a teacher; calculating that in this way I might be sought for in other places, where influential men would carry my project before some legislature, for the sake of obtaining a good school.

My exertions meanwhile, became unremitted and intense. My school grew to seventy pupils. I spent from ten to twelve hours a day in teaching, and on extraordinary occasions, as preparing for examination, fifteen; besides, always having under investigation some one new subject which, as I studied, I simultaneously taught to a class of my ablest pupils. Hence every new term some new study was introduced; and in all their studies, my pupils were very thoroughly trained. In classing my school for the term of study, which was then about three months, I gave to each her course, (being careful not to give too much) with the certain expectation, that she must be examined on it at the close of the term. Then I was wont to consider that my first duty as a teacher, required of me that I should labor to make my pupils by explanation and illustration *understand* their subject, and get them warmed into it, by making them see its beauties and its advantages. During this first part of the process, I talked much more than the pupils were required to do, keeping their attention awake by frequent questions, requiring short answers from the whole class—for it was ever my maxim, if attention fails, the teacher fails. Then in the *second* stage of my teaching, I made each scholar recite, in order that she might *remember*—paying special attention to the meaning of words, and to discern whether the subject was indeed understood without mistake. Then the *third* process was to make the pupil capable of *communicating.** And doing this in a right manner, was to

*"This threefold process, in some studies, as the Philosophy of the Mind, of which an entire view should be taken, requires the whole term; in others, as in geography and history, parts may be taken, and the pupils made thorough in each as they go along. In mathematics the three steps of the process are to be gone through with, as the teacher proceeds with every distinct proposition. But still, there will, in every well-instructed class, be this three-fold order prevailing, and during the term, requiring a beginning, a middle, and an end; the first of the term being mostly devoted to teaching, and the middle to reciting, and the last to acquiring a correct manner of communicating" [Editor's note in the 1861 publication].

prepare her for examination. At this time I personally examined all my classes.

This thorough teaching added rapidly to my reputation. Another important feature of a system, thus requiring careful drill and correct enunciation, was manifested by the examinations. The pupils, there acquired character and confidence. Scholars thus instructed were soon capable of teaching; and here were now forming my future teachers; and some were soon capable of aiding me in arranging the new studies, which I was constantly engaged in introducing.

Here I began a series of improvements in geography—separating and first teaching what could be learned from maps—then treating the various subjects of population, extent, length of rivers, &c., by comparing country with country, river with river, and city with city,—making out with the assistance of my pupils, those tables which afterwards appeared in Woodbridge and Willard's Geographies. Here also began improvements in educational history. Moral Philosophy came next, with Paley for the author, and Miss Hemingway for the first scholar; and then the Philosophy of the Mind—Locke the author, and the first scholars, Eliza Henshaw, Katharine Battey, and Minerva Shiperd.

The professors of the college attended my examinations; although I was by the President advised, that it would not be becoming in me, nor be a safe precedent, if I should attend theirs. So, as I had no teacher in learning my new studies, I had no model in teaching, or examining them. But I had full faith in the clear conclusions of my own mind. I knew that nothing could be truer than truth; and hence I fearlessly brought to examination, before the learned, the classes, to which had been taught the studies I had just acquired.

I soon began to have invitations to go from Middlebury. Gov. Van Ness, wishing me to go to Burlington, I opened my views to him. The college buildings were then nearly vacant, and some steps were taken towards using them for a Female Seminary, of which I was to be Principal, but the negotiations failed. In the spring of 1818, I had five pupils from Waterford, of the best families. On looking over the map of the United States, to see where would be the best geographical location for the projected institution, I had fixed my mind on the State of New York, and thought, that the best place would be somewhere in the vicinity of the head of navigation on the Hudson. Hence, the coming of the Waterford pupils I regarded as an important event. I presented my views to Gen. Van Schornhoven, the father (by adoption,) of one of my pupils,—who was interested, and proposed to show my manuscript to the Hon. J. Cramer, of Waterford, and to De Witt Clinton, then Governor of New York; and if they approved it, then the "Plan" might go before the legislature with some chance of success. Thereupon I copied the manuscript with due regard to manner and chirography; having already rewritten it some seven times, and thrown out about three quarters of what it first contained—then sent it to Gov. Clinton with the following letter:*

To his Excellency, De Witt Clinton,—

Sir—Mr. Southwick will present to you a manuscript, containing a plan for improving the education of females, by instituting public seminaries for their use. Its authoress has presumed to offer it to your Excellency, because she believed you would consider the subject as worthy of your attention, and because she wished to submit her scheme to those exalted characters, whose guide is reason, and whose objects are the happiness and improvement of mankind; and among these characters where can plans to promote those objects hope for countenance, if not from Mr. Clinton.

The manuscript is addressed to a legislature, although not intended for present publication. The authoress believed she could communicate her ideas with less circumlocution in this than in any other manner; and besides, should the approbation of distinguished citizens, in any of the larger and wealthier states, give hopes that such an application would be attended with success, a publication might be proper, and the manuscript would need less alteration.

Possibly your Excellency may consider this plan as better deserving your attention, to know that its authoress is not a visionary enthusiast, who has speculated in solitude without practical knowledge of her

---

*"We would observe, at this point, that the chirography of Mrs. Willard's letter, a copy of which now lies before us, is exquisitely neat, and boldly distinct. One element in her success, has been, no doubt, her beautiful penmanship, inherited from her father and carefully cultivated, as important to her educational objects" [Editor's note in the 1861 publication].

subject. For ten years she has been intimately conversant with female schools, and nearly all of that time she has herself been a preceptress. Nor has she written for the sake of writing, but merely to communicate a plan of which she fully believes that it is practicable; that, if realized, it would form a new and happy era in the history of her sex, and if of her sex, why not of her country, and of mankind? Nor would she shrink from any trial of this faith; for such is her conviction of the utility of her scheme, that could its execution be forwarded, by any exertion or any sacrifice of her own, neither the love of domestic ease, or the dread of responsibility, would prevent her embarking her reputation on its success.

If Mr. Clinton should not view this plan as its authoress hopes he may, but should think the time devoted to its perusal was sacrificed, let him not consider its presentation to him as the intrusion of an individual ignorant of the worth of his time, and the importance of his high avocations, but as the enthusiasm of a projector, misjudging of her project, and overrating its value.

With sentiments of the deepest respect, I am, Sir,

Your Obedient Servant,
Emma Willard
Middlebury, Vt., February 5, 1818.

This treatise is in reality the foundation of the Troy seminary. It will not be thought surprising that I awaited with intense feeling Gov. Clinton's reply. It came before I expected it, expressing his accordance with my views in his happiest manner. His message to the legislature soon followed, in which, referring to my "Plan" (though not by its title or author's name), he recommended legislative action in behalf of a cause heretofore wholly neglected. The Waterford gentlemen had made Gov. Clinton's opinion their guiding light. They were to present my "Plan" to the legislature; and advised that Dr. Willard and myself should spend a few weeks in Albany during the session, which we did. The Governor and many of his friends called on us; and I read my manuscript several times by special request to different influential members; and once to a considerable assemblage. The affair would have gone off by acclamation, could immediate action have been had. As it was, an act was passed incorporating the institution at Waterford; and another, to give to female academies a share of the literature fund. This law, the first whose sole object was to improve female education, is in force, and is the same by which female academies in the state now receive public money.

Teaching in the Little Red Schoolhouse

Lucia B. Downing

From Lucia B. Downing, "Teaching in the Keeler 'Deestrict' School," *Vermont Quarterly, A Magazine of History*, n.s., Vol. XIX, no. 4 (October 1951), pp. 233–40.

Although Lucia Downing (1868–1945), the author of this lively reminiscence, began her teaching career in 1882— nearly eighty years after Emma Hart—she faced similar challenges. In a farm village, a plucky fourteen-year-old could still be mistress of an entire school. Free to enforce discipline and design the curriculum, Lucia Downing evidently thrived under the responsibility entrusted her. "Boarding out" (living with the family of a pupil) afforded her a welcomed escape from the identity of "little sister," and the work revealed her future career. She graduated from the University of Vermont in 1889, and taught in Vermont and Pennsylvania before her marriage.

Still sits the schoolhouse by the road,
A ragged beggar sunning;
Around it still the sumacs grow,
And blackberry vines are running.

It is still standing—the little red schoolhouse where I, a little girl barely fourteen, began my career as a teacher; still standing, though with sunken roof and broken windows, a solitary reminder of the days of long ago. No longer does its door's worn sill resound to the clatter of copper-toed boots; no longer does its smoking box-stove drive pupils and teacher out into the frosty air; never again on a summer's day will the passer-by hear the droning sound of the ab-abs, or the singsong recital of the multiplication table. The children, if there are any now in the old "Keeler Deestrict," clamber into a bus and ride merrily away to a central seat of learning five miles distant. "Time rolls his ceaseless course!"

In the days of my adventure, Vermont had no law restricting the age or youth, of a teacher, but shortly after my experience, and possibly consequent thereto, the state passed a law making sixteen the earliest age at which one might begin what Thompson, who probably never taught a day in his life, calls

Delightful task! to rear the tender thought,
To teach the young idea how to shoot.

In our little town, the duties of a school superintendent were not burdensome, nor the position lucrative, and for many years our superintendent was the village doctor (Dr. L.C. Butler), who was probably the best-educated man in town, not even excepting the minister! The doctor could easily combine the two occupations—I had almost said "kill two birds with one stone!" For instance, he could visit the school on Brigham Hill when he had a patient up there, and save a trip up a steep hill with narrow, rocky road, which even to a Ford presents difficulties to this day. The doctor lived about two miles out of the village (Page's Corners) in a lovely old colonial house, once used as an inn and a popular Mecca for horseback parties in the good old days. There was a schoolhouse—red, of course—just across the road, and the doctor could drop in there any time. But to the teachers in outlying districts it was a decided advantage to have a doctor for supervisor. The teacher always knew if any one in the neighborhood was sick, and she could keep watch of the road. When old white Dolly, drawing the easy low phaeton, hove in sight, there was time to furbish up a little, and call out a class of the brightest pupils!

The doctor had vaccinated me when a little girl came from Canada with symptoms of that dreaded disease, small pox, and all the parents were calling him in. And he had brought me through measles and chicken pox, and his wife was my Sunday

School teacher, and I was not a bit afraid of him. So when my sister, already a teacher, went to take another examination, the spring I was thirteen, I went along too, and said to the doctor, who was only a superintendent that day, that, if he had enough papers, I should like to see how many questions I could answer. The doctor smiled at me, and gave me an arithmetic paper for a starter. It proved to be easy, for it brought in some favorite problems in percentage, which would be an advantage to a merchant, as they showed how to mark goods in such a way that one could sell below the marked price, and still make a profit. I guess all merchants must have studied Greenleaf's *Arithmetic!* There was either a problem under the old Vermont Annual Interest Rule, or we were asked to write the rule. As it covered a half page in the book, writing it out involved some labor. I felt quite well pleased with my paper, and then proudly started on Grammar. I knew I could do something with that, for I loved to parse and analyze and "diagram," according to Reed and Kellogg. In fact, my first knowledge, and for many years my only knowledge, of "Paradise Lost" was gleaned from a little blue parsing book, and I have always been puzzled to know whether "barbaric" modifies "kings" or "pearl and gold":

High on a throne of royal state, which far
Outshone the wealth of Ormus and of Ind,
Or where the gorgeous East with richest hand
Showers on her kings barbaric pearl and gold,
Satan exalted sat.

Next came Geography. Though I had never traveled farther than Burlington, I knew, thanks to Mr. Guyot and his green geography, that Senegambia was "rich in gold, iron ore and gum-producing trees." (I always supposed it was "spruce gum," so popular before gutta-percha and licorices were combined and put up in slabs.) History and Civil Government were pretty hard for me, but next came Physiology, and I made the most of my bones and circulatory system, hoping to impress the physician. But it was in Theory and School Management that I did myself proud. I discoursed at length on ventilation and temperature, and, knowing that "good government" is a most desirable and necessary qualification for a teacher, I advocated a firm, but kind and gentle method, with dignity of bearing. In giving my views of corporal punishment, I related a story I had read of the Yankee teacher who was asked his views on the subject. He said, "Wal, moral suasion's my theory, but lickin's my practice!". When I reported at home that I had told that story, my Father laughed, but Mother expressed deep disgust.

When I compared notes with my sister, in regard to my answers, I began to feel that I did not know as much as I thought I did! An anxious week followed, and I haunted the post office. Finally, one morning, there was an envelope addressed in Dr. Butler's scholarly hand, but it bore my sister's name, and there was none for me. I was heartbroken—evidently my record was so poor that he was not going to tell me how I stood. But, as my sister opened her envelope, out fluttered two yellow slips—two certificates, entitling the recipients to teach in Vermont for one year. And one was in my name! I cannot recall any subsequent joy equal to what I felt at that moment—even a college diploma and a Phi Beta Kappa key, in later years, brought less of a thrill.

Of course, the eight or ten districts in town were already supplied with teachers, and no doubt that was why I was given a certificate, instead of a mere statement of standing. But one day my chum (Lena Brown) told me that in her Grandfather Keeler's district they planned to open up the old schoolhouse, unused for years because there were no children. Now there were at least four, of school age, and a school was demanded. She said the committeeman was Mr. Nichols (Charles Nichols), a friend of my father, and I insisted that he be interviewed. Thinking it was the "big girl" Father was talking about, Mr. Nichols talked very encouragingly, but when he found it was I who thus aspired, he laughed scornfully. Although Father told him I had a certificate, and was really bigger than the "big" one, the case looked hopeless. Sometime later he came to the house, and I happened to be the only member of the family at home. After various circumlocutions he told me that I might try it. He said they could not pay much, as there probably would be only four scholars, and said he would let me know when school would open and where I should board—"boarding-around" was gone by at that time. I was the happiest person in town that night, but later I heard he had said to others that, with so few scholars, it didn't matter much anyway—and I made up my mind to do or die.

Before the term opened I had a birthday and attained the mature age of fourteen, but, in spite of unusual height for my years, I really did not look very old, and my chief anxiety was to acquire the appearance that for many years now I have made every effort to avoid! My skirts were fearfully short, and though Mother let out the last tuck and hem, they only reached to the tops of my buttoned boots, and, unless I was careful in seating myself, there was a glimpse of my stockings that no modest young woman, especially a teacher, should permit! However, Mother sewed a watch-pocket in my little dresses, and gave me her watch, a lovely little Swiss, with wide-open face, and there was a gorgeous long chain. You can't think how much dignity was added thereby! The next difficulty was my hair, heavy and long, and the only way I could fix it was to make a long, thick, childish braid. But, after many experiments, I achieved a way of folding it up, under and under, tying it close to my head, and I thought it resembled a real pug.

It was to be a fall term, and it probably opened late in August. The morning dawned when I was to begin "the glorious adventure." Father harnessed old Diamond—he was just my age, but what is old age for a horse is youth to a human being—and I came out with a little black bag, borrowed from Mother, and wearing my blue gingham dress. I had insisted on wearing that one, because it was a half-inch longer than any other. I can visualize it now—rather tight at the waist, fortunately for the watch-pocket, with ruffles at the bottom.

I was supposed to board in the family of a Mr. Vespasian Leach, a former merchant, who, like many such, had retired to a farm. As we jogged along, we met Mr. Leach taking his milk to the cheese factory, and he told us that, owing to sickness, they could not take a boarder. My father expressed his regret, and, with fine old-fashioned courtesy, said he had counted on my being looked after by these old friends. Presently we met Mr. Nichols, and he said that I was to board in *his* family. Father said he was delighted to know that, and he would not worry about me at all. After we passed along I said, "Why, Father, you told Mr. Leach how sorry you are, and now you tell Mr. Nichols how glad you are." I do not recall his explanation, except that it sounded very reasonable, and that was my first lesson in diplomacy. I see now that there was no dishonesty in my father's mind or language.

Well, we journeyed on, passing the schoolhouse on the way to the Nichols farm. I don't know how I felt—that is one of the things I can't remember! I was to go home week-ends, though of course we called it "over Sunday," and it looked to me like a long, long week. Mr. Nichols was a wealthy farmer, with a grown-up family; and one son, with his wife and two babies (only one baby the first week), lived at home. There were menservants and maidservants galore, and we all sat down to most marvelous meals at a long table in a big dining-room. And what wonderful food! Picture it, even if you have not had the experience, and have not the imagination, of an Ichabod Crane! We did not have exactly the things to eat that made the pedagogue's mouth water in anticipation, but in retrospection it seems that nothing could be so good again as what was daily set before us. We did not have a young roast pig, but we had delicious home-smoked ham and tender roasts, and milk-fed chickens and honey with biscuits rich with cream, and then all the fruits and vegetables that early fall makes possible on a rich "interval" farm, besides plenty of eggs and cream and butter.

Then, too, I was treated like an honored guest, and given the "spare room" with blue walls and curtains, and was always addressed as "Teacher"— much to my satisfaction. I had really worried over that matter, for to call me Miss B. was absurd, and I feared I might be addressed by a familiar nickname, or pet name, which was most undignified. But, with the new title, my self-respect increased amazingly, and also my *conceit*. After four o'clock I was free from school duties, and I enjoyed the family life, playing with the two babies, or listening to the little parlor organ, played by some member of the family, and often there was a song by the son. I remember how he sang "Finnegan's Wake," and the song about the man from India, who ate ice cream and could never get warm again.

From nine to twelve and from one to four I was supposed to spend in the schoolhouse, and I can't see how I ever managed to put in the time—six long hours every day—with four pupils! Most of the time there were only four (four—all named Leach—two families), but one morning the number was increased. I was startled to see a young lady in trailing gown (how I envied her) approach and ask if she might come to school, adding that she loved me, just seeing me go by the house! She brought with her a little purple primer, with such lucid and inspiring sentences as, "Lo, I go! See me go up." She had learned to read out of that antiquated book before I was born, but in the intervening years reading had become a lost art, and she was ready to begin all over. It was a wonderful help to me in killing time, for each day we could go over and over the same thing, never too often to please her, as she stood by me and picked out the sentences, letter by letter.

But I still wonder how I put in the time. I did not knit or crochet, for I had heard of teachers who had made trouble for themselves by so doing. I was not skilful at drawing, and I couldn't sing much, being like the old woman who knew just two tunes—"Old Hundred" and "Doxology"! and when each pupil had read and ciphered and spelled and passed the water and recessed and recessed and passed the water and spelled and had a lesson in geography and read and spelled, there was usually an hour before I dared dismiss them. I sometimes carried my watch key to school and turned the hands ahead, but that took me home to the committee-man's too early. Parents, what few there were, I suppose were glad to be relieved of the care of their offspring, and no one ever suggested a shortening of the hours. I had to earn my salary! We had few books, and my principal memorizing had been confined to the Westminster Catechism with its one hundred and seven long answers, but I knew a few poems, and I taught the children all I knew. I devised what I thought was a wonderful set of "Instructive Questions and Answers," suggested by a *New England Primer* that had come down in our family, but I did not limit the field of instuction to matters Biblical, attempting rather to cover the entire realm of knowledge in art, science, history, literature and what you will.

My pride suffered several falls. I did not have very good discipline, for one thing. Then, when I was proud of my success in teaching a boy to read by the word method, just coming into use, I ventured to suggest that words were made up of letters, and began to point them out. He said, "Yes, I knew my letters last year, and that's why I know how to read." Then there was one *big* boy who was *peeved* because I would not allow him the same privilege as the little ones who always wanted to kiss "Teacher" good night. And my oldest pupil took a dislike to her teacher, as sudden and as inexplicable as her erstwhile fondness.

The glorious autumn days flew by, and the ten weeks' term was drawing to a close. One of the most arduous tasks was "keeping the register," and the consequent figuring up of averages at the end of the term. There was the total number of days' attendance by all pupils; the average attendance per day, which would have been a fine record, except for the defection of the oldest pupil, and the number of days' attendance per pupil. My sister showed me how to do all those things, but there was a vital question that I was obliged to leave until the last moment, namely, the amount of salary received. Except that it would be a small salary, the subject had never been mentioned. I was worried; just suppose I did not get enough to pay my board! I really had eaten a great deal, and I knew Father would not want to pay my board, even if he had the money. Waiting until the last possible moment to finish my register, I approached Mr. Nichols after one of the fine dinners we always had. When I spoke of my difficulty in completing the register, he looked worried—maybe he had heard of those averages! But, as I told him my *real* difficulty, he looked relieved, and smiled, as he said, in his delightful, cultured Yankee drawl, that the *district calculated* they could afford to pay three dollars and a half a week, to cover salary and board, the proportion to be determined by the committeeman, and he had decided to give me two dollars a week for my work, and take only a dollar and a half for board, which, I may say, was a most generous arrangement, in view of everything!

But the last days of school were busy ones. I drilled the scholars on the pieces they were to speak—I can remember one of them now, "Little Dan"—and I told the children how important it was that they should behave well the last day, if never before or later. And school ended in a blaze of glory, a vast and terrifying audience having assembled—entirely out of proportion to the number of pupils. There were fond parents, and grandparents, and aunts and uncles and cousins thrice removed. I think there were twenty-five visitors and only four scholars, but the children did very well. They went through some specially prepared lessons in the various subjects they had been studying; they spoke their pieces without prompting, and they went glibly through the "Instructive Questions and Answers," though if I had made a slip and asked the questions out of order, the results might have been disastrous. They might have said that Vermont is the largest state in the Union, or that George Washington had sailed the ocean blue in 1492, or that Rome was built by Julius Caesar, but I do not recall that any such contretemps occurred. I do fear, however, that "Teacher," herself, was at that time a bit uncertain as to whether the *I. Watts* who wrote hymns was the *J. Watt* whose mother had a teakettle. Everything went off well, and I presented the children with cards, for which I had borrowed the money from my sister, and my pupils and their friends said goodbye, and I went proudly home with twenty dollars, the remuneration for ten weeks of toil. But never before or since has that sum of money gone so far. I went to Burlington the next week, and I bought blue flannel for a dress, a photograph album, a cage for my canary, a beaver hat, and numerous small things, besides paying up for my cards.

I went back to school, picking up my work at the Academy, and I felt rather superior to my classmates. When spring came, I was flattered to be asked to go back and teach another term. I was told that children had moved into the neighborhood, some had become of school age, and some had even been born, in the hope of going to school to me! I went back, and completed my second term as a teacher while I was fourteen. I had fifteen scholars, and probably more salary, though I do not remember. As a matter of fact, I do not recall much about that second term and the other terms I taught there and elsewhere during my school and college course. But the incidents of that first term are still vivid in my mind after nearly half a century. It was an unusual experience, and the events of each week were told over at home, and repeated to any one who would listen, as I did a "round, unvarnished tale deliver." In the telling I have not exaggerated or drawn upon my imagination, but as I call the old time back, memories rush upon me, and I can visualize the scene, and it is all as fresh as if it had happened yesterday.

Remedy for Wrongs to Women

Catherine Beecher

From Catherine Beecher, *The Evils Suffered by American Women and American Children: The Causes and the Remedy* (New York: Harper & Bros., 1846).

An early (1846) and significant document proposing that teaching is woman's "true" profession was the "Address on the Evils Suffered by American Women and American Children," by Catherine Beecher (1800–1878). Stylistically florid by today's standards, the excerpts that follow convey the exhuberence and drama Beecher brought to her subject. The daughter of a minister—the calling also followed by her seven brothers—Beecher assumed an exclusively Christian ethic and audience. Her "Address" was not so much an argument as a series of assaults on the moral sensibilities of that audience. Her intention was to promote her favorite scheme, that of sending women teachers to open schools "at the West" (that is, in Ohio, Illinois, Iowa, and Wisconsin). Beecher believed that "Christian female teachers" could save two million children growing up in ignorance, and at the same time remedy the depression of "our sex" by setting a model of "healthy and productive labor." Through the Board of National Popular Education, several thousand teachers did go West in the 1840s and 1850s, and normal schools were founded in Wisconsin, Iowa, and Illinois.

For the history of women in teaching, however, the interest of this article lies not in the mission to the West, but in Beecher's assertion that women, not men, should educate children, and that teaching should be regarded not as

drudgery, but as "the noblest of all professions." Despite her
advocacy of self-sacrifice and her anti-suffrage position,
Beecher envisioned for women a domestic sphere that gave
them, rather than men, power to shape society.

Address

Ladies and Friends:

The immediate object which has called us together, is an
enterprise now in progress, the design of which is *to educate
destitute American children, by the agency of American women.*
It is an effort which has engaged the exertions of a large number
of ladies of various sects, and of all sections in our country, and
one which, though commencing in a humble way and on a small
scale, we believe is eventually to exert a most extensive and
saving influence through the nation.

Permit me first to present some facts in regard to the situation
of an immense number of young children in this land, for whom
your sympathies at this time are sought. Few are aware of the
deplorable destitution of our country in regard to the education
of the rising generation, or of the long train of wrongs and
sufferings endured by multitudes of young children from this
neglect.

The last twelve years I have resided chiefly at the West, and
my attention has been directed to the various interests of
education. In five of the largest western states I have spent from
several weeks to several months—I have traveled extensively
and have corresponded or conversed with well-informed gentlemen and ladies on this subject in most of the western states. And
I now have materials for presenting the real situation of vast
multitudes of American children, which would "cause the ear
that heareth it to tingle." But I dare not do it. It would be so
revolting—so disgraceful—so heart-rending—so incredible—
that in the first place, I should not be believed; and in the next
place, such an outcry of odium and indignation would be aroused
as would impede efforts to remedy the evil. The only thing I can
safely do is to present some statistics, which cannot be disputed,
because they are obtained from *official documents* submitted by
civil officers to our national or state legislatures. Look then at

the census, and by its data we shall find that *now* there are nearly a million adults who cannot read and write, and more than *two millions* children utterly illiterate, and entirely without schools. Look at individual states, and we shall find Ohio and Kentucky, the two best supplied of our western states, demanding *five thousand* teachers each, to supply them in the same ration as Massachusetts is supplied. *Ten thousand* teachers are now needed in Ohio and Kentucky alone, to furnish schools for more than two hundred thousand children, who otherwise must grow up in utter ignorance.

To exhibit some faint idea of the results of such neglect, let me give an extract from a private letter of a friend of mine, on a journey of observation in regard to education in one of these states, which was addressed to his children.

Could you, my dear daughters, see what I in my journeys so often see, the poor of your own sex and age, limited in wardrobe to one sordid cotton garment, without education to read a word, without skill to make or mend a garment, without a sufficient variety of proper food to unfold their forms to any perfection, lank as greyhounds, and their clothes hanging upon them like dresses upon a broomstick, and yet possessed of all your native love of dress, your quick capacity and your sprightliness, I do think you would behave better, be more humble, study harder, and feel more kindly to the poor than you ever have done. And yet what is all this to having the mind darkened, the feelings hardened, and the interests of the soul neglected, as is the case with many thousands around me? My heart bleeds at the irreligion, abject poverty, filth, and wretched vice which everywhere prevail. But my Heavenly Father enables me to hold on, and I am tolerably well: yet I cannot say that I am cheerful; it is too intolerable, and my spirits sink. The Methodist circuit riders are doing something, and have pitched upon the very plan I had thought of, that of having *traveling schools* among the most sparsely settled districts. Oh that our Heavenly Father may bless my mission, and that light may enter here!

This presents only a glance at the forlorn and degraded state of large portions of our country where education is totally neglected. A picture almost as melancholy is presented when we examine into the shocking abuse of young children in some of those states which are doing the most for education. The state of New York, for a few years, has been making exemplary efforts to raise her common schools from the low state in which they were found. In every county of the state a salaried officer devotes his whole time to the improvement of the common schools in his county, and every year he sends an account of them, to be presented to the legislature by the state superintendent.

The following is extracted from the general report made up by the general superintendent from these reports of the county superintendents for the year 1844.

The nakedness and deformity of the great majority of the schools, the comfortless and dilapidated buildings, the unhung doors, broken sashes, absent panes, stilted benches, yawning roofs, and muddy, moldering floors, are faithfully portrayed; and many of the self-styled teachers, who lash and dogmatize in these miserable tenements of humanity, are shown to be low, vulgar, obscene, intemperate, and utterly incompetent to teach anything good. Thousands of the young are repelled from improvement, and contract a durable horror for books, by ignorant, injudicious, and even cruel modes of instruction. When the piteous moans and tears of the little pupils supplicate for exemption from the cold drudgery or the more pungent suffering of the school, let the humane parent be careful to ascertain the true cause of grief and lamentation. . . . No subject connected with the cause of elementary education affords a source for such humiliating reflection, as that of the condition of a large portion of the school-houses visited. Only one-third of the whole number were found in good repair; another third in only comfortable circumstances; while *three thousand, three hundred and nineteen* were unfit for the reception of either man or beast. Seven thousand we found destitute of any playground, nearly six thousand destitute of convenient seats and desks, and nearly eight thousand destitute of any proper facilities for ventilation; while *six thousand* were destitute of outdoor facilities for securing modesty and decency!

And it is in these miserable abodes of filth and dirt, deprived of wholesome air or exposed to the assaults of the elements, with no facilities for exercise or relaxation, with no conveniences for prosecuting their studies, crowded on to comfortless benches, and driven by dire necessity to violate the most common rules of decency and modesty, that upward of *six hundred thousand* children of this state are compelled to spend an average of eight months each year of their pupilage! Here the first lessons of human life, the incipient principles of morality, and the rules of social intercourse, are to be impressed upon the plastic mind. The boy is here to receive the permanent model of his character, and imbibe the elements of his future career. Here the instinctive delicacy of the young female, the characteristic ornament of her sex, is to be expanded into maturity by precept and example. Such are the temples of science, such the ministers under whose care susceptible childhood is to receive its earliest impressions! Great God! shall man dare to charge to *thy* dispensations the vices, the crimes, the sickness, the sorrows, the miseries and brevity of human life, who sends his little children to a pest-house fraught with the deadly malaria of both moral and physical disease? Instead of impious murmurs, let him lay his hand upon his mouth, and his mouth in the dust, and cry unclean!

It must be remembered that this is the dark side of the picture. Were it my object to show how much New York excels most other states in her care of education, I should speak of her noble school system (one of the best in the world), her liberal provision for school libraries and apparatus, her well-endowed normal school, the many philanthropic citizens who labor in this cause, the great success that has crowned their efforts, and the very superior teachers and schools so often found in that state. But my object is to show how much neglect and abuse there is *where most is done.* How much worse then must it be in those states where less is attempted! New York has done so much that she is not ashamed to search out her defects and publish them, that they may be remedied. Those states which are behind her in efforts, have a still more fearful reckoning yet to come.

How must it look to those benevolent spirits who minister to these despised little ones of our country, whose whole career for eternity depends upon their training in this life, living among civilized and even Christian people, so neglected, so utterly contemned, that anything on earth secures more attention and interest than the work of rearing them to virtue and heaven! Christian women are sitting in the reach of their young voices, twining silk, working worsted, conning poetry and novels, enjoying life and its pleasures, and not lifting a hand or spending a thought to save them. Thus it is that two millions of American children are left without any teachers at all, while, of those who go to school, a large portion of the youngest and tenderest are turned over to coarse, hard, unfeeling men, too lazy or too stupid to follow the appropriate duties of their sex....

I wish now to point out certain causes which have exerted a depressing influence upon our sex in this land; for we shall find that the very same effort, which aims to benefit the children of our country, will tend almost equally to benefit our own sex. The first cause that bears heavily on our sex is, the fact that in our country, the principle of *caste*, which is one of the strongest and most inveterate in our nature, is strongly arrayed against *healthful and productive labor.*

To understand the power of this principle, see what sacrifices men and women make, and what toils they endure, to save themselves from whatever sinks them in station and estimation. And this is a principle which is equally powerful in high and low, rich and poor. To observe how it bears against healthful and productive labor, let any woman, who esteems herself in the higher grades of society, put the case as her own, and imagine that her son, or brother, is about to marry a young lady, whose character and education are every way lovely and unexceptionable, but who, it appears, is a *seamstress,* or a *nurse,* or a *domestic,* and how few are there, who will not be conscious of the opposing principle of *caste.* But suppose the young lady to be one, who has been earning her livelihood by writing poetry and love stories, or who has lived all her days in utter idleness, and how suddenly the feelings are changed! Now, all the comfort and happiness of society depend upon having that work properly performed, which is done by nurses, seamstresses, chambermaids, and cooks; and so long as this kind of work is held to be degrading, and those who perform it are allowed to grow up ignorant and vulgar, and then are held down by the prejudices of caste, every woman will use the greatest efforts, and undergo the greatest privations, to escape from the degraded and discreditable position. And this state of society is now, by the natural course of things, bringing a just retribution on the classes who cherish it. Domestics are forsaking the kitchen, and thronging to the workshop and manufactory, and *mainly* under the influence of the principle of *caste;* while the family state suffers keenly from the loss. Meantime the daughters of wealth have their intellectual faculties and their sensibilities developed, while all the household labor, which would equally develop their physical powers, and save from ill-health, is turned off to hired domestics, or a slaving mother. The only remedy for this evil is, securing a proper education for all classes, and making productive labor honorable, by having all classes engage in it.

The next cause which bears severely on the welfare of our sex, is the *excess of female population* in the older states from the disproportionate emigration of the other sex. By the census we find in only three of the small older states, *twenty thousand* more women than men, and a similar disproportion is found in other states. The consequence is, that all branches of female employment in the older states are thronged, while in our new states, domestics, nurses, seamstresses, mantua-makers, and female teachers are in great demand. In consequence of this, women at the East become operatives in shops and mills, and at the West, men become teachers of little children, thus exchanging the appropriate labors of the sexes, in a manner injurious to all concerned.

Meantime, capitalists at the East avail themselves of this excess of female hands. Large establishments are set up in eastern cities to manufacture clothing. Work of all kinds is got from poor women, at prices that will not keep soul and body together; and then the articles thus made are sold for prices that give monstrous profits to the capitalist, who thus grows rich on the hard labors of our sex. Tales there are to be told of the sufferings of American women in our eastern cities, so shocking that they would scarcely be credited, and yet they are true beyond all dispute.

The following extracts, from some statistics recently obtained in New York city, verify what has been stated.

There are now in this city, according to close estimates, *ten thousand* women who live by the earnings of the needle. On an average, these women, by working twelve or fourteen hours a-day, can earn only *twelve and a half cents*, with which they are to pay for rent, fuel, clothes, and food.

Here follow the prices paid for various articles of women's work at the clothing stores, and then the following:—

A great multitude of women are employed in making men's and boy's caps. We are told by an old lady, who lives by this work, that when she begins at sunrise and works till midnight, she earns *fourteen cents a-day!* That is, *eighty-four cents* a week, for incessant toil every waking hour, and this her sole income for every want! A large majority of these women are American born; some have been rich, many have enjoyed the ease of competence; some are young girls without homes; some are widows; some the wives of drunken husbands. The manner in which these women live; the squalidness, unhealthy location and nature of their habitations; their total want of recreation, or of intellectual or moral improvement; their forlorn situation in all respects, *may* be imagined, but we assure the public, that it would require an extremely active imagination to conceive the reality. When winter comes they are destitute of means to obtain fuel or warm clothing, while their work is often cut off, and then they have no resource but the poor-house, or the pauper ticket; and in this misery they have been often found so given over to despair, at repeated rebuffs from overdriven officers, that they have resolved to starve without further effort. . . .

Let us now turn to another class of our countrywomen— the *female operatives* in our shops and mills. Unfortunately, this subject cannot be freely discussed without danger of collision with the vast pecuniary and party interests connected with it. I therefore shall simply *state facts,* without expressing the impressions of my own mind.

Last year, I spent several days in Lowell, for the sole purpose of investigating this subject. I conversed with agents, overseers, clergymen, physicians, editors, ladies resident in the place, and a large number of the operatives themselves. All seemed disposed to present the most favorable side of the picture; and nothing unfavorable was said except as drawn forth by my questions.

In favor of this situation it was urged, that none were forced to go, or to stay in the mills, and therefore all must believe themselves better off there than in any other situation at command; that owners and agents incur great pains and expense to secure the physical comfort and intellectual and moral improvement of the operatives; that much care is used to exclude vicious persons; that great pains are taken to secure respectable women to keep the boarding-houses; that the board and lodging provided are at least comfortable; that the state of society and morals is good, and is superior to what many enjoy at home; that the *esprit du corps* of the community guards its morals; that there is much good society among the operatives, as is manifest from the great number who have been school teachers; that the bills of mortality show that there are fewer deaths in proportion than in other country places; and finally, that the night schools, Sunday schools, and faithful labors of the clergy secure great advantages and most favorable results....

Let me now present the facts I learned by observation or inquiry on the spot. I was there in mid-winter, and every morning I was wakened at *five*, by the bells calling to labor. The time allowed for dressing and breakfast was so short, as many told me, that both were performed hurriedly, and then the work at the mills was begun by lamp-light, and prosecuted without remission till twelve, and chiefly in a standing position. Then half an hour only allowed for dinner, from which the time for going and returning was deducted. Then back to the mills, to work till seven o'clock, the last part of the time by lamp-light. Then returning, washing, dressing, and supper occupied another hour. Thus ten hours only remained for recreation and sleep. Now eight hours' sleep is required for laborers, and none in our country are employed in labor more hours than the female operatives in mills. Deduct eight hours for sleep and only *two hours* remain for shopping, mending, making, recreation, social intercourse, and *breathing the pure air.* For it must be remembered that all the hours of labor are spent in rooms where lamps together with from forty to eighty persons, are exhausting the healthful principle of the air, where the temperature, both summer and winter, on account of the work, must be kept at 70°, and in some rooms at 80°, and where the air is loaded with particles of cotton thrown from thousands of cards, spindles, and looms....

As to the *wages,* the average is found to be $1.75 a week; but they are paid by *the job,* so that all are thus stimulated to work as much as possible every day, while prizes are given to such overseers as get the most work out of those they superintend. Thus everything goes under the stimulus of rivalry, ambition, and the excitement of gain, leading multitudes to sacrifice health for money. Thus it is said that the hours of labor are not more than the majority of the operatives desire, while sometimes even the regular hours are exceeded, to the great discontent of the over-worked and feeble minority. As to the large sums deposited in the Savings' bank, it is found that, of six thousand women, less than one thousand have made such deposits, and the *average* of such deposits do not amount to but about $100 for each depositor for three years of such hazardous toils....

Now, without expressing any opinion as to the influence, on health and morals, of taking women away from domestic habits and pursuits, to labor with men in shops and mills, I simply ask if it would not be *better* to put the thousands of men who are keeping school for young children into the mills, and employ the women to train the children?

Wherever education is most prosperous, there woman is employed more than man. In Massachusetts, where education is highest, five out of seven of the teachers are women; while in Kentucky, where education is so much lower, five out of six of the teachers are men.

Another cause of depression to our sex is found in the fact that there is no profession for women of education and high position, which, like law, medicine, and theology, opens the way to competence, influence, and honor, and presents motives for exertion. Woman ought never to be led to married life except under the promptings of pure affection. To marry for an establishment, for a position, or for something to do, is a deplorable wrong. But how many women, for want of a high and honorable profession to engage their time, are led to this melancholy course. This is not because Providence has not provided an ample place for such a profession for woman, but because custom or prejudice, or a low estimate of its honorable character, prevents her from entering it. *The educating of children, that* is the true and noble profession of a woman—*that* is what is worthy the noblest powers and affections of the noblest minds.

Another cause which deeply affects the best interests of our sex is the contempt, or utter neglect and indifference, which has befallen this only noble profession open to woman. There is no employment, however disagreeable or however wicked, which custom and fashion cannot render elegant, interesting, and enthusiastically sought. A striking proof of this is seen in the military profession. This is the profession of *killing our fellow-*
(text continued on page 48)

The Teacher "Becomes" a Woman

1: Emma Willard, founder of Troy Female Seminary (1821), devoted her life to educational equality for women.
2: "Standards of America," 1897. By the close of the nineteenth century, as this image makes evident, the public schools had become one of the nation's most important institutions. Behind most desks were female teachers.
3: "The Schoolmistress," 1853 engraving. In the early popular consciousness, the teacher was often a dour-faced "old maid" with a switch; the stereotype persists today.
4: "The Country School," 1871. This Winslow Homer painting suggests another cherished American concept, the ideal, one-room school governed by a pure and gentle, self-sacrificing schoolmarm.

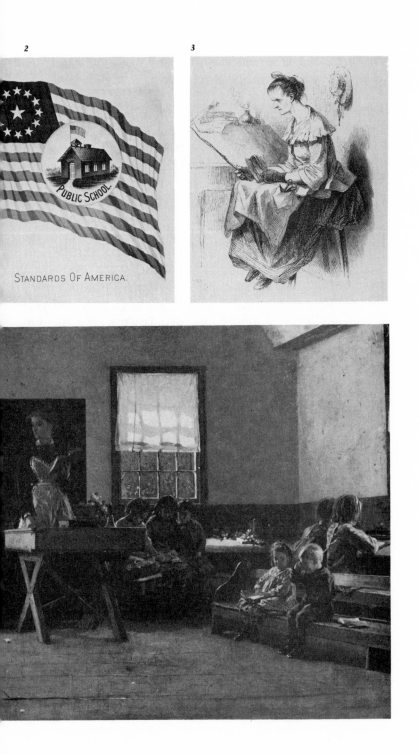

STANDARDS OF AMERICA.

creatures, and is attended with everything low, brutal, un-christian, and disgusting; and yet what halos of glory have been hung around it, and how the young, and generous, and enthusiastic have been drawn into it! If one-half the poetry, fiction, oratory, and taste thus misemployed had been used to embellish and elevate the employment of training the mind of childhood, in what an altered position should we find this noblest of all professions!

As it is, the employment of teaching children is regarded as the most wearying drudgery, and few resort to it except from necessity; and one very reasonable cause of this aversion is the utter neglect of any arrangements for *preparing* teachers for this arduous and difficult profession. The mind of a young child is like a curious instrument, capable of exquisite harmony when touched by a skillful hand, but sending forth only annoying harshness when unskillfully addressed. To a teacher is commit-ted a collection of these delicate contrivances; and, without experience, without instruction, it is required not only that each one should be tuned aright, but that all be combined in excellent harmony: as if a young girl were sent into a splendid orchestra, all ignorant and unskillful, and required to draw melody from each instrument, and then to combine the whole in faultless harmony. And in each case there are, here and there, individual minds, who, without instruction, are gifted by nature with aptness and skill in managing the music either of matter or of mind; but that does not lessen the folly, in either case, of expecting the whole profession, either of music or of teaching, to be pursued without preparatory training.

Look now into this small school-room, where are assembled a collection of children, with a teacher unskillful in her art. What noise and disorder!—what indolence, and discontent, and misrule! The children hate school and all that belongs to it, and the teacher regards the children as little better than incarnate imps!

Look, again, into another, where the teacher, fitted by nature or trained by instruction and experience, is qualified for her office. See the little happy group around their best-beloved friend—their *beau ideal* of all that is good, and wise, and lovely! How their bright eyes sparkle as she opens the casket of knowledge and deals out its treasures! How their young hearts throb with generous and good emotions, as she touches the thrilling chords she has learned so skillfully to play! What neatness and order in all her little dominion! What ready obedience, what loving submission, what contrite confession, what generous aspirations after all that is good and holy! She spends the pleasant hours of school in the exercise of the noblest powers of intellect and feeling. She goes to rest at night, reviewing with gratitude the results of her toils; and as she sends up her daily thanks and petitions for her little ones, how does the world of peace and purity open to her vision, where, by the river of life, she shall gather her happy flock, and look back to earth, and on through endless years, to trace the sublime and never-ending results of her labors. Oh, beautiful office!— sublime employment! When will it attain its true honors and esteem?

There is another class of evils, endured by a large class of well-educated, unmarried women of the more wealthy classes, little understood or appreciated, but yet real and severe. It is the suffering that results from the *inactivity of cultivated intellect and feeling.*

The more a mind has its powers of feeling and action enlarged by cultivation, the greater the demand for noble objects to excite interest and effort. It is the entire withdrawal of stimulus from the mind and brain that makes solitary confinement so intolerable that reason is often destroyed by it. Medical men point out this want of worthy objects to excite, as the true cause of a large class of diseases of mind and body, that afflict females of the higher classes, who are not necessitated to exertion for a support, especially those who have no families. And the greater the capacity and the nobler the affections, the keener is this suffering. It is only small and ignoble minds that can live contentedly without noble objects of pursuit.

Now, Providence ordains that, in most cases, a woman is to perform the duties of a mother. Oh, sacred and beautiful name! How many cares and responsibilities are connected with it! And yet what noble anticipations, what sublime hopes, are given to animate and cheer! She is to train young minds, whose plastic texture will receive and retain each impress for eternal ages, who will imitate her tastes, habits, feelings, and opinions; who will transmit what they receive to their children, to pass again to the next generation, and then to the next, until a *whole nation* will have received its character and destiny from her hands. No imperial queen ever stood in a more sublime and responsible position, than that which every mother must occupy, in the eye of Him who reads the end from the beginning, and who, forseeing these eternal results, denominates those of our race who fulfill their high calling "kings and priests unto God." Kings, to rule the destiny of all their descendants—priests, by sacrifices and suffering to work out such sublime results!

Now every woman whose intellect and affections are properly developed is furnished for just such an illustrious work as this. And when such large capacities and affections are pent up and confined to the trifling pursuits that ordinarily engage our best educated young women between school life and marriage, suffering, and often keen suffering, is the inevitable result. There is a restless, anxious longing for they know not what; while exciting amusements are vainly sought to fill the aching void. A teacher, like myself, who for years has been training multitudes of such minds, and learning their private history and secret griefs, knows, as no others can, the great amount of suffering among some of the loveliest and best of the youthful portion of our sex from this cause. True, every young lady *might*, the moment she leaves the school-room, commence the exalted labor of molding young minds for eternity, who again would transmit her handiwork from spirit to spirit, till thousands and thousands receive honor and glory from her hands. But the customs and prejudices of society forbid; and instead of this, a little working of muslin and worsted, a little light reading, a little calling and shopping, and a great deal of the high stimulus of fashionable amusement, are all the aliment her starving spirit finds. And alas! Christian parents find no way to remedy this evil!

The next topic I wish to present, and which has been brought to my observation very often during my extensive travels, is, the *superior character* of my countrywomen and the great amount of influence that is placed in their hands....

It is the immediate object of this enterprise now presented, to engage American women to exert the great power and influence put into their hands, to remedy the evils which now oppress their countrywomen, and thus, at the same time, and by the same method, to secure a proper education to the vast multitude of neglected American Children all over our land.

The plan is, to begin on a small scale, and to take women already qualified intellectually to teach, and possessed of missionary zeal and benevolence, and, after some further training, to send them to the most ignorant portions of our land, to raise up schools, to instruct in morals and piety, and to teach the domestic arts and virtues. The commencement of this enterprise, until we gain confidence by experiment and experience, will be as the opening of a very small sluice. But so great is the number of educated and unemployed women at the East, and so great the necessity for teachers at the West, that as soon as the stream begins to move, it will grow wider and deeper and stronger, till it becomes as the river of life, carrying health and verdure to every part of our land.

If our success equals our hopes, soon, in all parts of our country, in each neglected village, or new settlement, the Christian female teacher will quietly take her station, collecting the ignorant children around her, teaching them habits of neatness, order, and thrift; opening the book of knowledge, inspiring the principles of morality, and awakening the hope of immortality. Soon her influence in the village will create a demand for new laborers, and then she will summon from among her friends at home, the nurse for the young and the sick, the seamstress and the mantuamaker; and these will prove her auxiliaries in good moral influences, and in sabbath school training. And often as the result of these labors, the Church will arise, and the minister of Christ be summoned to fill up the complement of domestic, moral, and religious blessings. Thus, the surplus of female population will gradually be drawn westward, and in consequence the value of female labor will rise at the East, so that capitalists can no longer use the power of wealth to oppress our sex. Thus, too, the profession of a teacher will gradually increase in honor and respectability, while endowed institutions will arise to qualify woman for her profession, as freely as they are provided for the other sex. Then it will be deemed honorable and praiseworthy for every young and well-educated woman, of whatever station, to enter this profession, and remain in it till pure affection leads her to another sphere. Then a woman of large affections and developed intellect will find full scope and happy exercise for all the cultivated energies conferred by heaven, alike for her own enjoyment and the good of others.

This will prove the true remedy for all those *wrongs of women* which her mistaken champions are seeking to cure by drawing her into professions and pursuits which belong to the other sex. When all the mothers, teachers, nurses, and domestics are taken from our sex, which the best interests of society demand, and when all these employments are deemed *respectable,* and are filled by *well-educated* women, there will be no supernumeraries found to put into shops and mills, or to draw into the arena of public and political life.

In various places, in every section of our country, associations of ladies are formed, or are being formed, to aid in this enterprise. Beside these, quite a number of individual ladies of wealth and benevolence have contributed one hundred dollars each, for the support of missionary teachers. The plan adopted in many cases is, for an individual lady, or association, to raise one hundred dollars, and place it in the hands of the Central Committee for Promoting National Education, now organized at Cincinnati, to aid in the location of a missionary teacher, who will then correspond with those who have thus aided her. By this method, an interest will be created and sustained between those benefited and their benefactors.

In raising funds for this enterprise, another method has been adopted in which I myself feel a peculiar interest, for reasons which I beg leave to state. For twenty years I have had charge of a female seminary, first at Hartford, Conn., and afterward at Cincinnati, during which time, nearly a thousand young ladies came under my care; some from every state in the Union, and most of them from the more wealthy classes. The prostration of health for several years, has led to protracted journeyings, which have extended through most of the states of the Union, and thus I have been made acquainted with the domestic history of my former pupils, and that also of many of their friends. I have thus been led to apprehend the deplorable amount of suffering endured in this country by *young wives and mothers*,especially in the more wealthy classes, from the combined influence of poor health, poor domestics, and a *defective domestic education.* The prosperity of our country is constantly increasing the number of those who wish to hire, while it is diminishing the number of those willing to go to service. In the newer states, where domestics are most needed, the deficiency of female population renders it almost impossible to hire nurses or domestics; and when they are obtained, they are, in most cases, only the awkward and ignorant foreign domestics, who must be taught almost everything. The vexation, anxiety, and hard labor, that come upon a young housekeeper from this cause, are incalculable and endless. And in most cases these young housekeepers have never acquired physical strength for these labors by any previous habits of domestic exercise. To this evil, in a great multitude of cases, is added a debilitated constitution or destroyed health. Says Von Raumer, a late German tourist, "all travelers admire the beauty of the women in the United States, but at the same time they say that they soon grow old, and lose their beauty. And certainly I have seen no country in the world where among so many handsome women, there were so many pale and sickly faces." On the contrary, American travelers speak with delight of the full health and ruddy vigor of English matrons, and allow that these are but rarely seen at home.

A perfectly healthy woman, especially a perfectly healthy young mother, is so infrequent among the more wealthy classes, that it may be regarded as the exception, and not as the general rule. And the number of those whose health is crushed before the first few years of married life are passed, would seem incredible to one who has not investigated the subject. And few can realize what distress, discouragement, and sorrow are the inevitable consequences when the wife and mother is a perpetual invalid. And few are aware how many motherless children through our land, are bewailing a love which can never be restored.

To ill-health and poor domestics, in a great majority of cases, is added, *total inexperience and ignorance* in all the most difficult duties of a wife and mother. A woman who, by instruction or practice, is mistress of her domestic profession, can perform duty with half the labor and anxiety that come upon an inexperienced novice. And how many thousands of young, inexperienced girls are every year taken from school, or the resorts of gay pleasure, perfectly ignorant of all they most need to know, and as utterly incompetent to fill the complicated offices of wife, mother, nurse, or housekeeper, so cruelly imposed, as they would be to take charge of a man-of-war!

These difficulties are often heightened by the low and depraved character of a great portion of those who act as nurses for young children. One single vulgar, or deceitful, or licentious domestic may, in a single month, mar the careful and anxious training of years. Under the control, and in the constant society of such a nurse, to whom the feeble and inexperienced mother must give up her child, the indelible impressions on character and habits are made, not by the refined mother, but by the lowbred or vicious hireling, while the parents through life bewail an evil they strive in vain to repair.

It is probable that one-half of the evils experienced from changing or incompetent domestics result from the fact, that young ladies are not trained for their profession. They know not how to train those who are incompetent; they know not how to systematize, or to direct the labor of those who are competent. They know not how to escape the thousand mistakes and perplexities, from which instruction and experience would save them.

Permit me to draw one sketch, not from fancy—alas! I could point to many, who would claim that it was an incident of their own early domestic history.

See that young mother, sitting by the disturbed slumbers of her sick infant, while her puny elder boy is fretting for his morning meal. She has passed a sleepless night, is sick and weary, her only domestic has forsaken her, her hair is disheveled, her dress discolored, her countenance pale and haggard.

That was the bright young girl, who, four years ago, had not known sorrow, the darling of her father, the pride of her mother, the pet of her brothers, and the cynosure of fashion and pleasure. She had read in novels and magazines, that marriage was the climax of woman's happiness, and when the noblest and most beloved wooed her to enter this fairy-land with him, she joyfully gave her hand.

And now she is sitting in mute desolation, recalling her past brilliant career, her mother's love, her happy home. And now she returns to her present lot: feeble health, sleepless nights, anxious days, no nurse, cross and incompetent domestics, sick children, no comfortable food, a house all in disorder. Troubled days and sleepless nights have irritated the nerves of both husband and wife, hard words have passed, and now—oh, bitterist of all! she is imagining that the love for which she gave up all and suffers all, is chilled, cold, or departed. Her child moans and weeps, but fever and inexpressible suffering have dried up the fountain nature opened for its relief, and her inexperienced hand has nought but unhealthful food or baleful drugs to still its cries. She wishes she were dead, thinks of ways to end her woes and her life, till thoughts of her forsaken babes bring the balmy tears of a mother's love, and she rises to pursue her hopeless and melancholy task. Ill-fated child! It is *thy parents* who have planted the thorns that so keenly wound! What have they done to prepare thee for thy most difficult and most sacred duties? Look at the long train of teachers, masters, and schools! Not a word, not a thing has been afforded to guard from so sad a fate! I do not present this as the ordinary lot of young mothers. Heaven forbid! but I present it as what is so often to be found, especially where nurses and domestics are scarce, that many a mother has reason to expect that the sad reality may some day be met in her own daughter.

When I so often see gay young girls, in one short year changed to the pale and anxious wife, directing a complicated household, managing wayward domestics, nursing a delicate infant, trying to accomodate to a husband's peculiarities, and harassed by a thousand cares; and then have seen too how gently, how patiently, how bravely they give up gay pleasure, and bend to their heavy toil: I know not whether most to pity or to admire! But I have known so much sickness, sorrow, and discouragement among the young mothers of this land, that I seldom see a young bride led to the altar, without a pang of the heartache. Would to

God that the mothers who are now training their daughters for their future hard lot, could see this subject aright, how greatly they would modify their course!

"Civilizing" the West

Mary E. Adams, Ellen P. Lee, Mary S. Adams

From National Board of Popular Education Collection, Connecticut Historical Society, Hartford.

Mary E. Adams, Ellen Lee, and Mary S. Adams (no relation) were among 481 teachers sent west by the Board of National Popular Education. The idea for the Board was Catherine Beecher's. She believed that women could find dignified and godly work as Christian teachers away from the populous Eastern cities. With Williiam Slade, former governor of Vermont as its director, the Board raised funds publicly, trained teachers in four-week sessions in Hartford, Connecticut, then placed them "at the West." Beecher clashed with Slade early in their collaboration, and left the Board to attempt to establish schools for training teachers in western cities.

The three letters that follow are among many from young women teachers who went west under Board auspices, preserved in the National Board collection along with brief autobiographical statements the women submitted with their applications. Quotations from these statements appear in the headnotes to each of the three letters. While the letters bear witness to the teachers' loneliness, nostalgia for the more graceful and commodious living quarters of New England, and ill health—twenty-one teachers died during the first decade of work—they also attest to the teachers' understanding of the need for their services. Each letter makes clear the writer's

*firm belief that she was doing God's work as an evangelical
Christian, altering her community in exactly the ways
Beecher and Slade had desired.*

Mary E. Adams

*From Bangor, Maine, Mary E. Adams attended a "select school
for girls" where she studied Latin, algebra, history, philosophy,
French, drawing, painting, and music. She attended Mount
Holyoke Female Seminary for one year. After a conversion
experience there, she returned home, as she stated in her
Board application, "with a heart yearning to do & suffer....
Desire to visit the Western Country to see something of the
world we live in." Mary E. Adams stayed on to "colonize" the
West, marrying and settling there permanantly with an Indian
agent she met during her first year of teaching in Missouri.*

Summer, 1853, Neosho, Missouri

Friday morn left Springfield, for a ride of seventy five miles
over the best road between Boonville and this place. Saturday
eve, about five o'clock, just three weeks from the day we left
Hartford, I was introduced into this famous town of Neosho. It is
a small place with a population of four hundred. There are seven
stores and a Court House besides the dwelling houses, which are
neither very numerous or very magnificent. The people are kind
and friendly, but very ignorant of which they are well aware, and
are trying now to give their children the advantages they have
never enjoyed. The have provided us with good seats since I
came, and the school room is now very well fitted to seat sixty or
seventy scholars or will be the next session, and I doubt not the
seats will all be filled. My school at present numbers but twenty
chairs, and I have enough to keep me busy. I commenced school
the 13th of June and in just one month from today, the summer
term closes. I have had a rather trying time this summer. The
weather has been very warm, and I have not been well since I
came. I have dismissed school twice on account of sickness. Then
I came here under rather trying circumstances. Miss Savage had

gained the love of her pupils as no other ever can do, and it was very hard for them to give her up. She had been very lenient towards them the last session more so than she should have been, and her indulgence has made the task of governing them much harder than it otherwise would have been.

But as yet I have met with no open opposition nor do I think I shall. At first the people thought I was *too young* to come here to take Miss Savage's place, but I think they have changed their opinion of late.

I must bring this to a hasty close, for it is time it was in the Office. I intend writing to you again before the Class leaves, if I can get any time. Remember me to Miss Ferry, and tell her a letter from her would be *very acceptable* here in the "far West." After my negligence in writing to you, I deem it almost presumption to ask an answer, but should you have time, and feel disposed to write, I shall be very happy to hear from you. In one month from today, I shall be free for a time [?] at least. I am very much fatigued and can but wish it was even now closed. But a month will soon pass. Then I design having a picnic which arrangement pleases the young ladies very much.

I have written in very great haste, so I beg you will excuse all errors, and believe me

as ever yours, affect'ly
Mary E. Adams

Ellen P. Lee

Ellen P. Lee was a member of the eleventh class (1851) of the Board of National Popular Education. From Princeton, Massachusetts, she was one of eight children in her family. After the death of a younger brother, she had a conversion experience and joined the Baptist Church. She taught six-month school terms from age sixteen on, then decided to go west because she desired to do good: "In the school-room I feel perfectly at home." She governed men and young boys more forcefully than previous male teachers, by her own account—thus forcing the community to relinquish its prejudice against women teachers.

Hamilton County, Indiana
January 6, 1852

Dear Friends,
It is with pleasure that I comply with your request to write to you. I have just commenced the second term of my school here, so that I am able to judge pretty correctly of my prospects in this place.

It is a new settlement here, it being only fifteen years since the first person settled here. But the settlement is quite large, and thickly settled.

Nearly all live in log-houses. The people are kind to me, very kind; they are peaceful, honest, intelligent naturally, but have not had an opportunity for improving their minds; so that they are very ignorant. I have not seen a well-educated person; many of the adults can neither read nor write, and some cannot tell one letter from another, and do not care if the children cannot. There are nine preachers here, and scarcely one can read a chapter in the Bible correctly; and I have heard most of them preach; they are not at all like New England ministers and it is often a cross to hear them preach: but I hope some of them are good Christian men, who try to perform their duty, and not only preach, but practice what they preach. The religious societies here are United Brethren and New School or Antimason Methodist, the latter hold meetings in the house where I teach, and these I attend. They separated from the Episcopals on account of secret societies.

They have meetings every Sabbath, and preaching quite often; also meeting during the week evenings.

Just before I came here, a Sabbath School had been organized, and they had purchased a library of some more than 100 volumes; when I came they were on the point of giving it up. Those interested at first had got discouraged because they had failed to interest others. The school was conducted in a novel manner; no one here ever saw a school of the kind before, and considering this, and the qualifications of the teachers, they did well. I thought I could not get along without the Sabbath School, and they consented to try it longer.

We have now divided it into classes. I am obliged to take

charge of all the females, there being no one else who can; and sometimes I have a great number, and of course can not do as I would: and beside they depend on me to assist the others, but I enjoy it much; in this way some can be taught, who can be taught in no other way. It now seems prosperous and the interest increasing; sometimes the house is nearly full of children. Some of the parents who at first felt no interest in it, say they would rather give up anything than the Sabbath School. I hope the interest will continue to increase, and that it will prove a blessing to the neighborhood.

I came here unexpected by the people, they not having heard from Gov. Slade, but I was received kindly. My school was not very large at first, but it has gradually increased, 'till I have now about 50 [?] pupils most of whom are between the ages of 14 and 22. There has been no school here before for more than a year, and have never had a teacher who could do more than read, write and cipher a little; and these he did very imperfectly, so that my scholars are very backward but they are eager to learn, bright, active, attentive, and obedient, and learn very fast. I have a large number of young men between the ages of 18 and 21; they are very respectful, and obedient. I think I have gained the respect and affection of all my pupils, so that their obedience is cheerfully given. When I came here, there was a prejudice against female teachers; they had always employed men, and had never had a school six weeks without trouble, and they thought of course, if a man could not govern their boys, a woman could not; but I was allowed to take my own course, and I gave them only one rule, that was—Do right. And by awakening their consciences to a sense of right and wrong, and other similar influences, I have succeeded much better than I expected, and have had to use no other influences than kindness. The parents have been interested to visit the school, and I find this the best way, and the surest way to interest them. I commence school with devotional exercises which I think have a good effect on the school during the day; this is something which has never been done here before. In my school I am content, and happy for I hope I am doing good, but I am entirely deprived of sympathy, and good society. I have no human being here, in whom I can confide, or who possesses kindred feelings with mine. But there is one to whom I can go; were it not that I can cast all my care on God, and go to his Word for sympathy and consolation, I should be unhappy. I am also deprived of many New England comforts, and nearly all its privileges, but when I think that I am giving a privilege to others, which they have never enjoyed I think I ought not to complain. But although I sometimes sigh, and long for christian sympathy, and the privileges I once enjoyed, and feel lonely when I think of home, and friends, yet I am happy. I hope I have a friend who is always near and if I can in my way be useful I shall be happy. Pray for me, that my coming here may not be in vain. I should be pleased to hear from you.

Yours truly, Ellen P. Lee

Mary S. Adams

Mary S. Adams was a member of the fourteenth class (1853) of the Board. She left home at age fourteen, and had "depended upon my own exertions for livelihood and education." Her mother died when she was three, and her father remarried. She attended Cherry Valley Academy near her home in Otsigo County, New York, and attended Mount Holyoke Female Seminary for a year and a half before going west. In this letter, she voiced her objections to the traditional practice of having a teacher "board round"; evidently, she wanted a room to call her own. Despite her "small religious experience," Mary S. Adams started a Sabbath school where none had existed previously.

Calhoun, Henry Co. Mo. June 28, 1853

My dear Miss Swift,*
I wish I could see you now for I feel somewhat troubled, and should like more of your valuable advice. When I first came into Calhoun I providentally met with Mr. Smith at the hotel where the stage left me; and he very kindly offered to bring me to this neighborhood, a distance of four miles.

*Nancy Swift, who directed the teacher-training program.

He left me at the house of Mr. Knox, but said to them when he went away that he thought I had better board at Mr. Merritt's. They replied that they should like to have me remain with them, but expected me to board with either of the three families of my employ that I might choose to. This was on Wednesday— Friday I called at Messrs. Merritt's and Bell's and decided to board with the former; as I could have a room with them, in a quiet, retired part of the house, that pleased me very well; and there was an air of comfort and neatness about them not observable at the other places. And besides Mr. M. has but four chldren while each of the others have eight. Accordingly on Monday following, I came here expecting to remain during the year. Last week Mr. B. came to me and said he thought it time that writings were drawn* between my employers and myself, and wished to know what my calculations were about boarding—said he expected me to "board around." I told him what had been said to me, and that it would be a disappointment for me to do otherwise, as I had just got settled and was feeling at home at Mr. Merritt's. Nothing more was said about it at this time—two or three days after, he came to the school house with Mr. Merritt to draw writings after these were completed, Mr. Bell turned to me and said that all was settled now excepting the matter of board. I repeated what I had before said and told him in addition that I did not feel under obligations to "board around" as it was well understood by them before the application for a teacher was made what your requirements were and that nothing was said about it in that. Yet not withstanding, I should be willing to accomodate him, but did not feel able to walk so far, when teaching—he lives a mile from school, and would expect me to do my own washing, as he keeps no help—"Well" said he, "I want it understood now that I shall pay nothing for boarding when there is no reason why you should not board at my house. You look big and stout, and it seems like you might walk two miles well enough." He said much more that sounded about as kindly, but as I said nothing in reply, excepting that I thought I ought to be allowed to judge for myself concerning my own abilities, he got tired of talking alone and went away.... It would be very unpleasant for me to board

*A contract signed.

at Mr. Bell's even if he lived nearer. He can not let me have what I consider a decent room. His four oldest children are over fifteen years old, and attract much company, especially on the Sabbath....

Now I wish you to tell me what I ought to do. I do not feel as strong here as in N.E.—the climate is so warm that it overpowers me, and I need all the quiet and rest that I can have out of school. I have written you a long chapter about my trials, longer than I intended to. I will now say a few words about the pleasant things in my condition.

I commenced teaching the first Monday after I arrived, with fifteen scholars—the number has increased to twenty-one— and applications have been made for the admittance of six more. I am very much pleased with my school. I never before saw children so much interested in learning, and so desirous to please me. The parents visit me every week, and seem to partake of the spirit of the children.

Mr. Bell told me the last time he was in that I was just such a lady as he wished to have teach his children—that they were learning mighty fast and "thought a heap of me."...

Our school house to be sure, might be a better one, for when it rains the water comes in quite freely, but then the floor furnishes numerous facilities for it to run out again soon. My oldest scholars are a son and daughter of Mr. B. one twenty, the other twenty-two. I do not find any difficulty in teaching the Latin that is required here. Two weeks after I commenced teaching a day school, I opened a S. School there had never been one in the place before. The first day I had eight scholars, since then our small house has been well filled. The parents and children in this neighbourhood, and some young people from an adjoining one have come in so that we have had over thirty in all.... It seems rather hard that neither of the men are willing to open the School by prayer, but since they are not, I feel it is my duty to do so. They neither of them, have ever had family devotions....

There seems to be a great opportunity for doing good here the people are so willing to receive instruction. But I do feel very incapable of giving it. I have had so little religious experience myself. Pray for me that I may be taught of God how to teach and that my feeble efforts to serve Christ may be blessed to this

people. Miss Pratt spent a day with me last week. She is very
much beloved here—is a very devoted Christian. She sends
much love to you. I am sorry to add any to your numerous cares
by telling you of my boarding trials, but I felt that I needed advice
and knew of no other person whose counsel I should value so
highly as yours. Don't forget to give my love to Helen. Please
pardon the imperfections of this long letter and believe me,

Yours Aff[ectionately]
M.S. Adams

Preparing to Teach

Mary Swift

From Arthur O. Norton, ed., *The First State Normal School in America: The
Journals of Cyrus Peirce and Mary Swift* (Cambridge: Harvard University
Press, 1926).

*Only seventeen when she left Nantucket Island to join her
former teacher Cyrus Peirce at the first state normal school
in America, Mary Swift (1822–1909) kept a daily journal of
this historic experiment. Providing a first-rate record of
lessons in the academic disciplines, lectures on pedagogy, and
field trips, the journal rarely revealed her own thoughts—
except to test a theory. On March 14, for example, she
discovered that ice cream made her feel cool, "contrary to the
principles of Blakewell's philosophy." Throughout, and
extraordinary for the time, school activities attest to the
seriousness of the professional training. Distinguished
visitors lectured, the young women attended a board of
education meeting, and Peirce required them to hear each
other's lessons and to teach in the model school.*

*Evidently, this professional attitude had its effect. Swift
became a pioneering teacher of blind, deaf mutes at the
Perkins Institution in Boston, and wrote an influential book
on work,* Life and Education of Laura Bridgeman. *Hellen
Keller spoke of her as an inspiration. After Swift's marriage,*

she was a school committee member, and helped to found the Young Women's Christian Association in Boston. Until 1895, forty-six years after their first meeting in Lexington, Massachusetts, the twenty-five women in Mary Swift's class met for a yearly reunion.

The First Term, August 1–October 1, 1839

Agreeably to the wishes of our teacher, Mr. Peirce, I have purchased this book, which is to contain an account of the business of the school, & of the studies In which we are engaged...

After writing the above abstract [of the second Chapter of Combe's physiology] the remaining time on Saturday morning was occupied by Mr. P——in delivering a lecture to the pupils.— The subject of which was Normal Schools, their origin & the expectations of the Board of Education & of the Friends of Education in general. When our forefathers first came to this country, (he said) they saw the necessity of schools, and established those which we call Grammar Schools. As the population became more numerous, the demand for public schools increased, and various kinds have been instituted, from the High Schools down to the Infant Schools. A better idea of the number of these schools, can be formed, by considering that nineteen-twentieths of the children of the United States, receive their Education from them.—As our commerce increased, and the tide of emigration flowed more rapidly, the people found it necessary to do something for the support of the government, and knowing that it must devolve upon the rising generations, they turned their attention to the subject of Education. It was discussed freely, and Periodical Journals were established devoted to the subject.—Finally, the Board of Education was formed.... The legislature of Massachusetts were awakened, and by the assistance of private munificence, the school, whose advantages we now enjoy, was established. To us, therefore, all the friends of Education turn, anxious for the success of the first effort to establish such schools. For this success, we shall depend, chiefly, on three particulars: 1st on interesting you in the studies to which you attend & in the daily remarks; 2nd on the course of lectures to be given & 3d on the Model School.—

Thursday [8th.]. The lessons for this morn were N. Philosophy, Physiology, N. History. The subjects of the first were Light & Refraction. Our teacher explained the rule, that the intensity of light diminished as the square of the distance increased, in such a manner as to make it much more clear than it has been before in my mind.—The lesson in Physiology was very practical, & he made some remarks in connection with it, upon tightness of dress, apparently, thinking that it was the fashion at the present time to dress tightly. He has not probably heard that the wisdom or some other good quality of the age has substituted the reverse fashion for the time present....

Saturday [10th.]. After reading a portion in the Scriptures, Mr Peirce proceeded to give a Second lecture to the pupils.—The object of the lecture was, to show what the teacher is to do. The two grand divisions of the teachers work, are 1st, the discipline of the faculties, 2nd, the communication of instruction.—These appear to be synonymous, but the difference between them, may be made apparent by an example. Take the case of the lecturer; he understands his subject fully, and communicates facts to his hearers.—He, perhaps, carries most of the hearers along with him. They hear and understand, but it is without any exercise of the faculties of the mind. It is thus with the scholar: the teacher may talk upon his studies, and impart knowledge, but his faculties will remain unimproved.... The next subject to be attended to is the trials & pleasures of a teacher's life. The teacher always has one consolation: that the work in which he is engaged, is useful: on account of the good he may do. The advantages of education are too numerous to enumerate.... School education is at the basis of every profession. The business of teaching is not only honest but honorable: the ancients employed only their wisest men as teachers, for instance Aristotle, Plato, & Socrates. The wise of every age will honor the teacher. Females are peculiarly adapted to teaching: they possess more patience & perseverance, than the other sex, & if the moral cultivation of the school be attended to, they will find little difficulty in governing.

Sunday 11th. Left at one quarter before eight in the morn, to go to West Cambridge, in company with Miss Damon & Miss Stowe. Reached the place of destination at nine and one quarter, feeling very little fatigue. We went into the Sabbath School, & from there, to the Church. The minister, Mr Damon, was absent & Mr Richardson filled the pulpit. The text in the morning was "Unto every one that hath, shall be given & from him that hath not, shall be taken away, even that which he hath." In the afternoon "There are some among you who believe not." At half after six, we left to return; & at half after eight were in the academy, not feeling averse to taking a seat. The distance that we had walked was eleven miles.—

Wednesday [14th.]. In the P.M. spent an hour in writing home & after mailing the letter met Mr P. who gave us an invitation to attend the fair at the East Village. We accepted & had gone as far as the Monument House, when we met Mr Morse the preceptor of the High School in Nantucket.—He was intending to return to Boston in a short time & Mr P. stopped to speak with him, promising to overtake us before we got to the Village. He did so, and accompanied us up to the scene of action—Upon the hill called Mt. Independence was a building which appears to have been erected for an observatory—It was prepared for the refreshment table, and hung with evergreens. To contain the articles for sale large tents were made covered with canvass—adjoining this was a tent at right angles in which a long table was set for the entertainment in the eve.—There were many people from the nieghboring villages & all the tents were crowded—Groups were scattered among the trees and others were standing at the edge of the hill admiring the scenery around & below.—After viewing the fancy articles we entered the observatory & went into the upper part where Mr P. named many of the hills around & showed us the state of New Hampshire, & the commencement of the White Mountains. We also saw the ocean but it was at so great a distance that it appeared like mist over the land.—When we had become wearied with standing we descended to the refreshment room, where Mr P. treated us to ice-cream & cake—Contrary to the principles of Blakewell's Philosophy, we felt much cooler after eating the cream.—We sauntered through the grove & again through the tents, when it grew dark & we returned home, very well pleased with our afternoon excursion.—Went to tea with Mrs Muzzy in company with Miss Stodder's sister who had just come out from Boston.—

Friday [16th.]. This morn, Mr Peirce wished to try the experiment of having one of the scholars hear the recitation in N. Philosophy. Accordingly he gave to me the charge of the recitation. The feeling caused by asking the first question tended rather to excite my risibles,* but feeling the necessity of sobriety—I was enabled to play the teacher for a short time. I think that he can judge very little about our idea of teaching from the example which we give him in hearing a recitation for the manner in which it is carried on depends very much upon the interest felt by the teacher in the scholars & in their study.—To furnish a variety in conducting a recitation I think it will answer very well.

Saturday [17th.]. This morn after the recitation in Orthography,† & the solution of a few problems on the Globe, Mr P. gave his weekly lecture.... There are certain qualities which are very desirable to a teacher—not that he intended to say they were indispensible, but that they were very great additions. The 1st is Health—some leave other occupations as too laborious and teach a school, thinking that the trials of the school room are much less than those of any other station. Health is essential to the teacher, not only on his own account but for the sake of his pupils. To the sick, every trial is doubled.—Some suffering bad health are better teachers, than those enjoying good, but if the same person were possessed with health, he would be probably a much better teacher.—Personal deformity would be an objection not but that a dwarf or cripple *may* keep a better school than one formed with the most perfect symmetry, but it would be better that the children should have the beauties of nature presented to them, than the deformities. 2nd a fair reputation and good standing in community. If people speak slightly [sic] of you in the town in which you have a school, you will find your scholars will disrespect you.—4th, a well balanced mind, free from

---

*Make me laugh.
†The study of spelling.

eccentricities & from the infirmities of genius.—A person may have too much, as too little genius for a teacher.—5th a deep interest in children—she must feel an interest in whatever interests them; in their joys & their sorrows. Children readily perceive those who are interested in them, & feel hurt by coldness. 6th Patience, mildness, firmness, & perfect self control, are essential properties to every teacher. . . . Patience is requisite to meet the various trials which will beset you. You may not make so much impression by mildness in one instance, but in the end, much more will be accomplished. Mildness in manner, measures, language, countenance & in everything else.

Firmness is especially necessary, be firm to your plans; let your measures be the same each day—A teacher without these virtues, may be compared to a city without walls; which the enemy enters without opposition, & does what he chooses after entering. 7th nice moral discrimination, a high sense of moral responsibility, & accountability—The knowledge that you are accountable to a being superior to man, sustains you.—Teachers should be acquainted with their difficulties, and know how to surmount them. The government should be just, uniform, & impartial. All rules should be made so that the pupils can see they are for their good, & the reasons for making them should be explained. Teachers should be well acquainted with the branches they are to teach.—The next lecture will be upon the responsibilities of a teacher & School order & government.—

Wednesday [21st.]. This morn we recited the lesson in Philosophy & it appeared to be better understood than it was yesterday. This took up an hour & half & after recess we read our abstracts when there was a half hour before school closed. Mr P. gave us the question, Can the proper object of schools be secured without appeal to corporal punishments & rewards or premiums? to discuss & we each in order proceeded to give our opinions upon the subject—Mine is that it is very seldom necessary to appeal to corporal punishment & that rewards should not be given.—One or two agreed with me, & some approved of punishment & others not.—After conversing a while upon this subject it was nearly 12 o'clock & school closed.—

Saturday. [24th.]. After some reviews, Mr P. proceeded to give a lecture upon the subject of the Responsibility of the Teacher.—

To have some conception of this, remember that you are to influence the character, the future standing of the ten, fifty, or an hundred children who are committed to your care. Imagine each in his course through the world, & that your work will shape all their feelings, & the influence which they will exert through life. This will be imparted to those who are placed under their care, & thus your influence, instead of being confined to the hundred under your eye, will extend to thousands.—The situation, by taking this view of it, assumes a high responsibility—It is responsible in every stage, but chiefly so at the beginning. It is like a building; if the foundation is laid uneven it totters to the base, but if the contrary it will stand for ages. It is the same with physical, mental & moral education. If you instill false principles into their minds, your successors will have to root them out, before they can begin to act....

Saturday 31st. The last day of summer, & we have been here two months. 'Tis true that time waits for no man & it would appear that he had left us far behind but on taking a more favorable view of the subject we find that we have become initiated into the customs & rules of the school & thus have laid the foundation for future advancement.... After these remarks, [Peirce] proceeded to deliver his lecture, which was upon the subject of *School Order.* He commenced by calling our attention to the importance of the office of the teacher, with how many & various & invaluable interests it may connect us; if we are faithful how many will be rendered more happy by our instructions.—Follow each into life, notice his effect upon others & all his actions and after doing this we shall be able to answer the question "is not the relation of teacher one of unspeakable responsibility.—A good school must be orderly; whatever its object or title, or whoever its teacher may be. A school may be pleasant & forward, or even more than this, but order is necessary to make it a good one. The work of Education is a work of order. Order was Heaven's first law. The apostle directs that every thing should be done with order & the wise man associates the want of it with confusion. Look where you will, on celestial or terrestrial things; when you will in time past, present, or future & you will find it essential. If a man has failed, we hear, almost invariably, soon after, that his affairs were in a disorderly state. Death is put to all hopes of success without it. Oxygen is not more essential to vitality.—For your encouragement, I will add, that children, much as they like freedom, are fond of order & system. This is the cause of their admiration of regular figures, as the circles, & of their preference of such, when many are offered them. Consequently they are better suited by an orderly school, & if you would wish to please them, confine them to rules....

Tuesday [3d.]. The weather this morn appears more like the season than it has for some time, & the birds are singing merrily as if to hail the returning warmth. Upon such a morning one can but feel that their tasks are lightened and apply themselves more busily.—The lesson in Philosophy was repeated & to fix more permanently the latter part it was determined that we should review it.—The Physiology was well recited & the plan of asking questions will be very successful if everyone take as much interest as I feel. I think that we shall learn even more than by recitation if we express ourselves freely upon every subject....

Friday 6th. Political Economy—upon the division of labor. This is a very interesting study to me & I like the manner in which the author treats it very well. If he succeed as well in making every subject intelligible he must be an excellent teacher.—Will you, Mr P. tell us about the school at Barre— something about its numbers & c?—It will be pleasant to hear of the success of those engaged in a similar undertaking. The next exercise was Orthoepy* & after that Composition. The latter exercise consisted in reading aloud the pieces. Some seemed to feel very badly at being obliged to do it, but I think that it is about as easy to read one's ideas as to speak them as we do every day of our lives. It is only the associations connected with Composition that renders it so difficult to scholars as it almost invariably is.— After some comments upon the pieces in which Mr P. expressed himself pleased with the attempt he proceeded to give his lecture.—The subject of the remarks was School Government. This is necessary to every school. Teachers or scholars must govern; it must be a Monarchy Democracy or Republic. It is the same with a family as with a school, if the reins of government be

*The study of pronunciation.

put into the hands of the pupils or children, failure must be the
result. The most which can be done in a school is to admit the
scholars to a qualified participation. Let their opinion be asked
& let them assist the teacher in devising means for improving
the school as much as possible. But it is best to go no farther than
this. After you are convinced that the teacher must be governor
decide on what principles the government shall be based.

Monday Sept. 16. The school assembled again this morn, but
two of our seats were vacant. After reading from the Scriptures
Mr P. spoke of the erroneous views that were pervading the state
with regard to the conditions of entering the Normal School.
Some believe that the pupils must bind themselves to instruct a
certain number of years; while others carry the story farther, and
suppose that they are obliged to bind themselves to keep school
for their life time. Some that they must teach a public school and
others that the school must be in this commonwealth.—He told
us these that we may be able when we meet with any person
entertaining such opinions to contradict them & tell them the
true conditions.—He also told us of his intentions concerning a
Model school; that this would according to the plan marked out
be included in the third year, but that as we should probably stay
only one year he should interest himself immediately to procure
one upon which some of the scholars might operate.

Tuesday Oct. 1st. This day will close the term, & tomorrow we
shall be scattered in various directions.—Miss [——] took her
books this morn, and is intending to return to her friends, for the
want of means to defray the expenses of board. The exercises of
the forenoon, were N. Philosophy, Exercise in Worcester's
Dictionary, & Geometry. A gentleman & lady called, *she* looks
like a *"to be"* scholar.—P.M. What a poor guesser for a Yankee! The
gentleman was Dr. Howe the superintendent of the blind
institution in South Boston* & the lady one of his teachers.—
The exercises have been Rules for Spelling & Punctuation,
Problems on the Globe & Mental Philosophy & Algebra.—

Thursday December 26th. A day which the present Normalites
will probably have cause to remember for several *years, at
least.*—This morn is very delightful, and all are collected waiting

*Where Swift later became a teacher.

for the sleigh.—A few moments more, & we are seated & on our way to Mr. Dodge's to take a few in addition to the nineteen already there.—We were joined by Mrs D ——, Mrs Trusk & Mr D, & Mrs. P.—After a pleasant ride, got to Waltham & stopped at the door of the Central Tavern while the gentlemen made the necessary arrangements. Thence to the hall.... The first business transacted, was the reading of the Constitution.—Mr Dodge said that it was customary to choose a committee, for the choice of subjects for debate.—Messrs. Peirce, Hyde, Keith were chosen. A short time in which there was no business, passed and then Mr P. reported four resolutions, and fourteen questions or subjects for debate.—(My pencil & fingers refused to go fast enough to take these).—The report of the committee concerning the necessity of alteration in the common school system...The committee appointed to choose officers, now being ready to report, a motion was made, & seconded, to lay the question upon the table, & listen to the nomination.—It was accepted & the meeting adjourned till two P.M.—Returned to the hotel and after waiting a half hour we were summoned to dinner, it being advisable, as the gentlemen of the party (and I presume some of the ladies) thought to attend to the physical as well as the intellectual wants.—From dinner we went to the Factories for making cotton, which are worked by the Charles River. We entered the lower room which was [?] to Carding, the next above to Spinning, next to Weaving, and next to Dressing.—The noise of the Machinery was so great, that, at first, we were unable to hear each other speak.—The poor girls are now, more an object of my pity than ever before.—They generally looked very pale, & I should think, according to the principle of Physiology, must suffer much from lung complaints, on account of the particles of cotton constantly floating in the atmosphere.—Leaving the upper room, we descended to the basement, to see the water wheel.—From there to the banks of the river & then back to the Hall....

Tuesday Dec. 31st. The last day in the year, & the last day of the first six months, of my exile from home. On reflecting upon the pleasant connections formed here, it seems as if it will be nearly as difficult, to part with them as it was to leave our homes,—but we have six months more to enjoy their company,

& we will not anticipate trouble.—The exercises were N.
Philosophy, Combe,—Mental Philosophy & Book-keeping. In
the P.M. Reading in the Dictionary, N. History, M. Philosophy.—
In the P.M. Mrs P. called & after a very short recitation in M.
Philosophy, school was dismissed.—

And here is the end of the day, of the year, & of my journal, and
I will close it with the hope, that when my next is completed it
may show some slight improvement in the powers of Composition, and in Chirography.*—

The Schoolmarm

Anna Fuller

From Anna Fuller, "The Schoolmarm," *Pratt Portraits* (New York: G.P.
Putnam's Sons, 1892).

*This short story, one in a late nineteenth-century collection,
turns on woman's classic question—should she sacrifice work
for love? The spirited heroine, Mary Pratt, turns the question
around. "Would you give up your ranch and come and teach
school with me?" she asks her suitor. His reply, "That's not a
fair question," has a thoroughly modern ring. Well into the
twentieth century, in most states, female teachers—not
male—were forbidden to marry, presumably because, as moral
exemplars to the young, they had to demonstrate that a
married woman's sphere was the home. Thus, many women
faced Mary Pratt's dilemma.*

*The story touches indirectly on a second social injustice
encountered by women. The woman who chose teaching and
a life of "single blessedness" was often pitied and punished. A
"mother" to children to whom she did not give birth, and
with no man of her own, in the popular imagaination she
was supposed to grow into a jealous, intolerant "old maid."*

*Penmanship.

No biographical information is available on Anna Fuller, the author of the story.

A disagreeable sensation was caused throughout the entire Pratt family when Mary William announced her intention of "keeping school." Old Lady Pratt, who knew the history of the family ever since she came into it some sixty years before, could testify that no daughter of that highly respectable house had ever "worked for a living." An unprejudiced observer might have thought that Old Lady Pratt herself had worked for a living, and worked harder than any school-teacher, all through the childhood of her six boys and girls. But that, of course, was a different matter, as anybody must understand. A woman toiling early and late for husband and children was but fulfilling the chief end and aim of her being, but a woman who set out to wrest a living from the world, when she "need want for nothing at home," was clearly flying in the face of Providence.

"Well, Mary," she said to her grand-daughter, "you must not expect me to countenance any such step."

"Why not, Grandma?"

"Why not? Because I don't approve of young women gettin' dissatisfied with the sphere to which they've been called. That's why not."

"But I haven't been called to any sphere. Now that Bessie and Willie are almost as grown up as I am, mother doesn't need me any more, and I don't see why I'm not entitled to a change if I want one."

"If you want a change," said Grandma, promptly; "you'd better get married."

"Now, Grandma! You know well enough that I never had an offer. If I had, you'd have heard of it fast enough."

"And you don't deserve to have one," cried the old lady, with asperity, "if you go and *spile* everything by turning schoolmarm."

This was a sore subject with Old Lady Pratt. She, who was the sworn foe to single blessedness,* had constantly to hear that her own granddaughters had "never had an offer." It was not that they

---

*A nineteenth-century term signifying the choice not to marry; it had a positive connotation, unlike its counterpart, "old maid."

were less sought than other girls of their age, but early marriages had almost gone out of fashion since Grandma's day, and many a handsome girl might get to be well on in the twenties before a serious suitor made his appearance.

Mary William—so called to distinguish her from her Uncle Anson's daughter, who went by the name of Mary Anson—Mary William was at this time twenty-one years of age. Her father, the hero of the family, had been killed at the first battle of Bull Run, six years previous. He had left his affairs, what there was of them, in such perfect order that his widow knew precisely what she had to depend upon—a fact on which all the Pratts laid great emphasis. But to know one's financial status, if that status chance to be extremely low, is scarcely compensation for hardships and privations, and Mrs. William Pratt used fervently to wish that there had been just sufficient inaccuracy in her husband's accounts to leave a margin of possibility that a windfall might yet occur.

Mrs. William Pratt was not a woman of much energy or resource. She had a few fixed ideas, one of them being that she could not consent to "come down in the world." Coming down in the world meant to her comprehension renting or selling the commodious, well-built house in which her husband had installed her during the days of their prosperity, and moving into smaller quarters. Her house was Edna Pratt's special pride. It was large and rambling, with a front hall which did not confine itself to the manifest mission of furnishing a landing-place from the stairs, but spread itself out into an octagonal space, wherein pillars stood supporting arches; a dim ancestral-looking hall, which could not fail to impress a stranger. But as strangers rarely visited Mrs. William Pratt, and as nearly all the frequenters of the house distinctly remembered its erection a dozen or more years previous, the hall did not make quite the baronial impression which might have been expected. Mary William, especially when performing the arduous duties of maid-of-all-work minus the wages, used to murmur within herself against all the spacious rooms, which seemed to have taken their cue from it. For she reflected that every superfluous square yard of floor meant just so much more carpet to sweep; that every inch of wood-work offered just so much more of a resting-place for dust.

Mary William was of the opinion that her youth had been deliberately sacrificed to the house, and pre-eminently to the pillared hall, and she secretly rebelled against it with all her might and main. Not work for her living, indeed? How many a time had the one "girl" of the establishment been dismissed on some slight pretext! How many a time had her "place" remained vacant, and while Mrs. William Pratt sat in the parlor or lingered among the baronial pillars, complaining to visitors of the inferiority and scarcity of servants, the unfortunate Mary William had stood scorching her face over the kitchen stove, or cleaning the set of elaborate *repoussé* silver, which lent such an air of distinction to their sideboard.

But Mary William was a young person of much determination and rather unusual intelligence, and while her hands grew rough and her temper just a little sharpened in the drudgery of her daily life, she saw to it that no rust should gather upon her excellent faculties. She had graduated from the high-school at the head of her class, and after her education was thus "completed," she managed with the aid of the public library, to do a good deal of solid reading and some studying. Mary William was not intended for a book worm, but she turned to books as being the most congenial and the least exacting society within her reach. She was not able to dress well and tastefully. She was not able to entertain her friends at home, being far too poor for such luxuries. Neither was she the girl to enjoy playing a subordinate part in life, and she felt keenly the social disabilities which her poverty imposed upon her. She had never been of a complaining disposition, and no one suspected her of any discontent with her lot. But in her own mind she had long contemplated a declaration of independence, to be made when she should come of age. This was to occur in July, but she had no intention of hurrying matters. When she came down to breakfast, however, on the very morning of her twenty-first birthday, she suddenly found it impossible to refrain from making known her plans.

"Teach school!" cried her mother, in a tone of ineffectual protest.

"Be a schoolmarm!" cried Bessie; while Willie, who was still subject to the redoubtable race of schoolmarms, gazed upon her with a mixture of awe and incredulity.

"I never heard of such a ridiculous idea," said Mrs. William Pratt.

"I don't see anything ridiculous about it," Mary retorted, giving vent to her feelings with unprecedented freedom. "I've been scrimping and pinching and slaving all my life, and now I want to try how it feels to have a few dollars of my own."

"A few dollars of your own!" cried her mother. "Why, Mary, what an ungrateful girl you are! Doesn't your Aunt Harriet give you twenty-five dollars every single birthday?"

"Yes, Aunt Harriet is very kind; but twenty-five dollars isn't what you would call an ample income."

"But you have more than that to spend, and your living not costing you a cent either!"

"No; neither does her living cost Bridget a cent"; and then Mary William stopped, and did not pursue the comparison, an act of forbearance which should be recorded to her credit.

Now Mrs. William Pratt, though a weak woman, and both vain and selfish, was much respected in her husband's family. All were grateful to her for having kept up appearances on so small an income, and the fact that this had been done at her daughter Mary's expense was not wholly understood, even by her sharp-eyed mother-in-law. Hence, when she raised a cry of indignation at Mary's revolutionary behavior, she was sustained by a full chorus of disapproval from the whole clan.

Nevertheless Mary carried her point. Her venture was successful beyond her hopes. She had not led her class in the high school for nothing. No sooner had she made known her intentions than she was offered the position of assistant in the grammar-school of her own district, with the munificent salary of $350.

Singularly enough, her actual engagement as a teacher wrought an entire change in the feelings of the family. It was like the first plunge into cold water. The family pride had shrunk from it, but a reaction set in almost immediately, and that same family pride experienced a glow of gratification that one of their number should be so capable and so well thought of....

Old Lady Pratt alone withheld her approval. The fact of Mary's having a little more money seemed to her to be of small consequence in comparison with the girl's "prospects." She was

made of sterner stuff than her descendants; she knew deprivation and hard work by heart, and she was not in the least afraid of
them for herself or for anybody else. Even when Mrs. William
Pratt told her that Mary had offered to pay three dollars a week
for the "girl's" wages, Old Lady Pratt remained obdurate.

"Nonsense, Edna!" she said, sharply. "It wouldn't hurt you a
mite to do your own work. You'd a sight better do it than to have
Mary turn out an old maid. There's Eliza Pelham, now. She acted
jest so when she was Mary's age, and she'll teach school to the
end of the chapter. She got so set in her ways and so high-flyin' in
her notions that the Gov'nor himself wouldn't have suited her.
You mark my words, Mary'll be an old maid, jest like Eliza. You
see 'f she ain't."

And if Mary herself had been asked, she would have been the
first to admit the reasonableness of her grandmother's predic-
tions. She had never been so happy in her life as she was the day
on which she stepped upon the platform at school and assumed
the responsibilities of "schoolmarm." Mary William loved to
teach, and she loved also to rule—an art which she understood to
perfection. There were some pretty black sheep among her flock,
but before she had had them a month they had learned a lesson in
wholesome discipline which seemed to them much more
incontrovertible than anything Murray had to say against
alliances between plural subjects and singular verbs, or any of
Greenleaf's arithmetical theories. The new teacher's success
made so strong an impression upon the school committee that
by Christmas-time Miss Pratt's name was mentioned in
connection with a $500 vacancy to occur the coming year in the
highschool. Meanwhile Mary revelled in her independence; and
if she thought of matrimony in connection with herself, it was as
a state of bondage to be avoided at any cost.

One pleasant day in April the young teacher had just
dismissed a class in compound fractions, and sat looking down
upon the motley collection of boys and girls arranged with
geometrical symmetry over the large room. She was aware of a
spirit of restlessness among them. There were more boys than
usual engaged in the time-honored custom of twisting their legs
in intricate patterns about the legs of their chairs, more girls
gazing dreamily at the budding tree-tops just visible through the

high windows. Mary knew by her own uneven pulse that the seeds were sprouting in the ground outside, and that the spring trouble was stirring in the veins of all that youthful concourse. Mary William was in some respects wise beyond her years, and she did not reprove the vagaries of boyish legs and girlish eyes. But she kept a careful watch upon them during the study hour which preceded the long noon recess.

Just before twelve o'clock she was surprised by the entrance of two well-dressed ladies who did not look quite like products of Dunbridge soil. As she went forward to meet them they called her by name, the more stately of the two introducing herself as Mrs. Beardsley, of Stanton. Mary William, though somewhat mystified, bade her guests welcome with a very good grace, saying that she was on the point of dismissing the school.

The dispersion of the fifty or more boys and girls was a matter of some ceremony—a ceremony regulated by a succession of strokes on the teacher's bell, and usually very strictly observed. At a certain critical point in the proceedings to-day, of all days of the year, the boys broke loose, and made a stampede for the door, the girls remaining in the aisles, with their arms crossed behind them—models of propriety before company. Mary William's face flushed brightly, and she struck the shrill bell three times in rapid succession. Instantly the rabble of unruly boys stood transfixed. Two or three of them who had already escaped into the sunshine came sneaking back at the peremptory summons, while Mary William's voice, with a bell-like ring in it, said: "Boys, return to your seats!"

When all the boys' seats were filled with more or less contrite occupants, the order of exercises was resumed on the part of the girls, who filed quietly out of the room. Then Mary turned to her guests in a disengaged manner, with the assurance that she was quite at their service. A momentous conversation ensued.

Mrs. Beardsley stated that she was the Mrs. Beardsley whose school for young ladies had so long maintained its reputation as the leading school for young ladies in the state. Miss Pratt had doubtless heard of Mrs. Beardsley's school for young ladies. Miss Pratt was very sorry, but she was totally ignorant of any young ladies' school whatever outside her own town.

Mary had the discrimination to perceive that Mrs. Beardsley was a thorough woman of the world, and that she thought extremely well of herself. Nevertheless, she listened with entire self-possession to the revelations which followed.

Mrs. Beardsley was in search of a teacher to fill the place in the coming year of a valued assistant about to retire. She had heard Miss Pratt well spoken of by her cousin, the Rev. Mr. Ingraham, of Dunbridge, and she had come, with her sister, Miss Ingraham, to interview Miss Pratt. Miss Pratt signified her willingness to be interviewed, asking permission at the same time to dismiss the culprits, whose durance she considered to have been sufficiently long. This time the dispersion was performed with a precision which an army sergeant might have envied. As the door closed behind the last round jacket, Mrs. Beardsley resumed the thread of her discourse:

"My requirements, Miss Pratt, are somewhat severe. My school has a reputation to sustain, which necessitates rather exceptional qualifications in my assistants. The sort of discipline, for instance, which you have just carried out so successfully with those rough boys, would be entirely out of place in a school whose members are young ladies from the first families in the state. Tact and worldly wisdom are essential in the government of such a body. Having no doubt of your acquirements as a mere teacher of the branches desired—namely, Latin and mathematics—I am disposed to dwell more especially upon my exactions of a social nature. A teacher in my school must have the good-breeding and the equanimity of a lady, and, pardon my suggestion, she must dress in perfect taste."

Mary flushed slightly, being conscious of the ugliness of her gown, which had descended to her from a cousin whose means exceeded her discretion in matters of taste.

Mrs. Beardsley, having paused a moment, that the full weight of her words might take effect, asked, "Do you feel, Miss Pratt, that you are fitted in every particular to fill such a position?"

The flush on Mary's face had subsided, and to her own surprise she did not flinch. She raised her clear hazel eyes to those of her catechist, and with a direct gaze, in which there was unmistakable power, she said, quietly, "Yes, Mrs. Beardsley, I do."

Mrs. Beardsley returned the girl's look with an accession of interest. The "woman of the world" was not a creature of impulse, but she was a student of character, and, without a moment's hesitation, she said, "I engage you."

"Thank you," said the new assistant, as though the conversation were ended.

Mrs. Beardsley and Miss Ingraham exchanged glances, and waited for Mary's next remark; but it was not forthcoming. Mary seemed for the moment to have forgotten herself. She was looking about the homely room where she had served her short apprenticeship, lost in wonder over her sudden good fortune. Mary William was deeply impressed by Mrs. Beardsley's personality. She had always wanted to have a taste of the "great world." She loved the amenities of life, she loved the power which social training gives, and to her unsophisticated mind it seemed as though a school presided over by Mrs. Beardsley—a school where were gathered the daughters of the "first families in the state"—must offer an opening through which she might get at least a peep into that same great world.

Finding her future assistant disinclined to take the initiative, Mrs. Beardsley said, "You have asked me nothing about terms, Miss Pratt."

"Oh yes! Terms!" answered Mary William, recalled to practical affairs, in which she felt no sentimental lack of interest.

"That is, of course, in a certain sense, my affair," Mrs. Beardsley resumed; "but I should be curious to know your ideas on the subject."

Mary looked at her shrewdly. "I suppose the salary would be proportionate to the requirements," she said.

"A very reasonable supposition," Mrs. Beardsley admitted. "Then we will come to the point. As only a small number of my pupils live in my family, I shall not require your services there. You will, therefore, be at some expense for your living, and I had thought of offering you"—she paused a moment to notice whether the girl looked eager, but Mary William gave no sign— "twelve hundred and fifty dollars. Should you think that a fair compensation?"

Mary's eyes sparkled. Touched by the generosity of such an

offer to a mere grammar-school teacher, she cried, impulsively, "I ought to be a better teacher than I am, to be worth all that to you."

Mrs. Beardsley was gratified, but she only said, "If you are not worth that, you are worth nothing to me."

Mrs. Beardsley had gone out in search of a "treasure," and she had found one....

All summer long Mary spent much of her time in fashioning tasteful garments, wherein to meet one, at least, of Mrs. Beardsley's requirements, and her needle went in and out as gayly as though set to music.

One day she stood before her mirror, arrayed in a claret-colored cashmere, which was to be her "Sunday gown" in the coming winter. There was a trimming of velvet ribbon which was highly effective, and the broad tatting collar was very becoming to the round white throat within it. Mary studied the dress with some satisfaction, and then she inadvertently looked up at her reflected face. For the first time in her life she was struck with her own good looks, and her eyes danced with pleasure. Mrs. Beardsley would be more likely to approve her, the school-girls would perhaps like her, if she looked like that. She smiled at herself, and the pretty teeth thus revealed added greatly to the favorable impression.

The first week in September—for schools began earlier in Mary William's day than in ours—Mrs. Beardsley's "treasure" arrived upon the scene, and took all hearts by storm. It would be difficult to say whether the exhiliration of her spirits made the new teacher charming, or whether her almost instant popularity was the secret of that same exhilaration. Such things go hand in hand. Certain it is that Mary William lived in a round of pleasures far more stimulating, and far more satisfying too, than the pleasures usually thus designated. She loved her work so thoroughly that its very difficulties but lent it zest. She liked the girls, and she regarded Mrs. Beardsley with the enthusiastic devotion felt by a subaltern for his superior officer.

And so the first school term went by only too swiftly, and the long Christmas vacation came as an unwelcome interruption. How much more unwelcome would it have been had Mary William known what it held in store for her! Nothing could have

been more unlooked for, nothing could have been to Mary more
unwished for, than the events which followed upon the arrival
from his Western ranch of the minister's son, Fred Ingraham.
When Mary returned home for the holidays, he had been in
Dunbridge scarcely a week, and had not yet ceased to be the
sensation of the hour:

Fred Ingraham came into her life with all the freshness and
insistency of a prairie breeze, which goes sweeping across level
leagues unhindered by any obstacle, unabashed by any contrary
currents. This minister's son, with his high-bred features and his
air of conscious power, belonged to the finest type of ranchman.
In him many of the best qualities springing from the old
civilization existed side by side with the spirit and vigor which
animate the pioneer. There was not lacking a touch of the
absolute monarch, such as your genuine ranchman was five-and-
twenty years ago. Being, then, a young man of ready decision
and of hitherto unalterable determination, no sooner did he
behold the little girl whom he had patronized in big-boy fashion
a few years previous, transformed into a surprising likeness to
his secretly-cherished ideal of a woman, than he fell precipitately
in love with her. There was no time to be lost in preliminaries,
and Fred pressed his suit with the courage and persistency which
might have been expected of an absolute monarch—to say
nothing of a Yankee boy accustomed to deal with rough
cowboys and pitching broncos.

Mary was at first thrown off her guard by the very suddenness
of the assault. She had been predisposed in his favor by all she
knew of the daring and independence of his course in breaking
loose from family traditions and choosing his own rough path in
life. She looked upon him as a kindred spirit, and they had many
a long talk and more than one walk together in the sparkling
Christmas weather before she took the alarm.

He had often talked to her of ranch life—so new and
interesting a theme in those early days, before the cowboy had
been tamed into print.

They were walking home together from the skating pond one
afternoon, their two pairs of skates rattling gayly together in her
companion's hand, making a pleasant metallic accompaniment
to his narration.

Suddenly he interrupted himself to say: "Mary, you would like ranch life immensely. I am sure of it. Don't you think you would?"

His words were harmless enough, but the sudden pleading urgency of his manner, and something new and intensely personal in his tone, startled her, and she instantly bristled.

"Oh, yes!" she said. "I've no doubt I should like it if I were a man. But it must be a hideous life for a woman."

Fred bore the rebuff manfully, though it felt as grating and as blinding as a sudden prairie sandstorm. He turned and looked at her as she walked erect and strong by his side. A more defiant-looking young person he had never seen, nor a more altogether desirable one. Good heavens! the very curve of her chin was worth dying for, and Fred drew a deep breath and swore within himself that she should yet be vanquished.

The rest of that day Mary tried vainly to believe that her panic had been foolish and uncalled for. But she knew better. She feared that it was unmaidenly and conceited; that she was deserving of all the worst epithets usually applied to a forward girl; but she knew as positively as though Fred had told her so in plain English that this remarkable strong-willed young man was planning to overturn her whole scheme of life, to wrest from her her precious independence, to make her life subordinate to his.

He, meanwhile, saw his opportunity slipping away with the fleeting vacation days; he knew that in a cruelly short time Mary would be once more intrenched in her beloved work under the protection of that much-respected dragon Mrs. Beardsley. But he also knew that her mind, if not her heart, was set against his suit, and he did not dare defy her openly. They met less frequently now, Mary having developed a talent for eluding him which was most baffling. . . .

All through those tedious days of wasted opportunity he never for a moment questioned his inalienable right in the woman of his choice.

Mary meanwhile did not consciously yield an inch. . . .

"Summer after next," she would say to herself, "I shall go abroad"; and she marshalled all the wonders and delights of Europe to the support of her resolution.

The last night of the old year—which was also the last night of her visit at home—was to be celebrated with a "social gathering" at the Rev. Mr. Ingraham's house. Mary was arrayed for the occasion in her claret-colored cashmere, intending to accompany her family to the very stronghold of the enemy, when a sudden misgiving seized her, and she decided not to go.

"You may say I have a headache, if you like," she told her mother.

"But, Mary, it will never do to leave you alone in the house. You know Bridget is going out, and we've let the furnace fire go down, and you'll take cold."

"I can light a fire in the hall grate," said Mary. "That will make the house warmer when you come in. Besides, I shall go to bed early."

She watched the blue flames dancing on top of the bed of coals, and the little rows of sparks running along the soot at the back of the chimney—"folks going to meeting," she had been taught to call them. Somehow the suggestion of a string of people all bound for the same place made her feel cross.

"Everybody's always doing just the same thing as everybody else. It is so tiresome! If nobody else had ever got married, Fred would never have thought of anything so foolish"; and then she laughed at her own childishness. She would have like to cry just as well as to laugh, but she usually drew the line at tears.

It must have been about nine o'clock when there was a sharp ring at the door-bell. Mary shuddered. Was it some midnight marauder? Alas! her forebodings were worse than that. Thieves and murderers she might perhaps know how to deal with, but there was an enemy more to be dreaded than they. The bell rang a second time reverberating loudly through the empty house before she answered it. Her worst fears were realized.

"Why, Fred, is that you?" she said, holding the door half open in a gingerly manner. "Did mother want anything?"

"No. It's I that want something. Aren't you going to invite me in?"

"Oh, yes! Come in. I was so surprised! How could you leave your party?"

"That was easy enough. I just walked out of the room.... May I get a chair?"

Mary had never known him to be so voluble, but she was not in the least reassured by his flow of words.

"What are you reading?" he asked, as he sat down on the other side of the fireplace.

Her fingers still clasped the red book, though she had not opened it for an hour past. At mention of it, she recovered herself.

"It is Murray's guide-book of Switzerland. Have I never told you that I am going abroad summer after next?"

"Really? How enterprising you are!"

"Oh, it can be easily managed. You know I have quite a princely income."

"Mary," he cried, abruptly, "give up your income, give up Europe, give up all those plans. Come with me! Not now—of course you couldn't—but next summer."

She shut her lips firmly together, and stared at the fire.

"See!" he went on. "I put it in the baldest words. I concede everything from the very beginning. I know you would be giving up everything you care for; I know I am asking a perfectly tremendous sacrifice."

"Would you make such a sacrifice for me?" she asked, in a hard, dry tone. "I love my way of life just as well as you do yours. Would you give up your ranch and come and teach school with me?"

"That's not a fair question, Mary. You might as well ask if I would wear girl's clothes to please you. You wouldn't respect me if I did."

"I don't agree with you at all," she said, sharply and argumentatively. It did not sound like her pleasantly-modulated voice. "I don't see that the sacrifice would be any greater for you than for me. My work and my ambitions are just as necessary to me as yours are to you. And you would never think of sacrificing yours for my sake."

"I'm not so sure that there is anything under heaven that I wouldn't do for you, Mary," he cried, impetuously. "But that is something you would never ask. You wouldn't be yourself if you did. Men sacrifice their lives for women, not their careers. It would not be in the nature of things for you to ask of me what I am asking of you."

He paused a moment, and then he was sorry he had done so. Her face was set and repellant. But she spoke before he could stop her.

"No, Fred, I can't do it," she said; "and please don't talk to me any more. Didn't mother say I had a headache?"

"As though I believed that! I don't believe you ever had a headache in your life. And supposing you have? What is a headache, I should like to know, compared to a heartache? If I can bear to hear you say no in that horrid cold voice, you can bear to hear me talk as long as I ever choose. Mary, you *shall* hear me, and I am going to tell you something that will make you think you hate me. You know that I love you with all my heart and soul. But it seems foolish to talk about that. Of course I love you. Who could help it? Cousin Letitia adores you, though she may not tell you so. Everybody adores you, simply because you are the most perfectly adorable woman that ever lived. But, Mary," and his voice sank to a lower key—"Mary, there is one thing you don't know, and that I am going to tell you—*you love me.*"

"How *dare* you say such a thing to me, Fred Ingraham?" cried Mary, springing to her feet, white with anger, her eyes flashing, her breath coming fast.

"I suppose it does sound like a brutal thing to say," he admitted, "here in the house, where everything is conventional."

He was also standing now, leaning back in the shadow against the chimney, watching Mary's face with the uncertain firelight on it. The lamp was behind her. She had not got her breath sufficiently to speak again. The red book had dropped to the floor, and her hands were clinched. As he looked at her a sudden pity came over him....

Then she lifted her face in the firelight. "Fred Ingraham," she cried, in a despairing tone, "I believe I do hate you—you are—so—cruel."

Fred looked at the tragic face, and an exultant light came into his own.

"It's a kind of hate I'm not afraid of, Mary," he said, and he held out his arms.

The shadows among the baronial pillars seemed to be swaying and wavering before her eyes and her own step faltered. But she went to him, because she could not help it. He kissed her, rather cautiously, and she made no resistance. A strange, delicious, poignant happiness overwhelmed her.

That night Mary cried herself to sleep for the first time since she was a little child. But in that beneficent storm of grief her last tottering defences were swept away. When, but a few hours later, the time of parting came, her valiant lover knew that her surrender was complete.

Mrs. Beardsley generously forgave her young cousin for robbing her of her "treasure," though, as her short period of possession went by, she learned still better to measure her impending loss. She permitted herself but one form of revenge, which, however, she always clung to. As often as she had occasion to write to him in after years, she never failed to address him as her "dear bandit."

As for Old Lady Pratt, though Mary had gone contrary to all prognostications, she was too much relieved to resent being put in the wrong. Her unfailing comment when the event was discussed in the family was: "Mary William's got more sense, arter all, than I giv' her credit for."

TWO: A Noble Work Done Earnestly

Yankee Schoolmarms in the Civil War South

AT THE OUTBREAK of the Civil War, as the Union Army moved into the South to suppress the rebellious Confederacy, news of the victory at Fort Sumter, South Carolina, quickened the passion of anti-slavery Northerners of every persuasion. In the most feverish spirit, Henry Stanton wrote some days after

Sumter, "I hear old John Brown knocking at the lid of his coffin and shouting 'Let me out,' 'let me out!' The doom of slavery is at hand. It is to be wiped out in blood. Amen."[1] Weary of years of talk, abolitionists rushed into action on behalf of the Union. For a man, there was a soldier's uniform and the test of battle; for a woman, there was relief work at home—bandage-making, collecting clothing, and raising funds to provide for four million slaves, many of them in flight toward the advancing Union Army.

And, as the first months of the war stretched on into a year, another choice developed for the adventuresome. Many slaves had fled their masters, or now lived in newly taken Union

territory. The freedmen (or contrabands*) congregated on the
coastal islands of Virginia, the Carolinas, and Georgia. Northerners, commissioned by the army, set out to help them through
the transition to freedom. Men came South to organize the
camps, set up a labor system, and see to the distribution of land,
but by far the most numerous in this movement South were
unmarried women (and some few men) who came to establish
and teach in "freedmen's schools." From the coast, schools spread
throughout the South, springing up wherever the Union army
had control. By 1870, five years after the end of the war, there
were about 7,000 teachers in the South, instructing some
250,000 black students.[2] The teachers left as a significant legacy
the graduates they trained who staffed the South's segregated
schools on into the twentieth century. And among the students,
too, was a new and numerous generation of free black leaders.

The story of the schoolmarms begins with the formation in
Boston, New York, and Philadelphia of societies to promote the
work of abolitionist missionaries. These societies, sponsored by
town or church groups like the very active American Missionary
Association, raised funds, sent barrels of supplies south, and
recruited and supported teachers of the freedmen. Their efforts
were coordinated and protected first by the Union army, then by
the Bureau of Refugees, Freedmen, and Abandoned Lands,
commonly called "The Freedmen's Bureau."

Typically, a woman teacher would hear a speech that extolled
the blacks' thirst for learning, and presented the challenge of
educating the race as a momentous social experiment. No
American had attempted the mass education of blacks previously; indeed the education of black slaves had been outlawed in the
South. The speaker's enthusiasm would precipitate a decision to
join this woman-dominated teaching mission, or what we can
call, in retrospect, the first civil rights movement.† Teachers'
credentials were scrutinized with rigor by groups such as a state

---

*So named by General Benjamin Butler, who "confiscated" blacks legally as
contraband or smuggled goods.
†Just one hundred years after the Yankee schoolmarms went South, hundreds of
Northern civil rights workers—many of them young, middle class college
women—went South once again to establish "freedom schools" for blacks and to
register voters. As a freedom school teacher myself, I knew nothing of this

teachers' committee. One Massachusetts official described the appropriate qualifications. "No mere youthful enthusiasm, love of adventure, or desire of change, will sustain a teacher through the labors and hardships of her work." She had to have "good health," "religious faith," "patriotism," and a superior education, for she was to form "the people who are to influence very largely [this country's] future, for good or for evil." Found wanting in these qualities, the teacher would be told sternly, "one may labor for the freedmen as truly in Massachusetts as in South Carolina."[3] Found worthy, with very short notice the young woman would be steaming down the coast on a boat filled with soldiers.

Young Mary Ames and her friend Emily Bliss were "typical."[4] After hearing Harriet Ware,[5] a returned teacher, tell of her experiences, they went straight to Boston to see the chief of the Freedmen's Bureau, and were enrolled. Although their families ridiculed their going and tried to stop them, ten days later an army wagon deposited them on a desolate piazza of an abandoned plantation on the South Carolina Sea Island of Edisto. The only whites for miles around, they were befriended by Sarah, a former slave who lived at the back of the "big house" with her husband and six children. She helped the pair seek out a dry space on the floor for sleep, shared with them her tin teacup, and helped secure them against rattlesnakes and Confederate spies. Thus began their careers as Yankee schoolmarms. One month after their arrival, Mary Ames wrote proudly in her diary, "Our books number a hundred and forty scholars, and from sixty to seventy are in daily attendance. Our evening school [for adults] on the piazza is well attended, and we enjoy our labors. All are respectful and eager to learn." A year and a half later, Mary made her final diary entry. "The owner of the house we had lived in... wanted to come back. There was no place for us, and in the last week of September 1866, we said good-bye to our Negro friends."[6]

previous female-dominated missionary movement. The civil rights workers of the 1960's faced the same dangers, carried out the same activities, and received support from sources similar to those of the Yankee schoolmarms. Like them, we taught, ministered, cured, and organized against a backdrop of racial hatred, extreme poverty, and violence.

These modest sentences give the bare outlines of a little known history of heroism, self-sacrifice, and self-fulfillment carried out by daughters of established families with Yankee names like Towne, Gardner, Chase, Holley, Putnam, Ames and Bliss. Active members of abolitionist groups and adherents of a range of Protestant sects, they left their "dear ones at home"[7] to live out political and religious beliefs rather than remain, as one recruiting pamphlet put it, "ornaments in their fathers' parlors, dreaming, restless, hoping. . . ."[8] The black community was their ready "field of work," teaching "a labour of love," and success "a harvest" so gratifying that it set in perspective isolation, physical hardship, and life-threatening dangers for which nothing in their previous experience had prepared them.

Writing by and about the Yankee schoolmarms is more plentiful than that about other teachers in this book. As members of a social change movement, they recorded daily events to convince Northern sceptics of their cause, and to inform benefactors. And isolated from family and friends, they wrote constantly to their dear ones. Many of their letters were published, many saved. The extensive American Missionary Association collection, for example, contains over 500,000 items, most of them letters from teachers. The teachers published at least a dozen books of reminiscence, were the subjects of articles by noted journalists and fiction by the black writers W.E.B.Du Bois, (1868–1963) and Charles Chestnutt (1858–1932). Through the 1890's, their memoirs enjoyed a vogue. By the turn of the century, however, the teachers became overshadowed by their own writings. Historians ignored the authors, but used their stories as evidence of particular values and behavior among former slaves. Section 2 of this volume is among a few recent analyses which reconstruct the experiences of the schoolmarms' themselves.

Fashioning Relationships:
Across the Gulf of Race and Class

"We have come to do anti-slavery work, and we think it noble work, and we mean to do it earnestly," wrote the teacher Laura

Towne in her diary a few days after her arrival on the South Carolina Sea Islands, in March 1862.[9] In quite another tone, an American Missionary Association teacher wrote home, "I have always been taught to abhor slavery, but never, until I came among its victims, did I know anything of the blasting effects of that system; and the more I became acquainted with these people, the more do I realize the great work that is to be accomplished before their souls are brought from natural darkness into the marvelous light of God's truth."[10] These statements of Laura Towne and her anonymous sister, the former plain-spoken and secular, the latter full of rhetorical flourishes in the style of the evangelical movement, share an emphasis on the word "work." Whether the teachers believed that ultimately they were doing God's work by awakening the religious spirit or doing democracy's work by preparing the freed people to be landowners, office holders, voters, and friends, they had made their decision to leave home with similar activities in mind—feeding the hungry, clothing and housing the refugees, and teaching reading and writing. This essential work compensated (the secular term) or atoned (the religious term) for the sin of having enslaved human beings, and for having kept them from improving their own condition. Once established in the South, most teachers, however motivated, adopted a common set of ideas about the capacities and destiny of the free people.

One must remember that among Northerners, abolitionists were far outnumbered by people persuaded that the intent of the Civil War should be not the end of slavery—policy toward blacks was a local, not a national concern—but unity of the United States. In a minority, even among *abolitionists*, most teachers declared themselves committed to immediate political equality, and supported the passage of the 14th amendment in 1866. Through the process of education—almost uniformly interpreted to mean inculcating New England Puritan qualities of piety, self-reliance, industriousness, sobriety, and thrift—they believed that the Negroes would rise out of degradation to assume the full citizenship of which they were capable.* Their

---

*Only the Unitarian teachers, Laura Towne and Elizabeth Hyde Botume, left explicit statements that I have found favoring black female suffrage—still by law more than half a century away, and, de facto, even further. See Towne selection, p. 171 and Botume selection, p. 163.

statments on *social* equality, however, are more difficult to
interpret in the late twentieth century. Anathema in the South
and controversial in the North, the term "social equality" meant
the abolition of class as well as race discrimination. It meant
friendship, intimacy, and marriage between the races. Seen in
historical perspective, the teachers' position on this issue was
also radical. Using the metaphor of progress from childhood to
adulthood or from barbarism to civilization, most said blacks
would quickly "earn" social equality. One teacher wrote that "the
freedman compared with the educated white man is a child
needing instruction and guidance. He needs to be protected for a
time against the unscrupulous and designing. But it will not be
well for him to be treated like a hothouse plant, the wider fields
of competition as well as toil shut out from him." The Northern
black teacher, Charlotte Forten, thought that the black people's
"shouts," "the barbarous expression of religion, handed down to
them from their African ancestors," were "destined to pass away
under the influence of Christian teachings."[11]

Declarations of ideology and nineteenth century metaphors of
progress, however, tell us far less about the teachers' racial
attitudes than do their daily activities in the black community.
In remarkable numbers the teachers seemed to have entered into
informal and respectful relationships with the freed blacks.
They acted out a fundamental anti-racism which represented a
radical shift from their Northern homes.

Usually, relationships were forged during the teacher's first
days in the South; neither she nor the newly freed people had any
rules for behavior then, but the work of establishing a school
required immediate interdependence. *The Freedmen's Bulletin,* a
monthly newsletter of a state association, tells a characteristic
story. A "brave woman" had established a school on the
plantation of a "gentleman of northern extraction." Rebels
quickly arrived to warn the teachers "to desist from 'nigger
teaching.'" They captured the teachers, and "set out, a black man
driving, and a Confederate Captain and Lieutenant riding on
either side of the vehicle." While the blacks sounded an alarm,
the driver went at a "tardy pace," to allow Union pickets to come
to the rescue. Finally, one teacher observed a weak spot in the
harness. She "snatched the lines, struck the horse smartly...and

broke the harness." In the delay, Union soldiers arrived and the rebels escaped. Soon the school was reestablished on a confiscated plantation. Thus, blacks and whites had acted together on behalf of blacks, and against all previous tradition.*

Less dramatic, but equally capable of fostering new relationships, was the respectful and caring way the newly arrived teachers went about preparing the black community for its first experience of self-determination. Ten days in the South, Laura Towne, trained as a homeopathic physician, wrote home from St. Helena Island in a tone of surprise, "I have begun my professional career. On the next plantation to this, a good many negroes are sick, and at church this morning a young man in charge...asked me to make some medicine for them. This afternoon I doctored the half dozen families who had measles and mumps." In the same day, she distributed $2,000 worth of clothing, stopped a young girl from whipping two children—"I told them I had come here to stop whipping, not to inflict it"— and taught her school as well.[12]

Teachers also reported explicit attempts to transform custom. The women dined formally with black friends, to many Southerners the most flagrant and outrageous insult to the old system, and tabooed enough in the North for Laura Towne to emphasize its naturalness in a letter. Another teacher told of a Thanksgiving meal where the twelve oldest contrabands of the village took seats at a dining table for the first time, instead of eating around the cooking fire, as in slavery times. The inspiration for the meal as she describes it, reveals that she catches herself writing as if she were a member of the black community. "We had peace if not plenty, and were contented, if not comfortable. By we I mean the black people."[13] An anti-slavery worker insisted that an old Auntie take a seat in the carriage while he rode on the back. Laura Towne even saw the value of play as an antidote to the old order. At the supply house, she had blacks order her around for the fun of turning the tables.

And there were more deeply symbolic acts. In 1870, Laura Towne and her life-long friend and co-worker, Ellen Murray,

*Maria Waterbury, a teacher sponsored by the American Missionary Society, told a similar story. She required black guards. See Waterbury selection, p. 113.

adopted Puss, a neglected black child. Laura wrote the "grand news" home describing Puss as "bright as a dollar. She has been my scholar for years."[14] Young Mary Ames broke another taboo of the old order. "One night Ben [a favorite child with whose family Mary lived] hung over my chair. He was uneasy, and I asked what troubled him. He whispered, 'Is the reason you don't kiss me 'cause I'm black?' I took him into my lap and held him til he slept."[15] No wonder one white Southerner said that these "Yankee bitches" were engaged in a fight for control of black minds, and that their most potent weapon was acting on their convictions.[16]

In sum, the teachers took a pragmatic view of equality—it was an end, and they were the means, the vehicle for the journey. The Quaker Chase sisters, Sarah and Lucy, criticized "enthusiastic philanthropists" who over-praised black achievement. That attitude was "giving undue praise to the barbarous teachings of slavery."[17] And the behavior of missionary Austa French on her arrival at Hilton Head, South Carolina, was a standing joke among the teachers. According to one account, this misguided lady had rushed from the boat upon a startled black woman who happened to be passing by. Embracing and kissing her, she had sobbed, "oh, my sister."[18] Far more typical was the straight talk of Elizabeth Hyde Botume, thirty years a teacher in South Carolina. When counseled by an enthusiastic philanthropist that she would insult old house servants if she asked them to wash clothes for her, she answered that "laundry work had not been my business: I came to teach the freed people to help themselves. Whatever they could do better than I, in so far, they were my superiors. In consideration of their previous 'condition,' I gave them my time and instruction, whilst I should pay regular wages for their labor. But I should expect good work, and no make-believe."[19]

Given the gulf of culture, class and race that separated them from black women, the teachers turned to each other for strength to carry on. In general, in the nineteenth century, by virtue of work and earned independence, teachers were set apart from other women, and formed an informal sisterhood. For the Yankee schoolmarms, sisterhood and teamwork were crucial to survival. Almost no one went South alone, and some like Ellen

Murray and Laura Towne, and Sallie Holley and Caroline Putnam lived and worked together for as long as forty years. The Towne diary and letters spell out what must have been a characteristic life-long interdependence. Laura Towne "cut capers of joy" when Ellen Murray arrived in the South and the two "talked all night nearly."[20] Later, however, Ellen Murray became violently ill just after another teacher had died. "I am in such a state of alarm and dread that I cannot read my medical books for crying and distress,"[21] wrote Towne in her diary. Her nursing, however, had its desired result, and Murray survived. Later, the two women bought a house and land which, from occasional comments, seems to have become like the Holley Putnam farm, a model for its vegetable garden, flowers, and healthy livestock.

Even teachers in the South for only a year or two recognized how necessary, in that strange and isolated environment, were letters and visits from kin and friends. These visitors could witness and reconfirm the significance of the work. The teachers formed a network throughout the South, and with friends and returned teachers at home. Elizabeth Botume's assistant, "Miss Fannie," had her sister, "Miss Lizzie," come to teach. Laura Towne's brother William not only provided her salary, he also came to do legal work on behalf of her community, and Ellen Murray's mother and sister moved in down the road. Mary Ames and Emily Bliss had family visitors who helped them teach— and criticized their housekeeping; and Charlotte Forten corresponded with Laura Towne, the Chase sisters, and others, once she had returned to Massachusetts. Only the introspective young black woman Charlotte Forten described suffering from self-doubt and loneliness. She had come South without a dear companion, and her isolation was accentuated by the discovery that her racial identity with the freed people did not compensate for difference in life situation.

The Schoolroom

If the teachers needed each other's company to negotiate the new relationships in the black community, in the schoolroom the "acceptable" inequality of student and teacher was a familiar and functional structure for exchange which no one needed to change. Here, the newly-freed people and their Yankee school-marms showed the best of themselves. Here, the women could *teach toward* equality, understandably less difficult than acting it out. Though perhaps more self-confidently assertive than some teachers, Anna Gardner, a Nantucket teacher in Charlottesville, Virginia, represented the sentiments of many. She had asked the editor of the *Charlottesville Chronicle*, a man with professed "deep interest in the welfare of the Negro race," to print diplomas for her school. He had replied in the negative: "Your instruction of the colored people...contemplates some-thing more than the communication of ordinary knowledge implied in teaching them to read, write, cipher, etc. The idea prevails that you instruct them in politics and sociology, that you come among us...as a political missionary; that you communicate to the colored people *by precept and example*, ideas of social equality with the whites." Anna Gardner retorted with New England firmness, "I teach in school and out so far as my influence extends, the fundamental principles of 'Politics, and sociology' viz:—Whatsoever ye would that men should do to you, do you even so unto them.' Yours in behalf of truth and Justice."[22]

It was, however, also typical for the schoolmarm to arrive full of questions about the intellectual capacity of the race, but that scepticism vanished when she stood before her pupils. Indeed, the moment of discovering the blacks' insatiable thirst for learning. amounted to a "conversion" experience for the teachers. Initially, a teacher would think of herself as a missionary to the lowly; then she would recognize that, as educator, she symbolized freedom to a people whose curiosity about letters had only been strengthened by Southern law which forbade teaching slaves to read and write. Prayers for the safety of the teachers, like those uttered by Maria Waterbury's students, however, stunned her:* she could wield a marvelous and almost frightening power in the classroom. The secular teacher Elizabeth Botume, chose to teach the Combahee people because they were considered "the

*See Waterbury selection, pp. 120–22.

connecting link between 'human being' and the 'brute' creation." But the response to her arrival converted her to an attitude of reverence for her students. "When I first came in sight of the house, the piazza was filled with men, women and children. I heard many exclamations of 'Dar, da him'; 'Missus comes fur larn we.... ' The men and women had only come to 'get their names put down,' as field-work was not done. Each one regarded it as an honor to be enrolled as a scholar. They all left with a new consciousness of their own individuality and personal dignity. I use this term advisedly. The poorest and most downtrodden of these people are self-respecting." Botume continues, "Before Christmas the field work was done.... Now children and parents, even old gray-headed people, hurried to the school-room.... 'Us want book-larning *too*, bad,' they said over and over again."[23]

An evangelical teacher based her "conversion" on the revelation of blacks' moral capacity. Writing after a year of service in Paducah, Kentucky, she recalled that initially she had

looked upon these dark, dirty, ignorant men and women, boys and girls—but a short time since abject slaves—and still the slaves of ignorance, with strange and peculiar feelings.

She continues,

I had not exalted ideas of the African race, though I had always regarded slavery as the one great blot on our National escutcheon, and would gladly have done anything in my power to break the fetters and set the enthralled free—to make them all they were capable of being. Here was an opportunity before me, not only to judge fairly for myself of their capabilities, but to guide these hardly treated, despised outcasts, as it were, not only in the ways of worldly wisdom, but in the way of truth and holiness. A few days showed me what power I could wield over their opening minds—far more ready to grasp good than I had imagined. //

At the moment of writing, she felt herself to be educating "noble men."[24]

Secular and evangelical teachers both designed their lessons, as one teachers' committee official said, "to spread New England education" of so high a standard that "no local government will be able to overthrow it."[25] That meant inculcating Puritan morality undergirded by McGuffey's reader and Noah Webster's spelling book. "The worst thing I could say to an unruly boy," wrote a teacher from Charleston, South Carolina in 1865, "was to tell them a Yankee boy would be ashamed to do as they were doing."[26] "I teach them not to say, 'I can't,' " wrote another.[27] Many measured success by a single standard—the student's renunciation of the most pernicious vice of slavery—lying.

For more detail about curriculum, there are many accounts of year end school exhibitions—celebrations of progress for the entire black community. Parents often received written invitations, and expressed themselves "proud for mad" when neat copy books were passed around, or children went to the blackboard to "calculate the price of two bales of cotton sold here at the market price per pound," and compared the price of the same two bales at New York, "deducting expenses [and] commissions." Besides exercises in grammar, math, geography, and reading, students recited poems about freedom, little girls and boys demonstrated—no doubt, to teach parents—cooking, cleaning, and animal care skills, and older students performed comic satires.[28]

The black teacher Charlotte Forten was not alone in having her children sing about the slave leader John Brown, or in lecturing them "on the noble Toussaint...to inspire them with courage and ambition."[29] Laura Towne taught about the "wisest country of old times, Egypt in *Africa*," and Lucy Chase taught reading from *The Lincoln Primer*, which pictured freedmen "dancing in honor of liberty."[30] Other teachers used *The Freedmen's Book*, a comprehensive anthology of black history and contemporary thought compiled by the feminist abolitionist Lydia Maria Child.

By most accounts, the children appear to have entered into an alliance with their teachers built not just on mutual respect, but on love. The racial and class difference may have even intensified the relationships. The children could only have been constantly surprised by their white teachers' dedication and friendship, while the teachers, took special moral pleasure in increasing the power of the feared race. When asked by a group of visiting journalists and benefactors for a message to take North, Elizabeth Botume's students said simply, "tell 'em we is rising." Botume despaired of the stupidity of another class of visitors

[margin handwritten note:] Taught a lot about freedoms

who "treat those who are poor and destitute and helpless as if they were bereft of their five senses." These would have been "undeceived...if they could have seen those children at recess...repeating their words, mimicking their tones and gestures."[31] The teacher Maria Waterbury reported that Sarah Mahoney, a college graduate from Michigan, used to say "the freedmen work was her husband and children," the metaphor meaning, one supposes, that the blacks among whom she worked held the place in her life reserved for family.[32]

Staying On

For about a decade, Northern school teachers continued to come South for an average stay of three years. But by the early 1870's, the picture of black Southern education was changing. Northern aid societies had not intended to build a permanent system of private education for blacks, and, in truth, some were beginning to lose the ability to raise funds for their cause. In addition, many schools were absorbed into the segregated public school system where young black men and women, graduates of freedmen's schools, formed the faculties. A new group of institutions—high schools and colleges to train a black leadership—had been developing under the guidance of Northern white men. Between 1865 and 1870, white men had founded Howard, Rust, Atlanta University, Hampton Institute, Shaw, Morehouse, Fisk, and Tougaloo. Each of these schools also taught primary, secondary, and normal subjects, and thus sought some women teachers, but many Northern women felt their work was over.

Anna Gardner, the outspoken sociologist who taught truth and justice, had a typical career for a secular teacher. A Nantucket Quaker, her home had been a station on the Underground Railroad. By the age of eighteen, she was a militant abolitionist. At age twenty-five, she had been instrumental in calling an anti-slavery convention on her island (1841), then at age forty-six (1862), she had traveled South with nineteen other teachers to establish a freedmen's school in New Berne, North Carolina. From 1865 to 1870, she taught in a second freedmen's school in Charlottesville, Virginia, then after a brief stint as a normal school teacher—the practice was to train and place black teachers as quickly as possible—she returned to Nantucket. There she took up a cause she had relinquished reluctantly during her teaching years—the advancement of women and suffrage.[33]

But another pattern in the careers of a small group of schoolmarms was emerging as well. This group of women continued to raise money privately in order to carry on their schools as of old. Those we know most about are Sallie Holley (1818-1893)* and Caroline Putnam, Oberlin graduates (1851), with a school in Lottsburgh, Virgina (1868-1893d);† Martha Schofield (1839-1916), first on the Sea Islands (1865), then in Aiken, South Carolina (1868-1916d); Elizabeth Hyde Botume in Beaufort, South Carolina (186?-189?); Cornelia Hancock (1840-1927), first a nurse at Gettysburg, then briefly with Laura Towne, and finally in Charleston, South Carolina (1866-1875), succeeded by Abby Munro (?-1905); Sara Ann Dickey at Mt. Hermon Female Seminary in Jackson, Mississippi (1875-1904d) (illiterate until age twelve, she worked her way through Mt. Holyoke and graduated at age thirty-one); and Ellen Murray and Laura Towne (1825-1901) at the Penn School (1862-1901d), succeeded by Rossa B. Cooley (1873-1949), Vassar graduate (until 1949d). These women constructed an unusual place for themselves in Southern life and culture, one they would never have imagined had they stayed at home continuing what one teacher called "that selfish way of half living that used to be 'jist tolable' to me."[34]

Unlike the male anti-slavery worker, these Yankee schoolmarms had not abandoned budding careers in the North to pursue abolitionist work, and often they had already made the crucial decision of a woman's life—not to marry. Thus, free of family and without paid work at home, they had liberty to stay South long past the time when young white men had returned to college, the law, or business. Furthermore, these proper middle class women had been taught to shun wordly achievement for its

---

*Birth and death dates given where known.
†These dates indicate year began working in school followed by year of leaving or death = d.

own sake. In the South, one could be modest, and achieving as well. Those women who grew to status with their schools sometimes almost coyly refused praise for their success. Independent female educators, they were graduating black students from their private schools on into the twentieth century, and their letters to friends, family, and benefactors continued to flow North testifying to the satisfaction in their work.

The histories of the ten or so independent schools indicate that the pairs of women who ran them became more than teachers. They carved enclaves of power for themselves.[35] They were partisans of black political leadership, activists and organizers who had come to enjoy the fray of the battle for civil rights and to identify themselves totally with the black Southern cause. Historical circumstance had given birth to a group of independent women, and Northern social convention had hindered neither their capacity to solve problems, to speak boldly in public, nor to endure physical dangers.

As Reconstruction collapsed and Ku Klux Klan activity heightened in the 1870s, the old hierarchy of authority revived—white men on top, then white women, black men, and finally black women. In the black community, the white teachers advised and defended the black men whose new franchise was threatened. Sallie Holley wrote in 1872 to a Northern friend, from her school in Lottsburgh, Virginia, "although the old rebels are earnestly trying to get *our* coloured men to vote for Greeley, I hold monthly Republican meetings in our schoolhouse, and don't mean single man shall vote for Horace Greely."[36] In 1876, Laura Towne saw that the South Carolinians intended to put an end to black education and participation in politics. After several black male political activists were dragged from their homes nearby, she used her national reputation as an anti-slavery worker to champion the blacks' cause in a letter to the liberal journal "The Nation." With her black male allies, she would fight to control "this yankinized region."[37]

Her letters and diary also tell a story of her local political activism—lobbying at the state level to *permit* blacks to pay taxes to fund their own schools, the passing of key school resolutions in St. Helena that she had written, and support and counsel for Robert Smalls, a black South Carolina congressman and civil war hero. She also continued to do much of the legal work to help blacks claim land for themselves. Laura Towne thrived in the battle, and declared, "I want to agitate, even as I am agitated."[38]

The record of the schoolmarms' activity continues on for decades, in a stable, regularized pattern. In the surviving schools, rituals such as the annual school district meeting, year's end exercises, the celebration of emancipation, the teachers' summering in the North and Fall return marked the habits established and maintained year after year. Those Northern benefactors committed to long-term support corresponded with Laura Towne or Sallie Holley over routine matters. The whereabouts of thirty-six dollars for teachers' salaries, the building of a new school house, marriages, a student honored by an invitation to attend Hampton Institute—these are among the subjects of the letters.

From the *Lyons Republican* came a description of The Holley School: "This is the centre around which everything else revolves; and whatever else may fail, this goes on uninterruptedly from year's end to year's end, an ever active centre of influence constantly operating upon this community in the diffusion of intellectual light.... " The personal satisfaction seemed just as great as the public influence. In May, 1871, just a week after her forty-sixth birthday, and after nearly a decade on the Sea Islands, Laura Towne declared, "I do never intend to leave this 'heathen country.' I intend to end my days here and I wish to."[39] She died at Frogmore, her home, at age seventy-one.

It is perhaps fitting to leave the final word about the schoolmarms to the eminent black scholar W.E.B. DuBois, who wrote a novel about them, and who continually praised their work in *The Souls of Black Folk*. The schoolmarm, said DuBois, was "the best of all" to come from the Freedmen's Bureau. "This was the gift of New England to the freed Negro: not alms, but a friend; not cash, but character...love and sympathy...which these once saintly souls brought to their favored children in the crusade of the sixties, that finest thing in American history, and one of the few things untainted by sordid greed and cheap vainglory...In actual formal content their curriculum was doubtless old fashioned, but in educational power it was supreme, for it was the contact of living souls."[40]

Missionary Maidens

Mary Clemmer Ames

From Linda Warfel Slaughter, *The Freedmen of the South* (Cincinatti: Elm St. Printing Company, 1869).

This vignette, written just after the end of the Civil War, when teachers were arriving in the South in large groups, typifies the romantic view of many journalists who wrote sympathetically about the schoolmarms. They portrayed the "nigger teachers"—an epithet used throughout the South—as martyrs embodying all the popular female virtues: grace, elegance, Christian piety, and fine intelligence. Writings by the teachers themselves, by contrast, portray human beings enduring daily discomforts and occasionally questioning their own ability to persevere.

Attributed to "the artist pen of Mrs. Mary Clemmer Ames," this piece is included in a book of essays and letters from teachers published by Linda Warfel Slaughter in 1869. The author of poetry published in Godey's Lady's Book, as well as other writings, Slaughter (1843–1911) had also been a teacher in Kentucky and Tennessee for two years after her graduation from Oberlin College.

Harper's Ferry, West. Va.,
December, 1866

Yesterday, looking from my window, I caught a glimpse of "animated nature," which quickened with new life the repose caught from the blending here of ruins, rocks, and rivers. What was it? It was a small procession of Yankee girls, just from the cars, coming into Harper's Ferry, to scatter through the valley of Virginia, as teachers of the freed-people. *That* was a sight you would have to come all the way to the old slave-lands to appreciate! There they were—"the teachers!" The teachers! for whom Virginians had the most chivalric contempt, and the few Northern hearts here the warmest greeting.

A troop of maidens, who, in some undefinable way, suggest Tennyson's "sweet girl graduates with their golden hair," although I am very sure that their tresses are not all of the hue of the sun. I see jaunty hats and natty jackets, gay scarfs and graceful robes. I see elegance, beauty and youth; all come to brighten the lot of the lowly, to deliver from ignorance and vice that victim race which our brothers with their blood delivered from chains.

Opposite my window they encounter a Virginian belle, arrayed in the splendor of a purple dress, a scarlet shawl, a green hat, and a blue vail. Her scornful eyes behold the object which of all others she despises most—"a nigger teacher." What is worse, she beholds more than a dozen "nigger teachers" all together. It is a dreadful, unbearable sight, is it not, my dear? I suppose I ought to be very sorry for you; but I am not sorry a bit. It is an affliction of great magnitude, to be sure, that your whilom servants should be taught by better and prettier teachers than you ever had in your life; but it is a humiliation which you will have to bear, and the only way that you can lessen it is to improve yourself.

This old house, once occupied by the superintendent of the armories is now used as the temporary abode of the superintendent of the freed-people's schools in the valley of the Shenandoah, the Rev. Mr. Brackett, of Maine. In a grand old room, defaced by war, yet brightened with pictures and books from home, overlooking the prospect which I just inadequately sketched, I saw yesterday a scene not to be forgotten. That lovely Sabbath afternoon no church-doors opened to the teachers! With their books in their hands, they surrounded this wide room, holding a simple service of their own A room full of youthful women, far from home and all its loves, sang the Lord's song in a strange land. Those old walls, which within the last five years had resounded so often to the oath and jest of dissolute men, now sent back the echoes of sweet womanly voices, through which loving hearts trembled as they sang,

Nearer, my God, to Thee,
Nearer to Thee.

Here was the red-lipped school-girl, just from school; here the young widow, holding in tearful love the memory of buried husband and child; here were women in the prime of matured power, with their rare beauty of sumptuous womanhood— women, whose elegance and grace and fine mentality would have lent luster to the highest sphere. Such were the teachers of the freed slaves, who sat and knelt together; whose soft eyes dimmed with tears as they sang the hymns of home, and prayed for the blessing of God upon their work. After making due allowance for all superficial enthusiasm and the romance which may be inseparable from the womanly nataure and missionary labor, who can measure the significance of the fact that hundreds of young, gifted and cultivated women from the North are now scattered through the South as teachers of its former slaves; and though much against their will, and almost contrary to their knowledge, teachers as well of the old-time masters?

All unconsciously to themselves, in their mere presence, these women are educators.

In Spite of Threats

In these three brief pieces, the first an account given by a Northern supporter of the teachers, the second and third, excerpts from the teachers' letters home, the force of the Yankee schoolmarm's motivation shines through. Like the schoolmarm heroine of Charles Chesnutt's short story "The March of Progress" (see pp. 189–199), the first teacher described below, Carrie Croome, came South in memory of a loved one—her husband slain by the rebels. The second teacher believed that she would avenge the deaths of thousands of Union soldiers at Andersonville Prison camp by answering violence with the building of a school. Such discomfort as the third teacher reports could only have been endured in light of the larger mission.

I. The Schoolhouse Shall Stand

From *The Freedmen's Record,* Vol. 1, no. 9 (September 1865).

Within the shelter of the tall turpentine-trees at Clumfort's Creek, far out in the wilderness, where no point of bayonet could guard it, rose the Puritan schoolhouse. The American Missionary Association had posted its advanced picket here, in the person of Rev. George W. Greene, who had no sooner established this Northern institution than it was entered and occupied by a cultured lady, whom the New-England Freedmen's Aid Society sent out from Boston. This was Mrs. Carrie E. Croome. The rebels had slain her noble husband while in command of his battery at South Mountain; and she would avenge his untimely death by teaching the ignorant negroes how to throw off the yoke which those dastardly rebels had put upon their necks. This was the sublime retaliation of the gospel. But how was it met?

The sight of a "nigger schoolhouse" was more than the chivalry could bear. It had not been occupied many weeks in quietness, before three ruffians, calling themselves "Confederate soldiers," but really guerillas, appeared in the night time, set the schoolhouse on fire, rudely summoned Mrs. Croome from her house adjoining it, and bade her hasten away before that also should be given to the flames. They threatened her with violence, and tried to extort the promise that she would never again teach "niggers" to read. But she bore herself with dignity and calmness, and so escaped their power. The loss of clothing, books, school furniture, and other property is slight, compared with the calamity which despoiled these people, hungering and thirsting after knowledge, of the instruction they prized so highly. They were indignant, angry, and sorrowful by turns, and are more than ever determined that the schoolhouse *shall* stand amid their forest homes, and that their children *shall* drink at the fountains of knowledge. The indefatigable Missionary Association has sent out the same agent, well furnished with materials, to rebuild, at Clumfort's Creek, the temple of learning. It will soon rise from its ashes. *And not a few of the negroes have purchased muskets, with which to dispute the right of the burglar and the assassin, when again he comes that way.*

Could any thing be more significant than is this incident, of the spirit which animates, on the one side the Union legions, and on the other the Confederate troops? The one diffuse knowledge, the other enforce ignorance; one would make the whole land bright with liberty and love, the other would pollute it with deeds of darkness and violence, and stain it with the blood of slaves....

II. Work While the Day Lasts

From Linda Warfel Slaughter, "Arrivals and Early Days," *The Freedmen of the South* (Cincinatti: Elm St. Printing Company, 1869).

Yes, we will let the teachers* tell their own story in little fragments of letters, written for the most part with no thought of publication. Sweet sisters, if at first you feel inclined to blame the hand that seemingly betrays your confidence, reflect that it is not yourselves but the grace given unto you that we would fain perpetuate, and you must, perforce, forgive.

Another teacher gives the following statement:

"This is *the* Andersonville of dreadful memory—a place made sacred by the dust of sixteen thousand martyred heroes—a place at whose mention patriotic hearts throb with new impulse; for here was wrought out most visibly the spirit of the system which has so cursed our land with its presence. Here our brave men were distressed, persecuted, *murdered*, and here we institute our plan of revenge.

"Our school began—*in spite of threatenings from the whites, and the consequent fears of the blacks*—with twenty-seven pupils, four only of whom could read, even the simplest word. At

---

*"Of the American Missionary Association" [Editor's note in the 1869 publication].

the end of six weeks, we have enrolled eighty-five names, with *but fifteen unable to read.* In seven years' teaching at the North, I have not seen a parallel to their appetite for learning, and their active progress. Whether this zeal will abate with time is yet a question. I have a little fear that it may. Meanwhile it is well to 'work while the day lasts.' Their spirit *now* may be estimated somewhat when I tell you that three walk a distance of four miles, each morning, to return after the five hours session. Several come three miles, and quite a number from two-and-a-half miles.

"The night school, taught by Miss R——, numbers about forty, mostly men, earnest, determined, ambitious. One of them walks six miles, and returns after the close of the school, which is often as late as ten o'clock. One woman walks three miles, as do a number of the men.

"On Sabbath mornings, at half-past nine, we open our Sabbath-school, which is attended by about fifty men, women and children who give earnest attention to our instruction. The younger ones are given to the charge of 'Uncle Charlie,' a good old negro who wants to do something to help. Miss R—— takes the women, and leaves the men to my care. As they are unable to read, we take a text or passage of Scripture, enlarge upon and apply it as well as we are able, answering their questions, correcting erroneous opinions, extending their thoughts, and endeavoring to bring their souls from nature's darkness to the marvelous light of God's truth. Their views of the sacredness of life, its object, or of true living, are extremely limited; they need instruction absolutely in *everything.*"

III. I Can Get Along

From *The Freedmen's Bulletin,* Vol. 1, No. 6 (May 1965).

Arrived—went about gathering scholars; have forty. Did well enough till it rained; since then have walked three miles a day, ankle-deep in thick, black mud, that pulls off my shoes.

Nothing to eat but strong pork and sour bread. Insulted for being a "nigger teacher." Can't buy anything on credit, and haven't a cent of money. The school shed has no floor, and the rains sweep clean across it, through the places where the windows should be. I have to huddle the children first in one corner and then in another, to keep them from drowning or swamping. The Provost Marshal won't help me. Says "he don't believe in nigger teachers—didn't 'list to help them." The children come, rain or shine, plunging through the mud—some of them as far as I do. Pretty pictures they are. What shall I do? If it will ever stop raining, I can get along.

From Northern Home to Southern Dangers

Maria S. Waterbury

From Maria S. Waterbury, *Seven Years Among the Freedmen* (Chicago: T.B. Arnold, 1891).

This hair-raising account from Maria Waterbury's Seven Years Among the Freedmen *establishes the two worlds of the Northern teacher—in the white world she is a hunted enemy, the potential victim of a lynching; in the black world, she is a savior, to be guarded constantly. Indeed, for many blacks the school was a powerful symbol of freedom, a visible sign of God's favor. Prayers like the one Waterbury includes here—that Jesus keep the school in "de holler ob [his] han" were typical. Like many teachers, Waterbury went North each summer of her service. Although the journey described here was more hazardous than most, it illustrates that to Southerners the white woman's egalitarian association with blacks meant that she lost her right to the respect due a woman. Research yields no information about Waterbury except that recorded in her book. She appears to have taught in the deep South—at least in Tennessee and Mississippi— during the 1870s.*

Journeying

"In perils by mine own countrymen."—2 Cor. xi. 26.

T he instructions of the missionary society, are, "go south about eight hundred miles, until you find the plantation school waiting for you." The last week of November two of us start from near Chicago. Our Saratoga trunks are heavy with books. Our friends in the northern churches, have sent us with many prayers and blessings, and our gray-haired pastor has given us letters of introduction to churches at the South, wherever we may find a home. We are to teach our first Freedmen's school, on a plantation, twenty-five miles from a railroad. From Cairo, Illinois, we go down the Mississippi, and across to Paducah, Kentucky. The marks of the bomb-shelling the town received in war time, are still visible. The houses are unpainted, gloomy-looking habitations, some of them with ball holes in them.

From the large steamer we have crossed the river in, we ascend the bluffs, and take the cars on the M. & O. railroad. All day we have been traveling with a party of southern ladies, who have been north to attend a wedding; one of them walks with crutches. We have been through the train in Illinois, distributing tracts,* and the sweet-faced lady on crutches, says to us:

"Oh! you have tracts. Yes, I'll take some tracts, and I'll join your company too. I'm a preacher's wife, and I do that kind of work sometimes."

"Indeed! Do you work among black and white both?"

"Yes; I tell 'em they're all bound for the same place. The grave'll soon hold us all."

Directly one of the southern ladies, two or three seats distant, says in a loud voice, "You'll soon see some nigger teachers. My husband says they all wear spectacles, and read newspapers."

We laugh in our sleeves to think the high-toned southrons sought our society, and don't dream they are traveling with hated nigger teachers; but we say nothing. . . .

We reach the end of our railroad ride at midnight, and find at the shed-like depot only a white man with a lantern, and a dozen

---

*Pamphlets on their religious doctrine.

half-grown colored boys dressed in cotton sacks and cast-off clothes of Union soldiers....

After a night at a country hotel, the women were sent off on a mule cart. The driver, discovering that he had been cheated by the stable keeeper, abandoned the women in the woods. They were rescued and taken to their destination; but there, relatives of their to-be host, refused the "nigger teachers" entry. Finally they arrived on foot at the planter's, spent the night, and the next day journeyed another six miles to their school site.

Arriving at the plantation, we find a store, a shop or two, a white school, and an immense building, used in slave times for a white boys' school. We are to have living rooms in the upper story of the large building, and school rooms in the lower. A colored woman is employed as cook for us; and at our first Sunday-school, the next morning, over a hundred black people, men and women, join in singing so grandly, that it brings tears to our eyes to hear the wonderful pathos of their music. The white planter believes the school will please the blacks, and be a means of helping him keep the better class of them to do his work. At the first Sunday-school, he brings his newspaper, and sits in the chapel near us to hear our instruction. They tell us he is a class-leader, and we ask him to open the school with prayer. He peers at us over his spectacles and says, "That's your business, ma'am," and we two teachers go on with the school, giving oral instruction, as not ten of the hundred before us can read.

In the afternoon we go to the first colored meeting we have ever attended. Five ministers are in the pulpit. The church building is far inferior to the barns at home. A young preacher, very black, reads from Revelation vi., of "an angel with a pair of *banisters* in his hand." The ignorant sermon is done, and the praying! oh! that is enough to pay us for our journey of eight hundred miles, mule rides, poor whites, and all. We are lifted on those prayers heavenward, and the songs reach to the depths of our souls. As the benediction is pronounced, the only white man in the large audience, wearing lemon-colored kid gloves, rises and says he has heard of a school to be opened for the people, that he has thought of teaching a school himself, and will begin in the morning.

The young preacher of the day, says, "We has got our teachers here, from de norf, with much trouble, an' de good book says, ef we put our hand to de plow, an' look back, we aint fit fur de kingdom. An' we is goin' tu stick tu our teachers."

But the war against us has begun, and we are threatened with many things. "The building will be burnt I fear," says the planter. "You all can come to my house for awhile."

In the upper story of the plantation house, we are guarded by freedmen, not daring to begin our school. Here we pass the Christmas holidays, cared for by the planter's family, and guarded at night by colored people, who build great bonfires, and we hear them in their night watches, talking, and sometimes singing. They are paying dear for their first attempt at starting a school. On Christmas morning before breakfast, a colored woman, bearing two glasses of egg-nog, comes up stairs, saying, "Mrs. S. sends her compliments, and wishes you a merry Christmas." We thank her and say, "Tell the lady we never drink anything of the kind."

The astonished girl does down, and again returns, saying, "The missus wants to know if you will take some wine." We tell her we never drank a glass in our lives, and ask her to excuse us, saying, "Our church at home has the temperance pledge, as a part of the creed."*

We pass the day writing, and towards evening, go down to chat a little with the family. The planter rises and begins telling us we needn't fear, as he has his gun loaded, and dogs ready, and if there is any fuss, he can stop it. We notice his gun standing in the corner of the room, and soon he begins to stagger towards it, so drunk he nearly falls down. Alas! this is our protection! We hope it is better with the freedmen, but find many of them too, have been drinking. The planter has a wine cellar, and to cheer them

*The national movement for abstention from alchohol—the temperance movement—attracted many women who were also abolitionists and supporters of woman suffrage.

up in their trouble, has taken one or two favorite ex-slaves into it, and dealt out liquors to them, and they have given to others, until many on the place are drunk.

We retire to our room, realizing that our "weapons are not carnal." Before the holidays are over, we see children drunk, for the first time in our lives. In a week we begin school, and immediately start a temperance society. Before the five months of school are closed, there are over a hundred members to our Band of Hope, and over thirty are hopefully converted....

A large brick house with a lovely garden in the rear, walks bordered with box, fig trees with green and ripe figs on them, tall pines down the walk, lovely roses, and climbing vines—one of the homes of aristocracy in slave times. The planter who lived here owned several hundred slaves. Now a family from the North reside here, and we two "nigger teachers" board with them. The family have been visiting twenty miles away for a day or two, and we teachers are keeping house for them, with a colored family of six persons living in the kitchens...and doing all the work for us. We are in charge of two colored schools a mile away. We have heard of the Ku-Klux being on their night raids of late, and this morning as the clock struck two, we heard a low whistle outside the gate, and Miss C—— and the writer woke the same moment, each saying to the other, "Did you hear that?" We struck a light, pulled down the shades of the windows, and hastily dressed, but not before we heard the tramp of heavy feet on the porch outside. Our room opened into another room kept for storage purposes, where was a large box of shelled corn. 'Twas the work of a moment for us to slip a package containing a large sum of money, that had been left by an officer under government, in care of the lady of the house, into the box of corn, and drag our Saratoga trunks against the door. The money was left in our care in the absence of the family, and for a moment we supposed the night riders had found it out; but afterwards learned they knew nothing of it, but were trying to impress upon the teachers, and northern family, the fact that "this is a white man's government."

Tramp, tramp went the feet, first on the north porch, then on the south, and ever and anon a whistle, and we expected them to
(text continued on page 120)

Missus Comes fur Larn We!

1: Laura Towne, with pupils Dick Washington ("my righthand man"), Maria Wyne, and Amoretta ("bright and sharp as a needle"), 1866. Among the first teachers in "freedmen's schools," Towne and her friend Ellen Murray continued teaching in South Carolina for the remainder of their lives.
2: Ellen Murray with pupils Grace and Peg, 1866.
3: Caroline Putnam, teacher of freed people from 1868 to ca. 1897.
4: Sallie Holley followed Caroline Putnam South in 1870; together they established the Holley School, in Lottsburgh, Virginia.
5: Visiting teacher Harriet Murray (sister to Ellen) with Elsie and Puss, 1866. Puss was adopted and reared by Laura Towne and Ellen Murray.

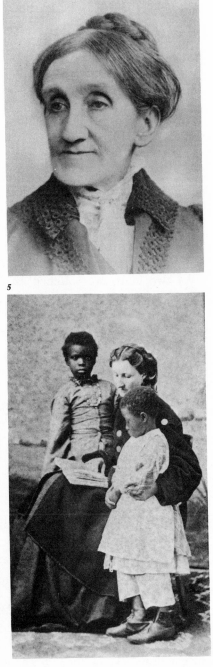

3

5

enter, but God heard our prayers for safety. We sat, one on each side of our little table, with our lamp lighted, and our Bibles in our hands, and read aloud the promises of our God, so mighty to save.

"As the mountains are round about Jerusalem, so the Lord is round about his people from henceforth even forever."—Psa. cxxv. 2.

"If two of you shall agree on earth, as touching any thing that they shall ask, it shall be done for them of my Father which is in heaven."—Matt. xviii. 19.

We said, "Lord, we *do agree*, and we ask that the intruders may not enter this room.

Together we repeated the same prayer, over and over, and soon one of us said, "I have the assurance that they *will not* enter." Tramp, tramp went the feet on the porch, and we heard them try the locks of the doors, and whistle to each other, and thus for over two hours we watched and waited, and only until the morning began to dawn, did they go to their carriages and ride away.

In the morning we saw the tracks of horses, and of many people. The next night a guard from the town, a mile away, came and staid on the plantation.

We afterwards heard there were two wagon loads of Ku-Klux, but they dared not enter to molest us, as they feared we were armed, and so we were, and guarded, too, for "the angel of the Lord encampeth round about them that fear him, and delivereth them." We had only proved God's faithfulness.

The Prayer Meeting

"How d'ye, ma'am! I cum tree mile dis mornin', tu tell ye de Lawd stood by me last night, an' he tell me you all *is safe!* He aint gwine tu let ye get 'sturbed by de white 'uns, honey. You jes go on teechin' de skule, an' de good Massa tote you in his bosom.

"I got shoutin' happy last night, an' my ole man says, 'Peggy, what ails ye?' I says, 'Ole man, wake up! de Lawd is yer! He done jes filled me, an' he aint gwine tu let dat are skule be broke up.' Honey, de Lawd jes showed me how he shet de lions' mouths, an' he got ye all in de holler ob his hand; dey can't touch a hair o' you heads. Hallelujah! Massar Jesus got sumthin' tu du wid dis skule. You jes go on teechin', honey. De Lawd dun sent de angels, tu stan' by ye. He cover ye wid his feathers."

A prayer-meeting—fifty black people—some gray-headed, who were stolen from Africa when they were infants; some whose mothers had been sold and run off to the sugar plantations, before they were a year old. Ah! how such had learned to pray. Now the school had been threatened by Ku Klux. A letter had been written to a teacher, with the picture of a white girl tied to a tree, and a man standing on each side, with an overseer's whip, laying strokes on her back. "On the side of their oppressors there was power." Under the picture was written, "This is the way we serve northern *'nigger teachers.'* Beware! lest you shere the same fate." This is not a fancy picture, reader, but an actual fact.

Old Aunt Emeline begins the prayer-meeting by singing in the old slavery wail, trotting her foot to keep time, and all join in singing, swaying their bodies from side to side, as if overwhelmed with grief:

'Rastlin' Jacob! an' I will not let thee go!
'Rastlin' Jacob! an' I will not let thee go!

Still wailing out the song, they fall upon their knees, and with sobs and prayers, tell Jesus about "dem people who's tryin' tu brake up de skule."

"Masser Jesus, put dy hand ober our teachers. Jesus, aint you de same God as took Jonah out ob de belly ob de whale? Shine in our hearts, Masser Jesus, and help us tu lub our enemies. Ain't you de same God as 'livered Dan'l from de den ob lions? 'Liver us, good Lawd, an' tote us in yo' bosom, an' hedge us 'bout, an' plant us out anew fur de kingdum. Masser Jesus, set down de right foot ob dy power *hea'!* an' keep dis skule in de holler ob you' hand. Cum dis way, Masser, an' bind us all in de bundle ob life". . . .

Going Home

Our first year of school is over. We have taught over two hundred colored people, only two lady teachers, of all ages, sizes, and colors, from jet-black to pure white-looking, and many of the

class called by the jet-black ones "yaller ones." We have lived in
an old school building, used for a white school in slave times,
now a harbor for rats by day, and dogs by night....

Now the school is done, and the people have come to say
good-by's. We are to start at four o'clock in the morning, for a
twenty-five mile ride....

Next in order is a prayer-meeting, to pray for our safe journey
home. They pray for everything we shall ever need, if we live a
thousand years. They remind Masser Jesus of all his promises.

"Lawd, don't ye say you'll stan' by dem as trusts in ye? Cum
right down yer now, Masser Jesus, an' take a walk troo dis
country, an' see what de debbil's duin' in de kingdom."

"Lawd, place blessings by de wayside fur our teachers."

"Tote 'em safe down de stream o' time, Masser Jesus, an' let de
ole ship o' Zion lan' 'em high up in heaven, an' crown 'em
dine"....

"The carriage is ready, ma'am." The children are giving us great
bouquets, and some give us cakes and candy, and the blacks
almost push each other, for the privilege of stowing our luggage.
The good-by's come between sobs and tears. Some reach up to
touch our hands, after we are seated in the carriage, and one calls
out, "My God, is they gone!"....

Three miles on our journey, and a halloo announces to us that
we are followed by one of our young men scholars—Robert, a
young Methodist Episcopal preacher, has determined to go
North with us to get an education. Some of the white people have
found it out, and all night he has been hunted by those who have
threatened to kill him. He rides a mule, has lost his hat, and left
all his books and most of his clothing behind. One of the
teachers pays his fare, and he comes on with us.

Jackson, Tennesse—the end of our first day's railroad travel.
No trains have passed out of this place for three days. There is a
strike on the road. Many passengers and trains are waiting. The
workmen claim they haven't had their pay for two years, and as
our train nears the depot, a committee of three or four men
loosen the engine, and run it into an engine house near by. Two
or three hundred of excited people are on the platform, and all is
confusion.

We go to the nearest hotel, and to another, and another, but everywhere are refused a night's lodging, or a meal of victuals. We go back to the train. Evening: Lamps lighted in the cars. Passengers, all but us, seem to have found some place for the night. Soon we hear the familiar title, *"nigger teachers!"* hissed out near us. The conductor tells us there are soldiers on board the train, who have come to guard the engines. He brings the head officer of the staff to us; we show him the commissions of the American Missionary Association recommending us to the protection of the government, and immediately we are under guard. Enter the postmaster on the train—a northern gentleman. He tells us the people of this place say *they have never surrendered.* Instantly he comprehends the situation. Some outside are calling out our names. Pounding on the cars, some one calls out,

"Miss W ——, Miss T ——, you'd better come out. There's goin' to be a nigger killed!"

The soldiers raise the window, and threaten to shoot the next man who moves his tongue against us. The postmaster, with his arms full of velvet cushions off the seats, followed by one or two colored helpers, proceeds to fit up the postal car, and soon orders our trunks into it, and we follow him out of doors, and around to the end of the car. The mob by this time has increased; but one soldier is behind us, another near by, and the brave postmaster is fully armed. He makes a way through the crowd, and we are locked into our quarters among the mail bags, and could sleep if we knew what had become of Robert, and if the mercury was not up to 90°, and the *fleas would keep still. . . .*

Just at dark, the fifth day of our imprisonment, a lady comes on board the train, guarded by a soldier. She has heard of our situation, and comes to invite us to spend the night with her, out in a house, half fallen down, where she lives alone. She is a teacher of freedmen; has a pass from Governor Brownlow, to go where she pleases, and pleases to stay in this place, because her only son, all she has left since the war, is a soldier, and quartered here.

We thought we had seen poverty before, but here is *abject poverty;* no comforts in her room, no Bible. Her education is so poor she can hardly talk correctly. She tells us she has never studied grammar; wants us to spend the night with her, and help her teach the school on the morrow. The woman, in her endeavors to have us enjoy our prison life, fairly outdoes herself; gives us her small couch, suitable only for one person, finds a blanket or two among the freedmen, brings a lamp and a few sticks, lights a fire, and asks us to read our Bibles and have family worship. Together we read, and draw water from the wells of salvation. God seems so near we don't either fear or feel lonely. The new-found friend rolls herself up in a blanket, lays her loaded revolver by her pillow, and lies on the floor at night, saying, "I've often done it since that war," and gives us two teachers her bed. Morning: Our food is provided by some of the freedmen—a few biscuits, coffee, and milk. We eat in singleness of heart, and are thankful. We have at least found Christian companionship, and we go into the school and teach for an hour or two; but soon a colored man comes to inform us we are being followed and are unsafe, and we go back to our car and remain another day under guard.

In the evening, a lady closely veiled, and guarded by a soldier, comes on the train to see us—a northern woman, bound for New York—a sympathizer with us. She proposes a walk around the fortifications. The next day, we three ladies, with a soldier following not far from us, go out to view the earth works and rifle-pits; not as much to see the lions, as to get fresh air. We are returning to our train, but on the way, stop at the hotel where the lady boards, and, for a few moments, rest in her room. The proprietor of the hotel, very soon knocks at the door, calls the lady into the hall, and tells her he will not have us in his house; and if she associates with *nigger teachers*, she must also leave his house. He says we ought to marry niggers, and quite a little more of that kind of talk.

We are now *three* ladies on the train, under guard. For nine successive days and nights we have endured the tropical heat, but our courage holds out. Many have been on the train to see us, much as we have seen animals exhibited in a menagerie. Men and women have come in and passed through the cars, looking at us, as if we were there for show. To all who would accept them, we have given tracts, and most of them go away reading. . . .

As all things come to an end in time, on the tenth day the strike is over. The train is about to pull out, when our colored young preacher makes his appearance. Some of the people have offered him twenty-five dollars to leave the teachers and stay with them; but he prefers to continue his journey northward, and is allowed to ride in the smoking car. Several hundred people are on the platform; as the train is to move on, some attempt to open the door, and find it locked. The soldiers are on duty, and safely we leave the Jackson friends, to meet them, perhaps, in another world. Who shall say where? "Inasmuch as ye have done it unto one of the least of these my brethren, ye have done it unto me"....

Sisters in the Service

Sarah Chase, Lucy Chase, Julia Rutledge

From Henry L. Swint, ed., *Dear Ones at Home* (Nashville, Tenn.: Vanderbilt University Press, 1966).

Quaker sisters from a prosperous Worcester, Massachusetts family, Sarah (1836–1911) and Lucy (1822–1909) Chase went South in 1863 as teachers appointed by the Boston Educational Commission. They served first in refugee camps on Craney Island, Virginia, then throughout the South. In 1866, in ill health, Sarah returned North, but Lucy taught in Richmond, Virginia, and Florida until 1869. Skilled administrators and organizers, these two, in letters to "dear ones at home," described their travels through the South to set up massive school systems, distribute supplies, and establish labor systems—activities uncommon for women.

Like other secular teachers, the sisters were less missionaries than organizers of the black community for self-government and self-help. Notable in this connection are Sarah Chase's argument for maintaining separate black schools, and the letter to Sarah from Julia Rutledge, a freedmen's school graduate in training to become a teacher. In eloquent language, the letter makes it clear that Julia Rutledge not only loved her former teachers, the Chase sisters, but had been guided and sustained by them in her

*own mission of carrying on the work of schooling black
children.*

*Richmond
April 18th [1865]*

Hurray!! The Peace—thank God!*
Though much exhausted with my morning task of governing and teaching (oral and with the black board) my *little* school
of *one thousand and* twenty-*five* children, who but a few days ago
were slaves—I will try to give you a few hints of my work since I
last wrote. It is useless to wait longer for leisure and freshness for
writing. . . .

Although the officers and newspapers say truly that no one
can get to Richmond, unless ordered—and such multitudes are
waiting in Washington-Norfolk and at Fortress Monroe for
passes—our party. . .through intimate acquaintance with the
leading officers here, got passes to come at once, to organize the
work in the beginning of the new regime—and constantly and
diligently have we labored through the day; and in the night I
have *thought* for coming time. Government can only give us
leave to *work*, but by ourselves we have got the field and labor
organized in less than ten days, in a manner that gratifies and
surprises us.

Never have I attended committee meeting more dignified and
to the point than the many we have appointed with the
leading men in the colored churches. At our first meeting a noble
looking and most intelligent deacon started up suddenly saying,
"I felt frightened for a moment seeing more than five colored
people together"—it being the law here that more than five must
never assemble without a white man was authorized to sit with
them. Not long ago, the white man they employed to sit in one of
their Sunday Schools stepped out on an errand and was detained
a little, and the whole school with its teachers was carried to
jail. . . .

We have already enrolled over two thousand pupils and expect
to nearly double the number before long. As soon as our teachers
come up and the schools are turned over to them, I shall open

*This was the day that the Confederate capitol fell, and the war ended.

employment offices and get manufactures under way—it is too soon yet—and most too soon for schools. The officers sent their wives passes to come up and had to telegraph them *not* to come. So of course the teachers cannot come for it is not yet safe. I have heard many threats, and these impetuous people are every day shooting or stabbing someone, so I want no one to come until these people are convinced they are under Govt. The delay is no disadvantage to the little ones, who can be taught to sit still & how to give attention, en masse—their brains can be roused and put in working order by general instructions and exercises, so that when they have their books and teachers they can make a better beginning and I feel that these mental gymnastics I give them will always make study easier for them. I have talked with them in all the churches and met them outside where they weep over me, call down blessings on my head, shake my poor hands so they keep lame so I can hardly hold my pen—as I pass some caressingly take hold of my raiment while some push back the crowd.—All this I well know is not for me but for "de good Norf people." And how much I wish these same good North people who have prayed and worked for the people here could join with them in their songs of joy and thanksgiving, as it has been my privilege in this, their day of jubilee. I have opened books in the different churches with headings of occupations where I register names—and soon expect to find very advantageous in getting work.

The colored people will need little help except in helping themselves. We are not going to make beggars of them. Will you please consult with your Society in regard to getting a box of straw & materials for braiding—and yarn & needles & other materials for manufacture. . . .

Savannah Wharf on "a stack" of boxes barrels & trunks
Dec. 1st 1865

Dear Mrs. May;*
Since I saw you, I have been almost like a bag of the wind; at no time sufficiently settled to report on "Winter plans."

*Member of Boston Committee on Clothing and Supplies.

   The last six weeks of our vacation were to have been given to
pleasant recreation, and farewell glances into beloved house-
holds in the northern cities, but a crying need for someone who
knew the lay of the land, to found a family* in Norfolk made us
turn our steps that way, instead; where we took a large empty old
house (but two doors from the one we occupied last season) and
fitted it up for the teachers. The day after we arrived, we
reopened all the schools belonging to our family, and held them
in a large church three weeks till other members came, teaching
regularly and faithfully all who were ready to come to school.
The schools are never full till Winter—all working, who are able,
as long as they can get "jobs"; many selling cakes and candies
about the streets. Each day the stragglers came in—and all took
hold, with a good will, to learn. Mr. Banfield† was the young man
sent out by the society to be gentleman of the house, and we
three worked together in converting the dismal, deserted old
place, into a pleasant home.
   As soon as the family came, we gave over the schools, and
opened two large schools at the Rope Walk, (the Refugee
Camp)—of which we had general supervision. I wish you could
have seen our grotesque, wild, lawless menagerie of a school, the
first few days, when it seemed as if the little "fliberty gibbets" had
arms and legs by the dozens; and all seemed to have more than
the lawful number of tongues—the third day, saw an orderly and
most interesting school; and I could hardly believe it had any
relationship to the first days gathering. These schools we held
while we remained; taking care of the old women's home, in
addition;—and fitting them up for Winter—visiting the familys
of the sick and needy; and attending to the wants of all old &
extremely destitute people, in the time not given to the school.
The enthusiastic welcomings of the people on our return, were
most touching as well as gratifying. They told us they knew we
were coming back; though we had told them we certainly should
not—when we left. "Wese been a praying for yer,—and prayin
you might come back to us; for you knowd our ways and trials as

*A Quaker expression meaning "working group."
†J. Stuart Banfield, a teacher from Dover, New Hampshire.

if you was of us, always; and peared like we could tell you, and you could understand & do for us, as no one else could" said they.

"Teachers are wanted in Georgia—only men—it not being agreeable, proper, or safe for ladies—Who'll go?" We reported ourselves as ready to start any time at a days notice & Nov. 20th Mr. Banfield, Miss Ellen B. Haven (of Portsmouth N.H. one of our family and a particular friend of ours) Lucy & I took the overland route for Savannah. Nine toilsome tedious days of tortuous terrible travelling brought us to this lovely (all but the dirt) city.

I marvel much that we are here alive—travelling as we did, day and night—the wheels getting on fire—axles breaking, frequent fording and occasional collisions—the roads, engines and cars, so much out of order. Most grateful too am I to be thus far on the road. Our final destination I know not, the agent of the State being in the interior and not answering our telegram (wh. probably do not reach [him?])....

Savannah is ravishingly lovely: all the streets are very wide—running entirely across the city, dividing it in squares, like Phila. a broad strip of green, with trees on both sides, runs through the centre of the streets—which also have shade trees over the sidewalk. High in the gardens hang the golden oranges, sending their sweet perfume afar, and drooping over the full blooming Camilla [sic], which gladdens the eyes through the Winter....

Columbus, Georgia
Feb. 5th 1866

Dear Mrs. May;
When I last wrote we had just opened a school at Savannah. There were already several schools opened there and Col. Sickles was administering the affairs of the Bureau in a most admirable manner, so it did not seem right to tarry in that charming city, though we could have found enough important work to fill every moment. Wishing to work where there was the most need (there being so many places where nothing has been done for the Freedmen, and where they are sorely persecuted), we came here, where a school house, built by the soldiers, had just been destroyed by the citizens and the feeling is intensely bitter

against *anything* northern. The affairs of the Bureau have been [f]rightfully mismanaged here; and our Govt has been disgraced by the troops who were stationed here. Now the troops are withdrawn, and the people are chafing at the presence of the Bureau and "a few pious and enthusiastic N.E. school marms:" "both must be cleared out of the place," says the daily press.

We have never seen any discourtesy in any of the citizens, but we know that we are generally *discussed* in circles; and many plans are proposed for "getting rid" of us.—We have glorious schools in full blast.—And I am so satisfied with the work here that nothing in the world could make me wish to be in another place, or doing anything else. In my own day school and night school, I have 140 pupils, who have made truly wonderful progress, in the five weeks I have been teaching....

With ever best wishes—singing at the plough.

S.E.C.

Monday April 2d [1866]

Dear Mr. May
Your welcome letter, *and* the money, came duly to hand. Lucy paid for the bbl. with other "contraband" freight we brought, with money she had for the purpose. In regard to "mixed schools," I regret that I am obliged to say, not what I *think*, but what I *know*; id est, they are an impossibility. I feel confident they would be of no benefit to the blacks in Md. Va. N.C. S.C. Ga. and Ala., consequently I cannot see how they will work well, in any part of the South.

No one is more anxious than I that the Southern whites should be elevated; but my life is consecrated to the blacks.

Since all are friendly to the whites, there is a certainty that their cause will not suffer. If the few friends of the Freedmen continue in their special field, I think they will be far better satisfied, in the end. Enough will be done for the whites, *without* the combination, and *far less* for the blacks, will be accomplished *through* it than is now. I think no one who has been in the field could differ from me. How long it took the enlightened North to make the experiment of mixed schools a success! I am not sure that they could yet be pronounced successful except in a few districts. Think how much the South is behind the North in civilization, and how much worse the feeling is between the whites and the blacks! Wishing well to *all* mankind, I have much desired to see a movement for the elevation of the Southern whites: (though I feel it no duty to take part in the work, their [sic] being plenty of people for it) and have had this matter on my mind throughout my Southern life and have talked Education and Industry to them whenever I have met them; and on my own responsibility urged them to go to the "Yankee Schools," knowing what a benefit it would be to the *blacks,* to be thus associated with the whites they are to have dealings with in future. But though the parents were "wishing their children had the advantages the Niggers were enjoying" they usually "would rather they'd die than go to school with the Niggers" or they said: "I never will get so low as to have my children learnin with nigs."

No matter how strict the rules, and wise and kind the teachers plans, for the comfort, and rights of the black scholar; the *feeling* of the whites expressed or not—*will* keep the sensitive African away; though he would willingly bear cold, hunger, and whippings if need be—to "get a little larnin." I know I. agrees with me, for she made no dissent, when I was talking; on the subject last eve....

With best wishes
S.E.C.

Normal School Va.
Oct 4th 1868

Dear Miss Chase
     I will venture to send you another letter hoping you will may get it   I have not heard a word from you for the last year wich keeps me in an anxious state   Dear Miss Chase I cannot tell you how very anxious I am to hear from you—if you get this letter I will send my picture as I promise it and would like you to have one   please if we are fortunate enough to take up our

corresponds again I would like very much to have a picture of you and Miss Lucy. I will give you an account of my self. I am here in virginia at school the school you wrote to tell me about paying my own way by working the girls work in doors and the boys on the farm the girls all have all the domestic affairs wash for the boys sow all the scrubbing to do

there are about 14 girls and 22 boys five from Charleston Mr Jefferson are one of the number I like it very much indeed we are very comfortably fix our chambers are neatly furnish cottage setts and every convienientcy we have water pipes in the house a baithing room.

I will tell you the rules the bell ring at half pass five allowing us half our to dress then it ring at six for breakfast tha allow five minutes if you are not there in time you are mark the bell ring at eleven for the boys to stop work and fix for dinner and school we dine at 12 clear up our dineing room and get in school by one we have school from one to five and then we recrute about a half our and the bell ring for evening prayers after prayers we go in to supper at half pass seven the bell ring for us to study we study untill half pass 8 the bell ring for us to get ready for bed at nine it ring for us to out the lights. and the best of it were have such a very kind Matron She tries in every way to make us happy each schollar love her and would not be happy without her She is a Miss Breck from Massachusetts. I hear from home pretty often Sarah did not come she is at home My sisters did not think wise for both of us to leave home the rebs have taken Mr Sumners school building at the corner of Morris and Jasper Court where we spent those delightful ours in the afternoon trying to gain kowledge tha have it for the Colored Children the picture you gave I had it very neatly frame in a guild fram I have sent to have it here with me

Louissia Elliott expect to come on very soon Louissia are one of your schollars. dear Miss Chase I am very anxious to see you I often wish you were here to teach I trust I will have the pleausure of seeing you once more. Should we not meet on earth may we meet in heaven where parting is no more give my best love to Miss Lucy   tell her I will write her next—

Good bye with a double potion of love.

Yours truly.
Julia A. Rutledge

Gordonsville, Virginia
Decr 14th '69

M iss Lowell,*
My kind, generous frd:
Excuses are said to be "lame"; but surely mine halt not; they are indeed sure footed. I am still alone!. . .

In the meantime, although my duties are onerous, I am delighted with my school. As I am alone, of course, the school is ungraded, and my classes are many; but I keep school until half past three; and, very often until four o'clock, and so I am able to add what I will call intellectual exercises to the ordinary exercises. I oblige every class to learn the meaning of all the important words in every-days reading-lessons; and I am daily gratified by their promptness and accuracy in defining the words, when they stand in class. I appoint, every morning, one from each class as interlocutor, and I oblige the whole school to listen to all the definitions; while all who can write, put upon their slates the words in their own lessons, with the definitions thereof. Time is demanded for that exercise, but it is indeed well spent. The children, all of them enjoy it. Most of them comprehend it, and their wits are perceptibly quickened by it. I have one class in the Fr'dm'ns Book which offers an amazing store of valuable words.† I frequently call the attention of the whole school to illustrations of the meaning of familiar words. I spend a good deal of time in teaching Arithmetic both Mental and Written. Many of the children add, almost without halting,

*"Probably Anna Lowell, of the New England Freedmen's Aid Society, Boston" [Editor's note in *Dear Ones at Home*].

†The reference is to Lydia Marie Child's *The Freedmen's Book.* See selection, p. 159

long columns of figures which I place upon the black-board, and many of them can mentally add, subtract, multiply and divide, units tens, and even hundreds, with readiness. I spend so much time upon these exercises that I can mark the improvement, which is rapid. I have three classes in Geography, and I give, daily, lessons to the whole school on Maps. All the children can navigate the Gulfs and Bays of the Globe, and they are now journeying with pleasure through the U.S., halting at the capital cities and sailing on the pleasant rivers. In addition to the defining exercise, of which I have told you, I hear the spelling and defining of the words above the reading lessons, and I also hear the whole school spell daily from a speller. . . .

Alone, too, I keep a night school. For awhile, I kept it five nights in the week, but generally I have but three night sessions. What little time these labors leave me is industriously seized hold of by the needy and sociable, who, having no love for the rebels about them, would fain seek help from me; and give me the reverence they love to bestow on a white skin.

Sincerely
Lucy Chase

Hard Work Every Day:
A New England Woman's
Diary in Dixie

Mary Ames

From Mary Ames,From *A New England Woman's Diary in Dixie* (Springfield, Ma.: Plimpton Press, 1906).

Perhaps more than any other writings, these simple diary entries of Mary Ames (1831–1903) (not the Mary Ames of the first selection) typify the flavor of daily life for an average

teacher. Ames and her friend Emily Bliss, natives of
Springfield, Massachusetts, spent fifteen months on the South
Carolina Sea Islands just at the end of the war, when supplies
were scarce, sickness and death stalked everyone, and whites
isolated as these women were, depended on the black
community for survival. These excerpts illustrate, among
other themes, the closeness that grew between the freedmen
and their Northern teachers.

Ames' Diary, written in 1865 and 1866, was published in
1906 in memory of her sister, and to provide a scholarship for
a black student to Hampton Institute, a black institution of
higher education founded in 1868 for the education of the
freedmen.

May 17 [1865]. A very warm morning. We find our half-mile walk
to school tiresome. A large school, sixty-six scholars, and rather
unruly. Poor Emily is not adapted to deal with such rough boys. I
am obliged to go to her aid and, stamping my feet and shouting
my commands, bring them to order. We are teaching the children
the days of the week, the months, and also to count.

Six new scholars. A woman came with a prayer-book, asking to
be taught to read it. We told her we would teach her willingly,
but it would be some time before she could read that. She was
satisfied, and as she was leaving, put her hand under her apron
and brought out two eggs—one she put in Emily's lap, the other
in mine.

May 18. The evening was delightfully cool. We had our first
evening school for men and women on our piazza. It was well
attended, all sitting on the floor and steps. One woman, who was
much bent with rheumatism, and seemed very old, said she was
"Mighty anxious to know something."

June 2. Mr. Everett is quite sick. We sent to the commissary for
the Government doctor, who had gone to Beaufort. Then we sent
to headquarters for Dr. Mason. He says Mr. Everett has typhoid
symptoms.

At school there were seventy scholars, who behaved pretty
well. A girl came just recovering from smallpox. She was
indignant when we sent her away, but we pacified her by telling

her she could come back in a few weeks. Going up to our bedroom we met on the stairs a rattlesnake. We screamed lustily, and Uncle Jack, Jim, George, and Zack* appeared. I jumped over it, and it fell through the balusters to the hall, where the men killed it. We find in our room many holes where it could have come up in the walls from the cellar. To-morrow we shall paper our walls with newspapers.

Sunday, June 4. No church going—too warm, and the walk too long for Sundays, as we are obliged to take it every week-day. We seated ourselves on the piazza to write letters. Soon a crowd of children were around us, all wanting books, and before we knew it we were teaching school. George and Zack came with the others. George is patient and promising. We are surprised at the ease with which he acquires the sound of words. He teaches his father after leaving us.

Sunday, June 11. Hottest morning we have had—not a breath of air. Dr. Mason advises us to leave the island as soon as possible—not safe for us to stay much longer. A woman who brought some cucumbers said she would make any sacrifice to serve us, who were doing so much to teach her children, who knew nothing but how to handle a hoe. George killed another rattlesnake under the plum tree,—they are after the figs—horrid creatures!

June 13 and 14. Intolerably hot days—rather cooler at night. Had a very large school, one hundred and one scholars—too many—cannot keep order with so many. I am well worn out before noon with shouting and stamping, for I am obliged to help Emily when she gets into difficulty. We stayed after school closed with three unruly boys, rough and tough customers, who confessed that they liked to tease us; but they were ashamed and promised to do better in the future.

Captain Storrs called. He told us there were five guerrillas at camp; they had been caught on the island, but there is no evidence to convict them and they will probably be set at liberty.

June 15. Hot, hotter, hottest! Impossible to go up to the church for school. The children came down to see why we did not

---

*Members of the black family with whom Mary Ames and Emily Bliss shared the house.

appear. We kept them and had school on the piazza; Emily there, and I down in the yard.

Mr. Blake brought whisky and remedies for Mr. Everett. He went to Beaufort for them, and nearly lost his life coming back. A storm arose, and the high wind blew their little boat thirty miles out to sea; if he had not had a small compass, he could not have got back. Mr. Blake gave us liberty to stop teaching when we like, and we have decided, as it is so fearfully hot and Emily's head troubles her so much, to have school in our house until we can go to the bay for our vacation.

June 16. Jim and Uncle Jerry have cleared out our big front room and arranged some boards on blocks for seats for the older children. The little ones can sit on the floor. Fifty came this morning. They are to bring stools—as many as have them—so we shall get on well.

Mr. Everett bade us farewell, riding off on his white beast; he seemed pretty weak. Mr. Redpath writes that we are to report to Mr. Pillsbury, as he himself goes North on the next steamer, and advises us to close our school. All the Charleston schools are closed, as there is much sickness; one northern teacher having died. He thinks we had better go North for our vacation. We cannot do that, for we should never return.

If our friends at home could only see our flowers! Cloth of gold roses and lovely Cape Jessamines. The evening was pleasant; the children sang to us and we told them stories,—Red Riding Hood, etc. They had never listened before to stories of any kind, and were most attentive.

June 19. We like the new school arrangement, for we do not get so warm, can wear loose sacks, and can spare our lungs.

When we feel tired, we sing, which they all enjoy. They particularly delight in singing "Hang Jeff Davis to a sour apple tree."

The children told us some of their experiences in slave life. One boy, Tom, showed us deep scars on his arms; said they were from severe whippings. When about eight years old, he rode a horse to a distant place, and lost the colt that was following; and of course was whipped.

Sunday, June 25. The sun came out and we had Sunday school in the school-room. I do the preaching and Emily attends to the

singing. She is highly amused at my teachings. What surprises
me is that they know so little of the life of Christ; not knowing
even of his birth, but they all are familiar with his sayings. They
all believe in a hell! I asked the children whom they love best.
Some answered "God"; Zack said,"Ma, she loves me and feeds
me."

[October 1865?] When Jim was sick, Sarah sent her baby to the
neighbors to be cared for, and devoted herself to the sick ones.
We did everything in our power, giving money and other things
to make them comfortable. Jim died the twelfth of September.
Sarah had succumbed to the same disease, and two weeks later
she died. The last time I saw her, she asked me to take her seven
children north to my "plantation." I promised to do all I could.

We told Judy, who had taken the baby, that we would clothe it
and pay her for its care, but she got tired of the child, and one day
left it at our house and slipped away. Rhoda begged me to keep it
and let her care for it, but I declined, knowing Mistress Rhoda
and myself too well to enter into such a partnership. One of our
neighbors, a young woman, took it for a time.

We consulted Mr. Alden about the children. George was old
enough to take care of himself. Zack was given to a woman, who
promised to treat him as her own. The younger children and baby
were sent, several weeks later, to the Charleston orphan asylum.

Mary Emily did not live long, nor did Charlotte, who was a
sickly little girl. Poor little Ben, the most affectionate of them all,
refused to eat, and died of homesickness the next winter.

My sister, who came down to visit us, carried Ann, aged seven,
and another little girl, Maggie Murphy, home with her. They
have lived in Springfield ever since...

[Fall 1865] When we made out the school report to send to
Boston, we were surprised that out of the hundred, only three
children knew their age, nor had they the slightest idea of it; one
large boy told me he was "Three months old." The next day many
of them brought pieces of wood or bits of paper with straight
marks made on them to show how many years they had lived.
One boy brought a family record written in a small book....

We had been inconvenienced by the lack of a chimney in the
schoolhouse. One day when, choking with smoke, we asked the

children if some of their fathers could not come and fix the stove, they began, "I haven't any father"—"I live with Aunty," and so on. We were surprised to learn how orphaned our school was. Eight of Captain Bacheller's men built a chimney for us. In return we gave each of them a book, which pleased them. They were fine-looking fellows and all of them could read....

[Winter 1866] A [government] horse was sent to Emily; we had the carryall and a buggy which came from home. We were altogether so comfortable that we invited my sister Elizabeth, my friend Mrs. French, and Emily's sister and her husband to visit us. They came in February; helped us with our school and criticised our housekeeping.

Robert and Rhoda had come with us from the bay. Rhoda was not the best of cooks, and now that she was "Striving for religion," she and Robert had to go to so many "Shouts" and dances that we moved them into the basement, so that they might not disturb us by their late hours.

Perhaps this "Striving" was the cause of her erratic cooking. We ate in silence the dried beef which she fried for breakfast, only wondering why the bacon was so queer.

Our friends, knowing that Emily was unusually fastidious, were surprised that we could live "In such a shiftless way." They said they "Would have things decent and the food properly cooked." We offered them the privilege of employing their New England energy in keeping house for us. One day was enough. At the end of it I asked my friend where she had been all day? "In the kitchen, holding up the stovepipe so that Lizzie could bake!"

They taught the alphabet to the little children who had forgotten it during the smallpox vacation, and they clothed the older ones, who went from the school to the house in squads of four or five, coming back completely metamorphosed, their mouths stretched from ear to ear with delight....

In May we moved to the bay with our school benches and books, and had a large school there, but a month later the Freedmen's Bureau was dissolved and we were notified that our services were no longer needed.... There was no place for us, and in the last week of September, 1866, we said good-by to Edisto and our negro friends.

A Black Teacher Goes South

Charlotte L. Forten

From Ray A. Billington, ed., *The Journal of Charlotte L. Forten* (New York: Dryden Press, 1952), and Charlotte L. Forten, "Life on the Sea Islands," *Atlantic Monthly* (May 1864), pp. 67–86.

One among a small group of black women and men who went South to teach in freedmen's schools, Charlotte Forten (1837–1914) left a revealing record of her experiences: a very personal, private journal, and a lengthy "public" essay which appeared in the Atlantic Monthly. *The two pieces of writing—which are not always in agreement—are interspersed, below, for contrast. It is not the essay, but the journal, which reveals that issues of racial prejudice and racial identity, along with concern about women, dominated Forten's emotional and intellectual life, drawing her sometimes-reluctant attention from the literary and cultural pursuits that she loved.*

The granddaughter of a prosperous Philadelphia sailmaker, she joined in the abolitionist work of her family. Forten's family educated her at home, in order that she might avoid the segregated Philadelphia schools. She completed her education at Salem State Normal School in Massachusetts, and was the first black to teach white children there. Charlotte Forten went South in 1862 to join Laura Towne (see selection, p. 170) on the Sea Islands. Teaching there tried her perfectionist nature, and apparently accentuated her sense of racial isolation; after a year and a half of service, she returned to Philadelphia. In 1878, she married Francis Grimké, the natural slave son of Henry Grimké and brother of Sarah and Angelina Grimké, noted proponents of abolition and women's rights.

From the Journal, 1854–1862

Salem, Massachusetts. Monday, Oct. 23 1854. At last I have received the long expected letter, which to my great joy, contains the eagerly desired permission to remain. I thank father very much for his kindness, and am determined that so far as I am concerned, he shall never have cause to regret it. I will spare no effort to become what he desires that I should be; to prepare myself well for the responsible duties of a teacher, and to live for the good that I can do my oppressed and suffering fellow-creatures....

Sunday, Jan. 18 1856. Dined with Mr. and Mrs. P[utnam]. We talked of the wrongs and sufferings of our race. Mr. P[utnam] thought me too sensitive.—But oh, how inexpressibly bitter and agonizing it is to feel oneself an outcast from the rest of mankind, as we are in this country! To me it is *dreadful, dreadful.* Were I to indulge in the thought I fear I should become insane. But I do not *despair.* I will not *despair;* though *very* often I can hardly help doing so. God help us! We are indeed a wretched people. Oh, that I could do *much* towards bettering our condition. I will do *all,* all the *very little* that lies in my power, while life and strength last!...

Monday, Nov. 15 1858. A gloomy, chilly, and, to me, most depressing day. We have our first snow. It is an earnest of Winter, which I dread more than I have words to express. I am *sick,* today, sick, sick at heart;— and though I had *almost* resolved to forbear committing sad thoughts and gloomy feelings to my pages, dear Journal, and have very rarely done so, yet, to-night I long for a confidant—and *thou* art my only one. In the twilight—I sat by the fire and watched the bright, usually so cheering blaze. But it cheered me not. Thoughts of the past came thronging upon me;—thoughts of the loved faces on which I used to look so fondly;—of the loved voices which were music to my ear, and ever sent a thrill of joy to my heart—voices now silent forever. I am *lonely* to-night. I long for one earnest sympathizing soul to be in close communion with my own. I long for the pressure of a loving hand in mine, the touch of loving lips upon my aching brow. I long to lay my weary head upon an earnest heart, which beats for me,—to which I am dearer far than all the world beside. There is none, for me, and never will be. I could only love one whom I could look up to, and reverence, and the *one* would never think of such a poor little ignoramus as I. But what a selfish creature I am. This is a forlorn old maid's reverie, and yet I am only twenty-one. But I am weary of life, and would gladly lay me down and rest in the quiet grave. There, alone, is peace, peace!...

Friday, Nov. 19. Went to town with Aunt H[arriet].... This eve. went to hear Mr. Curtis. I have rarely been so delighted with any lecture as I have been to-night with "Fair Play For Women." It is as much Anti-Slavery as Woman's Rights. The magnificent voice of the orator—the finest voice I have ever heard, his youth, beauty and eloquence, and the fearlessness with which he avowed his noble and radical sentiments before that immense, fashionable, and doubtless mostly pro-slavery audience,—all these impressed me greatly, and awakened all my enthusiasm. I *will not* despair when such noble souls as he devote the glory of their genius and their youth to the holy cause of Truth and Freedom....

Salem, June 22, 1862. More penitent than ever I come to thee again, old Journal, long neglected friend. More than two years have elapsed since I last talked to thee—two years full of changes. A little while ago a friend read to me Miss Mullock's "Life for a Life." The Journal letters, which I liked so much,—were at first addressed to an unknown friend. So shall mine be. What name shall I give to thee, oh *ami inconnu?* It will be safer to give merely an initial--A. And so, dear A. I will tell you a little of my life for the past two years. When I wrote to you last,—on a birght, lovely New Year's Day, I was here in old Salem, and in this very house. What a busy winter that was for me, I was assisting my dear Miss S[hepard] with one of her classes, and at the same time studying, and reciting at the Normal, Latin, French and a little Algebra. Besides I was taking German lessons. Now was I not busy, dear A? Yet it seems to me I was never so happy. I enjoyed life perfectly, and all the winter was strong and well. But when Spring came my health gave way. First my eyesight failed me, and the German which I liked better than anything else, which it was a real luxury to study had to be given up, and then all my other studies. My health continuing to fail, I was obliged to stop teaching, and go away. Went to Bridgewater, and in the Kingmans' delightful home grew gradually stronger. Then went to the Water Cure* at Worcester, where the excellent Dr.

*A popular treatment for women's ills, based on a program of baths, drinking of water, and rest.

R[ogers] did me a world of good—spiritually as well as physically. To me he seems one of the best and noblest types of manhood I ever saw. In my heart I shall thank him always. Early in September, came back from W[orcester] and recommenced teaching, feeling quite well. But late in October had a violent attack of lung fever, which brought me very, very near the grave, and entirely unfitted me for further work. My physician's commands were positive that I sh'ld not attempt spending the winter in S[alem], and I was obliged to return to P[hiladelphia]. A weary winter I had there, unable to work, and having but little congenial society, and suffering the many deprivations which all of our unhappy race must suffer in the so-called "City of Brotherly Love." What a mockery that name is! But over those weary months it is better to draw the veil, and forget....

Week before last I had a letter from Mary S[hepard] asking me to come on and take charge of S.C.'s [?] classes during the summer, as she was obliged to go away. How gladly I accepted, you, dear A., may imagine. I had been *longing* so for a breath of N[ew] E[ngland] air; for a glimpse of the sea, for a walk over our good hills.... We left P[hiladelphia] on Tuesday, the 10th; stopped a little while in N[ew] Y[ork].... Then took the evening boat, and reached here Wed[nesday] morn. Mrs. I[ves]* gave us a most cordial welcome; and we immediately felt quite at home...

Sunday, July 6. Let me see? How did I spend last week? In teaching, as usual, until Friday, on which, being the "glorious Fourth," we had no school, and I went to Framingham to the Grove Meeting.†

Ah, friend of mine, I must not forget to tell you about a little adventure I met with to-day. I was boarding with Mrs. R[?] a very good anti-slavery woman, and kind and pleasant as can be. Well, when I appeared at the dinner-table to-day, it seems that a *gentleman* took umbrage at sitting at the same table with one whose skin chanced to be "not colored like his own," and rose and left the table. Poor man! he feared contamination. But the charming part of the affair is that I, with eyes intent upon my dinner, and mind entirely engrossed (by Mr. Phillips' glorious words, which were still sounding in my soul), did not notice this

*President of the Salem Female Anti-Slavery Society.
†Annual Fourth of July meeting of the Massachusetts Anti-Slavery Society.

person's presence nor disappearance. So his proceedings were quite lost upon me, and I sh'ld have been in a state of blissful ignorance as to his very existence had not the hostess afterward spoken to me about it, expressing the wish, good woman—that my "feelings were not hurt." I told her the truth, and begged her to set her mind perfectly at ease, for even had I have noticed the simpleton's behavior it w'ld not have troubled me. I felt too thorough a contempt for such people to allow myself to be wounded by them. This wise gentleman was an *officer in the navy*, I understand. An honor to his country's service—isn't he? But he is not alone, I know full well. The name of his kindred is Legion,—but I defy and despise them all. I hope as I grow older I get a little more philosophy. Such things do not wound me so deeply as of yore. But they create a bitterness of feeling, which is far from desirable. "When, when will these outrages cease?" often my soul cries out—"How long, oh Lord, how long?"—You w'ld have pitied me during the last part of my ride back to S[alem] this afternoon. The first part of the ride—from B[oston] to L[ynn] in the horse cars, w'ld have been quite pleasant but for the heat. One has a good opportunity of seeing the surrounding country— traveling in this way. At L[ynn] we met the stage, or rather omnibus. We packed in;—thirty outside; the inside crowded to suffocation with odorous Irish* and their screaming babies;—the heat intense. Altogether it was quite unbearable. The driver refused to move with such a load. Nobody was willing to get off. And I think we must have been detained at L[ynn] an hour, till at last an open wagon drove up, and taking off part of the load, we started for S[alem]. We were altogether about three hours going from B[oston] to S[alem]. . . .

From "Life on the Sea Islands"

It was on the afternoon of a warm, murky day late in October that our steamer, the United States, touched the landing at Hilton Head. A motley assemblage had collected on the wharf,—

---

*Forten apparently shared a common ethnic prejudice of the times. The Irish were Boston's most recent immigrant group.

officers, soldiers, and "contrabands" of every size and hue: black was, however, the prevailing color....

From Hilton Head to Beaufort the same long, low line of sandy coast, bordered by trees; formidable gunboats in the distance, and the gray ruins of an old fort, said to have been built by the Huguenots more than two hundred years ago. Arrived at Beaufort, we found that we had not yet reached our journey's end. While waiting for the boat which was to take us to our island of St. Helena, we had a little time to observe the ancient town....

Little colored children of every hue were playing about the streets, looking as merry and happy as children ought to look,— now that the evil shadow of Slavery no longer hangs over them. Some of the officers we met did not impress us favorably. They talked flippantly, and sneeringly of the negroes, whom they found we had come down to teach, using an epithet more offensive than gentlemanly. They assured us that there was great danger of Rebel attacks, that the yellow fever prevailed to an alarming extent, and that, indeed, the manufacture of coffins was the only business that was at all flourishing at present. Although by no means daunted by these alarming stories, we were glad when the announcement of our boat relieved us from their edifying conversation.

We rowed across to Ladies Island, which adjoins St. Helena, through the splendors of a grand Southern sunset. The gorgeous clouds of crimson and gold were reflected as in a mirror in the smooth, clear waters below. As we glided along, the rich tones of the negro boatmen broke upon the evening stillness,—sweet, strange, and solemn:—

Jesus make de blind to see,
Jesus make de cripple walk,
Jesus make de deaf to hear.
  Walk in, kind Jesus!
    No man can hender me.....

Arrived at the headquarters of the general superintendent, Mr. S., we were kindly received by him and the ladies, and shown into a large parlor, where a cheerful wood-fire glowed in the
(text continued on page 148)

Sisterhood of Service

1: Living quarters, Holley School, 1890s. Background, on the porch, are Holley (left), Putnam (right), and a third teacher (center); foreground are other teachers posed with their scholars.

2: Holley School grounds. In an ox-drawn cart are Putnam and Holley, other teachers, and pupils. With assistance of black neighbors, Holley and Putnam built teacher residences and farm buildings as well as a schoolhouse. They also raised their own vegetables and cultivated flower gardens.

3: Entrance of the Holley schoolhouse, 1897. Third from right is Putnam, surrounded by scholars and graduates. Foreground is Elijah Ball, described by Sallie Holley as "U.S. mail contractor & carrier on a 9 mile route."

grate. It had a home-like look; but still there was a sense of
unreality about everything, and I felt that nothing less than a
vigorous "shaking-up," such as Grandfather Smallweed daily
experienced, would arouse me throughly to the fact that I was in
South Carolina.

The next morning L.* and I were awakened by the cheerful
voices of men and women, children and chickens, in the yard
below. We ran to the window, and looked out. Women in bright-
colored handkerchiefs, some carrying pails on their heads, were
crossing the yard, busy with their morning work; children were
playing and tumbling around them. On every face there was a
look of serenity and cheerfulness. My heart gave a great throb of
happiness as I looked at them, and thought, "They are free! so
long down-trodden, so long crushed to the earth, but now in their
old homes, forever free!" And I thanked God that I had lived to
see this day.

After breakfast Miss T.† drove us to Oaklands, our future
home. The road leading to the house was nearly choked with
weeds. The house itself was in a dilapidated condition, and the
yard and garden had a sadly neglected look. But there were roses
in bloom; we plucked handfuls of feathery, fragrant acacia-
blossoms; ivy crept along the ground and under the house. The
freed people on the place seem glad to see us. After talking with
them, and giving some directions for cleaning the house, we
drove to the school, in which I was to teach. It is kept in the
Baptist Church,—a brick building, beautifully situated in a
grove of live-oaks. These trees are the first objects that attract
one's attention here: not that they are finer than our Northern
oaks, but because of the singular gray moss with which every
branch is heavily draped. This hanging moss g rows on nearly all
the trees, but on none so luxuriantly as on the live-oak. The
pendants are often four or five feet long, very graceful and
beautiful, but giving the trees a solemn, almost funereal look.
The school was opened in September. Many of the children had,
however, received instruction during the summer. It was evident
that they had made very rapid improvement, and we noticed

---

*L. is Lizzie Hunn, Forten's traveling companion, a Quaker from Philadelphia
who came South with her father.
†Miss T. is Laura Towne. See selection, p. 170.

with pleasure how bright and eager to learn many of them seemed....

The first day at school was rather trying. Most of my children were very small, and consequently restless. Some were too young to learn the alphabet. These little ones were brought to school because the older children—in whose care their parents leave them while at work—could not come without them. We were therefore willing to have them come, although they seemed to have discovered the secret of perpetual motion, and tried one's patience sadly. But after some days of positive, though not severe treatment, order was brought out of chaos, and I found but little difficulty in managing and quieting the tiniest and most restless spirits. I never before saw children so eager to learn, although I had had several years' experience in New England schools. Coming to school is a constant delight and recreation to them. They come here as other children go to play. The older ones, during the summer, work in the fields from early morning until eleven or twelve o'clock, and then come into school, after their hard toil in the hot sun, as bright and as anxious to learn as ever.

Of course there are some stupid ones, but these are the minority. The majority learn with wonderful rapidity. Many of the grown people are desirous of learning to read. It is wonderful how a people who have been so long crushed to the earth, so imbruted as these have been,—and they are said to be among the most degraded negroes of the South,—can have so great a desire for knowledge, and such a capability for attaining it. One cannot believe that the haughty Anglo-Saxon race, after centuries of such an experience as these people have had, would be very much superior to them. And one's indignation increases against those who, North as well as South, taunt the colored race with inferiority while they themselves use every means in their power to crush and degrade them, denying them every right and privilege, closing against them every avenue of elevation and improvement. Were they, under such cricumstances, intellectual and refined, they would certainly be vastly superior to any other race that ever existed.

After the lessons, we used to talk freely to the children, often giving them slight sketches of some of the great and good men. Before teaching them the "John Brown" song, which they learned to sing with great spirit, Miss T. told them the story of the brave old man who had died for them.* I told them about Toussaint,† thinking it well they should know what one of their own color had done for his race. They listened attentively, and seemed to understand. We found it rather hard to keep their attention in school. It is not strange, as they have been so entirely unused to intellectual concentration. It is necessary to interest them every moment, in order to keep their thoughts from wandering. Teaching here is consequently far more fatiguing than at the North. In the church, we had of course but one room in which to hear all the children; and to make one's self heard, when there were often as many as a hundred and forty reciting at once, it was necessary to tax the lungs very severely....

In the evenings, the children frequently came in to sing and shout for us. These "shouts" are very strange,—in truth, almost indescribable. It is necessary to hear and see in order to have any clear idea of them. The children form a ring, and move around in a kind of shuffling dance, singing all the time. Four or five stand apart, and sing very energetically, clapping their hands, stamping their feet, and rocking their bodies to and fro. These are the musicians, to whose performance the shouters keep perfect time. The grown people on this plantation did not shout, but they do on some of the other plantations. It is very comical to see little children, not more than three or four years old, entering into the performance with all their might. But the shouting of the grown people is rather solemn and impressive than otherwise. We cannot determine whether it has a religious character or not. Some of the people tell us that it has, others that it has not. But as the shouts of the grown people are always in connection with their religious meetings, it is probable that they are the barbarous expression of religion, handed down to them from their African ancestors, and destined to pass away under the influence of Christian teachings. The people on this island have no songs....

*The white man John Brown (1800-1859) led a slave attack on the U.S. arsenal at Harper's Ferry, West Virginia. He was hanged for treason.
†Toussaint L'Overture (1743-1803), black leader of a revolutionary liberation movement in Haiti.

A few days before Christmas, we were delighted at receiving a beautiful Christmas Hymn from Whittier,* written by request, especially for our children. They learned it very easily, and enjoyed singing it. We showed them the writer's picture, and told them he was a very good friend of theirs, who felt the deepest interest in them, and had written this hymn expressly for them to sing,—which made them very proud and happy. Early Christmas morning, we were wakened by the people knocking at the doors and windows, and shouting, "Merry Christmas!" After distributing some little presents among them, we went to the church, which had been decorated with holly, pine, cassena, mistletoe, and the hanging moss, and had a very Christmas-like look. The children of our school assembled there, and we gave them the nice, comfortable clothing, and the picture-books, which had been kindly sent by some Philadelphia ladies. There were at least a hundred and fifty children present. It was very pleasant to see their happy, expectant little faces. To them, it was a wonderful Christmas-Day,—such as they had never dreamed of before. There was cheerful sunshine without, lighting up the beautiful moss-drapery of the oaks, and looking in joyously through the open windows; and there were bright faces and glad hearts within. The long, dark night of the Past, with all its sorrows and its fears, was forgotten; and for the Future,—the eyes of these freed children see no clouds in it. It is full of sunlight, they think, and they trust in it, perfectly.

After the distribution of the gifts, the children were addressed by some of the gentlemen present. They then sang Whittier's Hymn, the "John Brown" song, and several of their own hymns....

Christmas night, the children came in and had several grand shouts. They were too happy to keep still.

"Oh, Miss, all I want to do is to sing and shout!" said our little pet, Amaretta. And sing and shout she did, to her heart's content.

She read nicely, and was very fond of books. The tiniest children are delighted to get a book in their hands. Many of them

*John Greenleaf Whittier (1807–1892), American Quaker poet and strong abolitionist.

already know their letters. The parents are eager to have them learn. They sometimes said to me,—

"Do, Miss, let de chil'en learn eberyting dey can. *We* nebber hab no chance to learn nuttin', but we wants de chil'en to learn."

They are willing to make many sacrifices that their children may attend school. One old woman, who had a large family of children and grandchildren, came regularly to school in the winter, and took her seat among the little ones. She was at least sixty years old. Another woman—who had one of the best faces I ever saw—came daily, and brought her baby in her arms. It happened to be one of the best babies in the world, a perfect little "model of deportment," and allowed its mother to pursue her studies without interruption. . . .

Daily the long-oppressed people of these islands are demonstrating their capacity for improvement in learning and labor. What they have accomplished in one short year exceeds our utmost expectations. Still the sky is dark; but through the darkness we can discern a brighter future. We cannot but feel that the day of final and entire deliverance, so long and often so hopelessly prayed for, has at length begun to dawn upon this much-enduring race. An old freedman said to me one day, "De Lord make me suffer long time, Miss. 'Peared like we nebber was gwine to git troo. But now we's free. He bring us all out right at las'." In their darkest hours they have clung to Him, and we know He will not forsake them.

The poor among men shall rejoice,
For the terrible one is brought to nought.

While writing these pages I am once more nearing Port Royal.* The Fortunate Isles of Freedom are before me. I shall again tread the flower-skirted woodpaths of St. Helena, and the sombre pines and bearded oaks shall whisper in the sea-wind their grave welcome. I shall dwell again among "mine own people." I shall gather my scholars about me, and see smiles of greeting break over their dusk faces. My heart sings a song of thanksgiving, at the thought that even I am permitted to do something for a long-

*Forten made several trips away from the islands, then returned.

abused race, and aid in promoting a higher, holier, and happier life on the Sea Islands.

From the Journal, 1862–1863

Friday Oct. 31, 1862. Miss T[owne] went to B[eaufort] to-day, and I taught for her. I enjoyed it much. The children are well-behaved and eager to learn. It will be a happiness to teach them.

I like Miss Murray so much.* She is of English parentage, born in the Provinces. She is one of the most whole-souled warm-hearted women I ever met. I felt drawn to her from the first (before I knew she was English) and of course I like her none the less for that.

Miss Towne also is a delightful person. "A charming lady" Gen. Saxton calls her and my heart echoes the words. She is housekeeper, physician, everything, here. The most indispensable person on the place, and the people are devoted to her.... And indeed she is quite a remarkable young lady. She is one of the earliest comers, and has done much good in teaching and superintending the negroes. She is quite young; not more than twenty-two or three† I sh'ld think, and is superintendent of two plantations. I like her energy and decision of character. Her appearance too is very interesting....

Wednesday, Nov. 5. Had my first regular teaching experience, and to you and you only friend beloved, will I acknowledge that it was *not* a very pleasant one. Part of my scholars are very tiny,— babies, I call them—and it is hard to keep them quiet and interested while I am hearing the larger ones. They are too young even for the alphabet, it seems to me. I think I must write home and ask somebody to send me picture-books and toys to amuse them with. I fancied Miss T[owne] looked annoyed when, at one time the little ones were unusually restless. Perhaps it was only my fancy. Dear Miss M[urray] was kind and considerate as usual. She is very lovable. Well I *must* not be discouraged. Perhaps things will go on better to-morrow....

*Miss Murray is Ellen Murray. See selection, p. 170.
†Towne was actually thirty-seven.

We've established our household on—as we hope—a firm basis. We have *Rose* for our little maid-of-all-work, *Amaretta* for cook, washer, and ironer, and *Cupid,* yes Cupid himself, for clerk, oysterman* and future coachman. I must also inform you dear A., that we have made ourselves a bed, whereon we hope to rest to-night, for rest I certainly did not last night, despite innumerable blankets designed to conceal and render inactive the bones of the bed. But said bones did so protrude that sleep was almost an impossibility to our poor little body.

Everything is still very, very strange. I am not at all homesick. But it does seem *so* long since I saw some who are very dear, and I believe I am quite sick for want of a letter. But patience! patience! *That* is a luxury which cannot possibly be enjoyed before the last of next week....

Talked to the children a little while to-day about the noble Toussaint [L'Ouverture]. They listened very attentively. It is well that they sh'ld know what one of their own color c'ld do for his race. I long to inspire them with courage and ambition (of a noble sort,) and high purpose.

It is noticeable how very few mulattoes there are here. Indeed in our school, with one or two exceptions, the children are all black. A little mulatto child strayed into the school house yesterday—a pretty little thing, with large beautiful black eyes and lovely long lashes. But so dirty! I longed to seize and thoroughly cleanse her. The mother is a good-looking woman, but quite black. "Thereby," I doubt not, "hangs a tale."

This eve. Harry, one of the men on the place, came in for a lesson. He is most eager to learn, and is really a scholar to be proud of. He learns rapidly. I gave him his first lesson in writing to-night, and his progress was wonderful. He held the pen almost perfectly right the first time. He will very soon learn to write, I think. I must inquire if there are not more of the grown people who w'ld like to take lessons at night. Whenever I am well enough it will be a real happiness to me to teach them.

Finished translating into French Adelaide Proctor's poem "A Woman's Question," which I like so much. It was an experiment, and I assure you, *mon ami,* tis a queer translation. But it was good

---

*A staple of the teachers' diet was oysters.

practice in French. Shall finish this eve. by copying some of my Journal for dear Mary S[hepard]. . . .

This eve. our boys and girls with others from across the creek came in and sang a long time for us. . . .

The effect of the singing has been to make me feel a little sad and lonely to-night. A yearning for congenial companionship *will* sometimes come over me in the few leisure moments I have in the house. T'is well they are so few. Kindness, most invariable,—for which I am most grateful—I meet with constantly but congeniality I find not at all in this house. But silence, foolish murmurer. He who knows all things knows that it was for no selfish motive that I came here, far from the few who are so dear to me. Therefore let me not be selfish now. Let the work to which I have solemnly pledged myself fill up my whole existence to the exclusion of all vain longings. . . .

Monday Nov. 17. Had a dreadfully wearying day in school, of which the less said the better. Afterward drove with the ladies to "The Corner," a collection of negro houses, whither Miss T[owne] went on a doctoring expedition. The people there are very pleasant. Saw a little baby, just borne [sic] today—and another—old Venus' great grand-child for whom I made the little pink frock. These people are very gratiful [sic]. The least kindness that you do them they insist on repaying in some way. We have had a quantity of eggs and potatoes brought us despite our remonstrances. Today one of the women gave me some Tanias. Tania is a queer looking root. After it is boiled it looks a little like potato, but is much larger. I don't like the taste.

Thursday, Dec. 11 1862. Came home, and soon afterward, to my great grief, heard that poor Tillah's dear little baby was dead. It was really a shock to me; for only this morn. we thought the little creature seemed better. I hastened at once to the cabin. The baby had just died, and lay on old Nella's lap, looking as if it were sleeping sweetly. The poor mother sat by looking so very sad. My heart aches for her. During eight weeks she has been constantly devoted to this child—her only little girl—and we hoped she w'ld be rewarded by having it spared to her. But it has gone to heaven. It was one of the loveliest, most interesting babies I ever saw. We are going to bury it to-morrow, over at Polawany; I'm so sorry that William, its father, will not get to see it. It looks very lovely. Its death is a great grief to its mother and grandparents, and a sorrow to us all.

Friday Dec. 12. This morn. Mr. R[uggles] beaming with delight, informed me that there was a large mail in by the "Star of the South." I'm afraid I answered somewhat impatiently that I was disgusted with mails, and that I wasn't going to expect any more. I had been so often disappointed. Nevertheless I *did* expect, despite myself. I did hope for those letters this time. And when we heard that there were letters for us at The Oaks, we at once despatched our trusty Cupid there. With what a beating heart did I await his coming. Calm outwardly, but what a flutter of expectation within. I never sh'ld have thought that I sh'ld become so *insane* about letters.

At last Cupid came, and only *one* letter for me, and that not from home. It was entirely unexpected—from Mr. McK[im]. Certainly it was very kind in him to write to me. He reminds me that he expects to have a line from me. And indeed I ought to have written to him before. But I am *so* disappointed. Why do I not hear from Mary S[hepard]? I thought she w'ld certainly have written to me during her vacation. I am very much troubled at not hearing from her, and from H[enry]. Aunt M[argaretta] has probably written and put her letter in the box, which I suppose will not get here for a month. I am quite sick at heart to-night, and must go to bed....

Sunday, Dec. 14. What a night last night was! A night worth telling you about, dear A. We retired early. I was very sleepy, but what with the headache, the fleas, and Miss H[unn's] *tremendous* snoring I got very nervous, and it was a long time before I c'ld get to sleep. At last sleep came. It seemed to me that I hadn't slept more than ten minutes when I was awakened by what seemed to me terrible screams coming from the direction of the Quarters. Three or four times they were repeated, and then, with infinite difficulty I succeeded in awaking Miss Hunn. We both heard the shrieks repeated. I thought somebody was insane or dying, or that something terrible had happened. Sometimes I thought it might be that the rebels had forced a landing, and were trying to carry off the people. We were in a state of great alarm; and sleep was impossible. At last the sounds ceased. And then near day, I had a short and troubled sleep which did me no good. Consequently I felt rather wretched this morn. but the day was so beautiful [I] determined to go to church.

L[izzie Hunn] and I started, but met Mr. T[horpe]'s wagon in the lane, coming for us. How very kind he is. But I am hardly willing to be under such an obligation to a stranger. And yet we can't very well refuse. How very sad Mr. T[horpe] looked to-day. I know he must greatly miss Mr. Phillips, with whom he was so intimate. I pity him.

There were several new arrivals at church to-day. Among them Miss T[owne]'s sister—Miss Rosa T[owne]. She does not look at all like Miss Laura. Is very fair, and has light hair; an English looking person, as I told her sister. A Miss Ware was also there.... A lovely but good face....

Nearly everybody was looking gay and happy; and yet I came home with the blues. Threw myself on the bed, and for the first time since I have been here, felt very lonely and pitied myself. But I have reasoned myself into a more sensible mood and am better now. Let me not forget again that I came not here for friendly sympathy or for anything else but to work, and to work hard. Let me do that faithfully and well. To-night answered Mr. McK[im]'s letter, and commenced one to my dear A[nnie] about whom I feel very anxious.

There, dear A, I have forgotten to tell you the cause of our fright last night. Two of the colored soldiers had come to visit their friends who live across the creek. And they blew a kind of whistle that they have so that somebody on the opposite side might send a boat over for them. That was the shrieking we heard. And it seems we were the only people who heard it on the place. And yet it was heard across the creek. They must be sound sleepers here. The rebels w'ld have a good chance to land without being discovered.

Thursday March 24 1863. With Miss T[owne] came the latest arrival—Mr. Pierce—the former *pioneer* down here. His manners are exceedingly pleasant—I can't help acknowledging that, though I had a preconceived dislike for him, because I had heard that he said he "wanted no colored missionaries nor teachers down here." His conversation at table to-night was most entertaining and genial. But I shall take an early opportunity of asking an explanation of that speech. If he said that, of course there's no possibility of my liking him....

Sunday, July 26. Had a pleasant morning under the trees, near the water, while Dr. R[ogers] read Emerson to us. Then had a long talk with him, after which came to the very sudden determination to go North in the next steamer. It is necessary for my health, therefore, it is wiser to go. My strength has failed rapidly of late. Have become so weak that I fear I sh'ld be an easy prey to the fever which prevails here, a little later in this season.

A few week since I stopped going to the church finding it impossible to drive there longer through the heat of the day, and opened a small school for some of the children from Frogmore in a carriage house on our place. Most of the children are crude little specimens. I asked them once what their ears were for. One bright-eyed little girl answered promptly "To put rings in." When Mrs. H[unn] asked some of them the same question. They said "To put cotton in." One day I had been telling them about metals; how they were dug from the ground, and afterward, in review, I asked "Where is iron obtained from?" "From the ground" was the prompt reply. "And gold?" "From the sky!" shouted a little boy.

I have found it very interesting to give them a kind of object lessons with the picture cards. They listen with eager attention, and seem to understand and remember very well what I tell them. But although this has been easier for me than teaching at the church—where, in addition to driving through the hot sun to get there, I was obliged to exert my lungs far above their strength to make myself heard when more than a hundred children were reciting at the same time in the same room—yet I have found my strength steadily decreasing, and have been every day tortured by a severe head ache. I take my good Dr.'s advice, therefore, and shall go North on a furlough—to stay until the unhealthiest season is over.

At Sea—Friday, July 31. Said farewell to Seaside and its kind household, white and black, and very early this morn Lieut. W[alton]'s boy drove me to Land's End, whence we were to take the steamboat which was to convey us to the steamer at Hilton Head.

And here we are, homeward bound.

Emancipation's Primer: The Freedmen's Book

Lydia Maria Child

From Lydia Maria Child, *The Freedmen's Book* (Boston: Ticknor and Fields, 1865).

The Freedmen's Book, *compiled and edited by Lydia Maria Child (1802–1880), is an anthology of works written by blacks and white abolitionists. Used in freedmen's schools, it introduced former slaves (mainly adults) to the written black cultural tradition, and encouraged racial pride. Below are the book's Introduction, Table of Contents, and sample selections—a poem by Mingo, a martyred slave, and another by the noted black woman poet Frances E.W. Harper, entitled "Bury Me in a Free Land." These excerpts illustrate the inspirational intent of* The Freedmen's Book.

Child herself was a distinguished woman of letters, the author of novels, political essays on the rights of blacks and Native Americans, and, for two years, the editor of The National Anti-Slavery Standard.

To the Freedmen

I have prepared this book expressly for you, with the hope that those of you who can read will read it aloud to others, and that all of you will derive fresh strength and courage from this true record of what colored men have accomplished, under great disadvantages.

I have written all the biographies over again, in order to give you as much information as possible in the fewest words. I take nothing for my services; and the book is sold to you at the cost of paper, printing, and binding. Whatever money you pay for any of the volumes will be immediately invested in other volumes to be sent to freedmen in various parts of the country, on the same terms; and whatever money remains in my hands, when the book ceases to sell, will be given to the Freedmen's Aid Association, to be expended in schools for you and your children.

Your old friend,
L. Maria Child

Contents*

*"The names of the colored authors are marked with an asterisk" [Lydia Maria Child's note].

The Aspirations of Mingo

A slave in one of our Southern States, named Mingo, was
endowed with uncommon abilities. If he had been a white man,
his talents would have secured him an honorable position; but
being colored, his great intelligence only served to make him an
object of suspicion. He was thrown into prison, to be sold. He
wrote the following lines on the walls, which were afterward
found and copied. A Southern gentleman sent them to a friend in
Boston, as a curiosity, and they were published in the Boston

Journal, many years ago. The night after Mingo wrote them, he
escaped from the slave-prison; but he was tracked and caught by
bloodhounds, who tore him in such a shocking manner that he
died. By that dreadful process his great soul was released from his
enslaved body. His wife lived to be an aged woman, and was said
to have many of his poems in her possession. Here are the lines
he wrote in his agony while in prison:

Good God! and must I leave them now,
My wife, my children, in their woe?
'Tis mockery to say I'm sold!
But I forget these chains so cold,
Which goad my bleeding limbs; though high
My reasons mounts above the sky.
Dear wife, they cannot sell the rose
Of love that in my bosom glows.
Remember, as your tears may start,
They cannot sell the immortal part.
Thou Sun, which lightest bond and free,
Tell me, I pray, is liberty
The lot of those who noblest feel,
And oftest to Jehovah kneel?
Then I may say, but not with pride,
I feel the rushings of the tide
Of reason and of eloquence,
Which strive and yearn for eminence.
I feel high manhood on me now,
A spirit-glory on my brow;
I feel a thrill of music roll,
Like angel-harpings, through my soul;
While poesy, with rustling wings,
Upon my spirit rests and sings.
He sweeps my heart's deep throbbing lyre,
Who touched Isaiah's lips with fire."

May God forgive his oppressors.

Bury Me in a Free Land
By Frances E.W. Harper

Make me a grave where'er you will,
In a lowly plain or a lofty hill;

Make it among earth's humblest graves,
But not in a land where men are slaves.

I ask no monument proud and high,
To arrest the gaze of the passers by;
All that my yearning spirit craves
Is, Bury me not in a Land of Slaves.

New Rules for Black and White

Elizabeth Hyde Botume

From Elizabeth Hyde Botume, *First Days Amóngst the Contrabands* (1893; reprinted New York: Arno Press and the New York Times, 1968).

Practical about teaching and forthright in her views of race relations, Elizabeth Hyde Botume analysed her experiences after three decades in the South in First Days Amongst the Contrabands *(1893). The vignettes selected here counterpose the great significance of the educational work against the trials and small satisfactions of the classroom. The final remark—that blacks had "amazing" respect for the white race—is, of course, a point of disagreement among historians of the period.*

Botume was apparently active nationally on behalf of blacks—her name shows up as a participant in a conference on "the Negro question." Her few extant letters indicate that she also took an active interest in the women's rights movement, but research reveals little else about her, not even birth and death dates. She came from the Boston area, and may have returned there at the end of her life.

Slavery

People at the North knew but little of slavery as it existed in the United States seventy-five or even fifty years ago. It was a *terra incognita* to them. When brought face to face with the slaves, as they were during the war, it was like the discovery of a new race. I do not mean politically. Everybody knows something of the politics of the times. History gives us the facts. What was known of the slaves themselves? Had they any individuality? Were they, as we were often told, only animals with certain brute force, but no capacity for self-government? Or were they reasoning beings?

"I do assure you," once said a Southern woman to me, "you might as well try to teach your horse or mule to read, as to teach these niggers. They *can't* learn."

"Then," said I, "will you be so kind as to tell me why they made stringent laws at the South against doing what *could not be done!*". . . .

The negro mind had never been cultivated; it was like an empty reservoir, waiting to be filled. Under their calm exterior was always a smouldering volcano ready to burst forth. . . .

Not long ago I heard some negro women talking of old times over their sewing. One said,—

"My father and the other boys used to crawl under the house an' lie on the ground to hear massa read the newspaper to missis when they first began to talk about the war."

"See that big oak-tree there?" said another. "Our boys used to climb into that tree an' hide under the long moss while massa was at supper, so as to hear him an' his company talk about the war when they come out on the piazza to smoke."

"I couldn't read, but my uncle could," said a third. "I was waiting-maid, an' used to help missis to dress in the morning. If massa wanted to tell her something he didn't want me to know, he used to spell it out. I could remember the letters, an' as soon as I got away I ran to uncle an' spelled them over to him, an' he told me what they meant."

I was attracted by this, and asked if she could do this now.

"Try me, missis; try me, an' see!" she exclaimed. So I spelled a long sentence as rapidly as possible, without stopping between the words. She immediately repeated it after me, without missing a letter.

The children of this woman were amongst the first to enter a freedman's school during the war. They took to books as ducks take to water. The youngest, a boy, was really entered when a baby in his sister's arms, and was only allowed to remain because his nurse could not come without him. As soon as he could walk his mother complained he did not know anything. When he was three years old she was bitterly disappointed that he could not read.

"Why, if I had his chance," she exclaimed, rolling up her eyes and stretching out her hands, "do you think I would not learn!"

It goes without saying, that her children became good scholars. This youngest boy is now a leader amongst his own people....

Northern Friends

During this time my Northern friends, individually and collectively, were doing their utmost to help on the work "amongst the freedmen"....

The best gift of all was "Miss Fannie," who was forwarded to me just after New Year's, ostensibly to be my assistant. But I halt at the word, for she was everything to me, and to the poor people around me. Young, active, and enthusiastic, fresh from school, with all the new methods of study and teaching, she inspired an admiration and enthusiasm which fell little short of hero worship.... The first I saw of her she was standing in the schoolroom door radiant with delight. The children began to buzz, so I gave an extra recess; but they only gathered around the door on the piazza and gazed at us.

"Who da him?" I heard them say.

"Him's Miss Fonnie," said one girl, with superior knowledge, having heard me speak the name.

"Oh, but him's prime!" they declared....

Miss Lizzie

Now that field-work was over, all the contrabands flocked to the school, until the room was over-crowded. It took most of my time to enroll and place the newcomers. They appeared irregularly, and at all times and seasons.

"Please read me quick, ma'am; I'se hasty. I'se got a baby at home," said a big black woman. This is but a specimen of many other days. In vain did we struggle to bring order out of this confusion. In this dilemma Miss Fannie signalled to her sister,

"Come over and help us;" and in due time Miss Lizzie arrived.

That was a day of jubilee to the contrabands. The children, laughing and shouting, surrounded the house, and peeped into the windows. Miss Lizzie had to go out and be formally introduced before they dispersed. "Oh, but him jes' like Miss Fonnie," said Sally, a sometimes waitress.

In times of trouble the contrabands always came to their teachers for help and advice. Sometimes we were much embarrassed to know what to say or do. When I saw their implicit confidence in our knowledge and sympathy, I found it very hard to tell them I could do nothing.

A sick woman came to me one day, who was suffering from a serious organic trouble. After listening to her story, and getting all the facts, I said, "Auntie, that is beyond me. I really do not know what to do for you."

Her look of astonishment and dismay was really startling, as she exclaimed, "O missis! You'na can read books, an in course you knows more'na we."

Yes, I could read books, but they did not tell me everything. In fact, I soon discovered they told me very little of what I needed to know most.

The New Bell

I had expressed a wish for a bell for my schoolhouse, hoping to bring about a more regular attendance, with less delay. Immediately a Boston friend, who had been in the department, responded by sending me just what I needed. Oh, what a delight was this bell to the whole neighborhood! The children would collect around the house very early, and lie on the ground waiting and watching for it to ring. For a long time this was a mystery incomprehensible to them. They talked often to each other about "we bell," and seemed to feel as if each one had a kind of right of possession in it.

"Oh, but him can talk loud!" said the boys with delight. I told them all what the bell was for, where it came from, and who sent it. Without consulting me they immediately named the school for our generous friends, "Hooper School, A No. 1."

The children were allowed to take turns in ringing the bell; but this was a privilege only granted as a reward for good behavior....

A man and his wife stood together in a class to read. They were great stalwart creatures, black as ink. Their three children were in the class above them, having conquered words of one syllable.

As soon as the parents began to read, the children simultaneously darted to their sides to prompt them.

"Boy! daddy, boy! Him don't know nothing," laughingly said Dick, prompting him.

"Shut you mouf, boy! I only want to catch dat word, sure," the pleased father answered, scratching his head.

"Dem chillen too smart. I ain't know what to do wid' dem," declared the proud mother....

Quite different from them was a "Combee*" woman, who came to school daily with a baby in her arms and two boys by her side. They all stood up to read together.

These families were refugees. They have all returned to their old homes on the "mainland." Primus, one of the boys, has become a teacher and a preacher, and is the wise man of that neighborhood. His mother comes to see me once a year, and tells with pride of her boy's position, always speaking of him as an "A No. 1 scholar."

"Min' Chile "

Babies! There was a host of them, and it was not easy to keep them away from school. Even the tiniest creatures were brought along. Each child had its own nurse, and all wanted to be in school. So it was arranged that one girl should come in the morning and get a lesson, and then run home to mind child, and let the nurse come. But usually the one left behind would come on with the baby and wait around the house until relieved. She always brought with her a tin can with hominy for the child when hungry. It was not unusual for the little nurse to appear in her class as soon as it was called, having passed her baby along to

*From the area of the Combahee River.

any friend who was disengaged. There must have been some signal from the window, for a girl would ask "to step out for a minute," when the baby-tender would return in her place.

These babies needed but little care; even the youngest would eat hominy when hungry, and then go to sleep. I have seen eight and ten of these little black creatures asleep on the piazza at a time. Usually the nurse would take off her apron and spread it down for baby to lie on; that was all. But, at the best, babies were very confusing to the school. Finally, I engaged an old mamma to mind them during school hours. Now the little girls were happy. Each one brought her charge to Aunt Clara's house, and left it on her way to school. It was pleasant to look in upon this primitive nursery and see these pickaninnies sitting upon the well-sanded floors, or asleep in the corner....

About this time two little white girls presented themselves, and asked to be taken into school. They belonged to a good old Southern family, but were out of the reach of any other school. The children of their mother's cook had told them what we were doing, and they were eager to be enrolled. They came regularly, and were very happy, and made good progress. The youngest was in the same class with her little black playfellow, both learning to read; but the black girl started first, and so was ahead.

It was touching to see her zeal in trying to help on her white companion, and her manifest delight when her friend said anything particularly good.

But at the end of two months the little maidens told me with evident reluctance and regret, that they could not come any longer, "they were needed at home."

I suspected there were other reasons, so I called upon the mother, a most intelligent and refined woman. She confessed the Southern white people had "made so much fuss" because she allowed the children to go to a *"nigger school,"* she felt obliged to take them away. She regretted this, for the children played all the time with their colored companions. They had been brought up with them, but must grow up in ignorance rather than be allowed to study with them.

"I would not care myself, but the young men laugh at my husband. They tell him he must be pretty far gone and low down when he sends his children to a 'nigger school.' That makes him mad, and he is vexed with me," said the mother sadly.

We all greatly regretted that these bright young girls should be removed, and so lose the opportunity for study; but I could well understand the odium was too great to be resisted.

Nothing in the history of the world has ever equalled the magnitude and thrilling importance of the events then transpiring. Here were more than four millions of human beings just born into freedom; one day held in the most abject slavery, the next, "de Lord's free men." Free to come and to go according to the best lights given them. Every movement of their white friends was to them full of significance, and often regarded with distrust. Well might they sometimes exclaim, when groping from darkness into light, "Save me from my friend, and I will look out for my enemy."

Whilst the Union people were asking, "Those negroes! what is to be done with them?" they, in their ignorance and helplessness, were crying out in agony, "What will become of us?" They were literally saying, "I believe, O Lord! help thou mine unbelief."

They were constantly coming to us to ask what peace meant for them? Would it be peace indeed? or oppression, hostility, and servile subjugation? This was what they feared, for they knew the temper of the baffled rebels as did no others.

"And this is what we fight for?" asked the young soldiers.

The hatred of some white people for the colored race amounted almost to frenzy. It was by no means confined to the old Southerners, but was largely shared by Northern adventurers, a host of whom had followed the army.

It took time for the freed people to find out who were their true friends. But they gradually learned to discriminate. Their respect, however, for a white skin was amazing, and sometimes made us ashamed of our own race.

One of our colored men, who had been deceived, and grossly cheated, and ill-treated by one who was known as a missionary, recounting his troubles to me, exclaimed,—

"I declar', ma'am, he don't desarve to be a white man. He'll shuck han's wid his right han', an' fling a brick-bat at you wid his lef'."

A Good Life, Staying On

Laura M. Towne

From Rupert Sargent Holland, ed., *Letters and Diary of Laura M. Towne* (1912; reprinted New York: Negro Universities Press, 1969).

One of the very first teachers to go South, Laura Towne (1825–1901) joined "The Port Royal Experiment," a project begun in 1862 on the South Carolina Sea Islands to convince Northerners that blacks should be emancipated. A student of medicine, an accomplished administrator and teacher, and a forthright abolitionist, Towne appears to have dominated and inspired her group, and set an example for other teachers. These selections are chosen from among various, rich letters and diary entries to reveal one thread in Towne's story: the gradual shaping of a full and permanent life in the South with her friend and co-worker Ellen Murray. The two women had a home and gardens, a family life, a political life, and intense satisfaction in their work.

In 1948, the Penn School, founded by Laura Towne and supported by Pennsylvania Quakers, became a part of the segregated South Carolina public school system. Penn Center remains today as a black community center, providing legal services, and housing a nursery school.

Towne's Letters and Diary *are available in many libraries.*

I have felt all along that nothing could excuse me for leaving home, and work undone there, but doing more and better work here. Nothing can make amends to my friends for all the anxiety I shall cause them, for the publicity of a not pleasant kind I shall bring upon them, but really doing here what no one else could do as well. So I have set myself a hard task. I shall want Ellen's* help. We shall be strong together—I shall be weak apart.

*Ellen Murray, Towne's friend and co-worker, with whom she shared her life on the Sea Islands for forty years.

St. Helena's, August 20, 1862

I t is too bad that I have had lately so little time to write. But you may guess how hard it is by the sketch of a day that I will give you.

I get up about six and hurry down so as to have breakfast by seven for Captain Hooper to set out to the ferry for Beaufort. After that I generally have three or four patients, feed my birds, and am ready by nine for driving out to see my patients on five plantations— only one plantation or two a day, though. The roads are horrible and the horses ditto, so I have a weary time getting along, but it is enlivened by a little reading aloud, Ellen and I taking turns at driving and reading. We come hurrying home by two o'clock or a little before, using mental force enough to propel the whole concern—horse, carriage, and ourselves. We snatch a lunch and begin school. I have the middle class, Ellen the oldest and youngest. At four, school is out for the children. Ellen then takes the adults while I go doctoring down to the "nigger houses," or street of cabins. As soon as I get home (generally with six or seven little negro girls and boys—or babies—tugging to my dress and saying, "*my* missus"—the little things that can scarely speak each having chosen a favorite "missus"), I run up the flag and the men come for their guns. This is about six o'clock. They drill an hour or so, and then I take the guns again. They are kept in the room next to mine, under lock and key. Then I dress for dinner, and order it, or see to its coming upon the table in some presentable shape. Dinner takes till eight or half-past, or even, if Captain H. is detained, till half-past nine. I generally have several patients to attend to in the evening, and the rest of the time Ellen and I are kept busy folding papers for the medicines. We go upstairs so as to begin to undress at ten, and we are so sleepy that I often get sound asleep just as soon as my head touches the pillow. We both keep hearty and strong. The negroes say I am strong "too much." . . . I am not sorry that I did not accept the superintendency of the place, for it would be too much care of a kind that I do not like—accounts, pay-rolls, rations to be measured exactly, complaints to hear and satisfy,

(text continued on page 174)

An Enduring Legacy

1: Formal group portrait in a classroom of the Holley School.
2: Caroline Putnam wrote on the back of this photograph, "Corner of school room— Holley School, January, 1896. Christmas tree still standing." On the opposite wall of the classroom, above a draped flag, was hung a large banner with the motto "Equal Rights for All."
3: "A Visit to the Library of Congress," photograph by Frances Benjamin Johnston, ca. 1900. Out of the post–Civil War schools set up by Yankee schoolmarms came black graduates who went on to become teachers themselves, thus carrying on the work of schooling Southern black people.

1

authority to exert. I like my position as volunteer and would not willingly give it up.

The Oaks, St. Helena, December 10, 1863

Dear Family All:—It is hard for me and for us all, I know, that this letter is all of me that comes by this steamer. I can't bear to think of what you will say and how you will look when you get it. Don't be very angry with me (as I think you must be at first), but consider that I am not disregarding all your requests by my free will, but by really cruel circumstances, and that I am bitterly disappointed myself.

I had made every arrangement to go with Rina and Captain Hooper, and was making plans day and night for getting to you and thinking of nothing but the pleasure we should have. But since Miss Ruggles' death* I never dared to dwell with too much certainty upon our meeting at any set time, and it fairly made me tremble to see by your letters how much you were all setting your minds upon it. Though Ellen was still very ill when I wrote last, we had good hopes that she would be well enough for me to leave her by Xmas, and, from General Saxton down to the negro boys in the yard, everybody was helping forward my going. But on the twenty-eighth day of sickness, the quinine seemed to have lost its effect, or there was some unfavorable circumstance which brought on a relapse. I sent for Dr. Rogers. He thought she must have the wisest medical aid or there was little hope for her. I told him that she had no home at the North and was unwilling to go with me without, or even with, invitation from my friends. Then he said, "You must stay with her; she will die if you leave her." I asked whether he thought it would be long before I could go, and he said hers *must* be a tedious convalescence—that the responsibility and risk of taking her North made it better for me not to urge her going, but that he must warn me not to go away till she was in a different state from now. So I have made up my mind to it, and I do not dare to think of Xmas at all. I hope she will get well sooner than he thinks, for she has gone on famously for the last four or five days. I shall set out as soon as she is well

---

*Miss Ruggles, a young teacher who went South with her brother and worked in the schools, died within several months of her arrival.

enough to go to her mother and do without medicine. Meanwhile I turn Kitty's ring and say, "Patience!

Aunt Rachel's Village
St. Helena, February 7, 1864

Y our nice long letter reached me only to-day. That is the worst of our living here, letters are very long getting to us and come by very uncertain hands, and we never know when a mail is going out. I have to trust to chance for getting our mail to Beaufort. So do not be alarmed if a vessel sails with no word from me, the next one will probably bring double.

I see by your letter that you are quite dissatisfied about my decision to stay till next summer, but I am sure that if you were here you would think as I do and advise my waiting. First place, the voyage. If I go this spring, I cannot ask transportation again in the fall, for our dear, good General is now having perpetual trouble and annoyances by having his passes discredited, or disapproved or complained of because they are so numerous. Yet he is very careful to give furloughs and passes only once a year except in cases of necessity or urgency. Even if I asked and obtained the two leaves of absence, I dread four sea voyages in six months or so. I think I *must* go home during the next un-healthy season. I cannot stand the trial of it here another year. I am not afraid of being sick myself, but of having to nurse and doctor those who are. I am quite sure that if I go North this spring and am seasick, as I cannot help being, it will make me run the risk of the autumn rather than of the voyage, and so I want to make sure of being away from this place through another such season as the last was. Besides, if I go now, I must run North in a hurry and come back before I have half seen you, my whole time being taken up with preparations for coming back here. But in the summer I will stay three months, have a thorough change and renovation, and have some leisure with you.

I am really ashamed and sorry about writing home for boxes and giving you all so much trouble, taking your time which is so overcrowded. I shall need some dresses in the spring, but there were very pretty things in Beaufort last year, and Susannah can make them up. If they are old-fashioned, no matter, for I shall only see you in the mountains, and down here I shall probably see less company than we used to. I suppose you thought me unconscionable in sending for carpets and household things, but this is my home probably for the rest of my days, and I want to be comfortable in it. I have lived now for two years in the midst of makeshift and discomfort, and have often thought this winter that even servants at home were more nicely provided with domestic conveniences and things to save time and trouble. So I sent for a few things of my own; that is, I wanted them taken from our house, and in the sale or division of our household goods, charged to my account—such as the carpet. Our room is nearly as ill-built and open as a rough country stable. H.'s* stable is a palace to it, and, our only bit of carpet being on our parlor floor, we have bare boards in our rooms with the air rushing through every crack, and sunlight along every board plainly visible where the sun shines under the house. This is comfortless and cold as you cannot imagine, who have not had uncarpeted floors since you can remember. When we first came here, and for a time, these things were endurable, but year after year it is hard to live so. Besides, now that things are taking a more permanent form here, everybody's style of living is improving and we do as others do. You know what South Carolina fare is. We are just in the oyster hòle again, and have nothing else till we are sick of the sight of them. I was going to send home for butter, for we have had neither butter nor milk for some time—so much less than last year; but Mr. Ruggles says he will supply us. We had a cow sent to us and were happy, but she was a jumper—and our fence such as you might expect—and she jumped and ran, after our feeding her for three days and getting just one quart of milk. Her feed, too, was a heartbreak—we are not sure of it from day to day—none to be begged, borrowed or bought, so her escape was a relief. . . .

Thursday, November 17, 1864

I am getting my South Carolina health back—eat like a horse, sleep like a top, do any amount of work, and read nothing; that

*H. is Laura Towne's brother Henry Towne.

last is too bad and greatly to my regret. We have begun reading in
the carriage on our way to school....

Just think, you poor, freezing, wind-pierced mortals! *we* have
summer weather. The fields are gay with white, purple, and
yellow flowers, and with the red leaves of sumach and other
shrubs. Our woods are always green, and just now the gum trees
make them beautiful with red. *You* can't see a leaf! Chill
November! I pity you. But—but!—We are perfect recluses.

Ellen has gone to-night to Frogmore to see her friends and
family and I miss her terribly. I think I get less and less used to
doing without things—yet I am resolved to stick just here to
my work....

We are just enjoying my darling little stove, being able to eat
our meals in comfort and without involuntary mastication from
chattering teeth, for it has been too cold until within two days to
do without fires in the dining-room, a luxury we never could
have before. It, the stove, draws well. Our curtains are not yet up,
and I begin to fear they will not decorate our windows all winter.

You do not know how snug and homelike our parlor looks—
just large enough for two....

December 18, 1864

Merry Christmas to all.
Our new school-house is now being hurried forward pretty
fast, and we hope to get in by the first of the year. How happy we
shall be, nobody can tell who has not taught in a school where he
or she had to make herself heard over three other classes reciting
in concert, and to discover talkers among fifty scholars while
one hundred fifty more are 'shouting lessons, and three other
teachers bawling admonitions, instructions, and reproofs. Generally two or more of the babies are squalling from disinclination
to remain five hours foodless on very small and tippy laps—their
nurses being on benches too high for them and rather careless of
infant comfort in their zeal for knowledge....

I went to-day to see Maum Katie, an old African woman, who
remembers worshipping her own gods in Africa, but who has
been nearly a century in this country. She is very bright and

talkative, and is a great "spiritual mother," a fortune-teller, or rather prophetess, and a woman of tremendous influence over her spiritual children. I am going to cultivate her acquaintance. I have been sending her medicine for a year nearly, and she "hangs upon top me," refusing all medicine but mine. I never saw her till to-day, and she lives not a stone's throw off, so you may guess how hurried I am.

March 9, 1866

I send the enclosed picture of me with three of my pets. The big boy is Dick Washington, my righthand man, who is full of importance, but has travelled and feels as if he had seen the world. He is incorrigibly slow and stupid about learning, but reads bunglingly in the Testament, does multiplication sums on the slate, and can write a letter after a fashion. The little girl with the handkerchief on her head is Amoretta—bright and sharp as a needle. She reads fluently in the Testament, spells hard and easy words in four syllables, and ciphers as far as nine times twelve on the slate. The other child is Maria Wyne, who is very bright in arithmetic, but very dull and slow in learning to read. My face is burnt out so as to do justice to them. Amoretta's head kerchief is put on as the candidates for baptism wear them. . . .

June 1, 1867

The people are just now in a state of great excitement over their right to vote, and are busy forming a Republican Party on the island. At their first meeting they had an informal time; at the second there was some business done. Our school was invited to sing at this/one, and it seemed the main attraction. But two or three white men—one of them Mr. Wells—got up and said women and children ought to stay at home on such occasions. He afterwards sent us an apology, saying he had no idea of including us or our school, but only outsiders who were making some noise. Nevertheless, the idea took. To-day in church Mr. Hunn announced another meeting next Saturday. "The females must stay at home?" asked Demas from the pulpit. "The *females* can come or not as they choose," said Mr. Hunn, "but the meeting is for men voters." Demas immediately announced that "the womens will stay at home and cut grass," that is, hoe the corn and cotton fields—clear them of grass! It is too funny to see how much more jealous the men are of one kind of liberty they have achieved than of the other! Political freedom they are rather shy of, and ignorant of; but domestic freedom—the right, just found, to have their own way in their families and rule their wives— that is an inestimable privilege! In slavery the woman was far more important, and was in every way held higher than the man. It was the woman's house, the children were entirely hers, etc., etc. Several speakers have been here who have advised the people to get the women into their proper place—never to tell them anything of their concerns, etc., etc.; and the notion of being bigger than woman generally, is just now inflating the conceit of the males to an amazing degree. When women get the vote, too, no people will be more indignant that these, I suppose.

June 20, 1867

On June 15th we got up about five and went across the river to Old Fort Plantation, where the friends of Sarah Clark (Miss Botume* and Miss Sangford) live. There we met a large party of ladies and gentlemen from all the islands, and they had some fine games of croquet. We stayed all night and the next day Miss B. and the pretty Miss S. came home with us, spent the night, and on Monday came to our school. Mr. Nichols and the gentlemen there had a grand croquet party on Monday, and we did not get home till almost morning. This dissipation is quite new to us.

May 29, 1870

We have had our little upset. A rabbit sprang across the road just in front of Saxton's nose, and he shied. We were in a no-top buggy that had no railing even, and Ellen, who had the reins and was driving, was slung out under the wheel, which

*Elizabeth Hyde Botume. See selection, p. 163.

went over her waist. When I saw myself and the big, heavy old-fashioned wheel upon top of her, I screamed; and her fall and the scream made Saxton give two more great jumps into the woods. I had not the reins, of course, and could not guide him, so the second jump brought the wheel against the trunk of a felled tree, and the buggy turned a complete summerset with me under it. Saxton's old harness gave way and he trotted a little way, and then came back, anxious to find his "aunties." By that time Ellen and I were both up again. I caught Saxton, who came at my call, and Ellen picked up the ruins of our lunch-basket—her splendid lunch-basket!—and various other things. Ellen had a pain in her side that was so severe at first that I feared internal injury, but it is almost well now. I was only a little bruised here and there, and not hurt seriously at all....

Something far more important has happened to us. We have taken in a little child to live with us—perhaps to bring up. She is Miss Puss—about the worst little monkey that ever was. Topsy was nothing to her. She wrote to Rosie a short time ago. That poor child has been undergoing all sorts of ill treatment all winter from her father. She is a dwarf already, and he starved and beat her every day. She is one of the best scholars in my class; as bright as a dollar; always noticed by strangers for her intelligence, good reading, etc., but, under her father's management and direction, just as smart at lying and stealing. She often ran away to escape a beating, and almost lived in the woods. At last they locked up her clothes and made her go almost naked to keep her from coming to school, or going to some neighbors. One day this week she did not do the field work her father set her, so he told her to follow him home to be tied up and beaten. She dodged into the woods and came to me with a ragged little petticoat and an apron tied over her back. I told her she must go home and face the beating, and took her into the buggy, for she was exhausted with crying and starvation. We left her near home and she promised to go there, but she dodged again, her heart failing her when she saw the family searching for her. She spent that stormy night no one knows where, and meantime Ellen and I concluded to take her for poultry-minder at half a dollar a month and food, but not clothing. The father did not feel willing to let her come, but the mother would have it, so the next day as we went to school and saw her in a field eating blackberries, we hailed her and told her she was to come to Frogmore to live. You never saw such a delighted little creature. So far she is good as gold, but the time will come when we shall have our trials. She has been my scholar for years....

Our school exists on charity, and charity that is weary. If turned over to the state, no Northern colored person has a chance of being appointed teacher of a state school. There are too many here who want the places and the school trustees are not men capable of appointing by qualification.

May 7, 1871

Just think, forty-six years of age! Almost half a century and with so much history in it, too! United States free; Italy free; France where she must be, and Prussia where she ought to be. Russia free, too, from serfs. I have seen a good deal in my half-century.

May 14, 1871

I do never intend to leave this "heathen country." I intend to end my days here and I wish to.... Next year is to be positively the last [for Northern support], but I shall not give up teaching; I couldn't live without it now.

June 14, 1874

How I wish I could pop in upon you all, just get a good hug all around and back again to school! We are in such a state of preparation and drill that we feel we can't lose a single day, and much as we want rain, we look jealously at every cloud.

I have another day ahead that I have to prepare for. There is to be a meeting of the people to consider school matters, and I shall have to mount the platform and give some kind of account of my stewardship as clerk of the board of school trustees, besides having to recommend measures for next year, the amount of tax to be voted for, and the proper division of the money raised.

September 27, 1874

I think stormy times are always best near the sea—for beauty. None of you bathe, I suppose. I go in sturdily nearly every day with my dogs, and I find great invigoration from it. My swimming improves a little, but I tire very soon, and I am very careful not to do too much and spoil my fun by getting to be afraid of doing anything. It is my arms that get tired, and back. I can swim *with* the tide a good distance, but against it cannot hold my own. But the best swimmers, indeed the best *rowers*, cannot contend with the strong currents we have here. My Bruno and Tim are great company for me and stick close by my side all day, of course, but I never think of such a thing as being lonely, I am so busy. For three weeks now, and for a long time in the evening too, I have been mending school-books. W. helped me,* and indeed was so skilful at binding that he did most of it for two weeks; but now he is away, and I am patching torn leaves. Sometimes I put nearly a hundred patches in one book, so you may know the labor. I use thin paper and paste over the print. These books have been put away as worn out, but now that the fund is so nearly exhausted, we cannot afford new books, and *must* have some, so I have undertaken a heavy, tiresome job....

I have written to Mr. Cope† to say that as the Fund is nearly at an end, and my brother has so liberally provided for me, I will not take a salary any longer, but reserve it for the other teachers, so that the school may go on as it is for one or two years longer. He answered, saying that he had no doubt I took great pleasure in this arrangement, as I enjoyed before being a volunteer teacher so much, and apparently he was very glad to have the Fund spun out longer. Ellen is, of course, pleased at the prospect of continuance, and I thank Henry more for this than for any other thing I could get with his money—that is, for being able to live here, keep up this home, to feel sure of Ellen's staying, and of the school not being turned over to some teacher I could not agree with, or to some set of trustees who would do with it exactly what we wouldn't like.

*W. is Laura Towne's brother William Towne.
†Francis R. Cope, of Philadelphia, who acted as financial agent for the Penn School.

November 11, 1877

I f it were not for the almanac I should declare the last twenty years were only twenty months. Every year gets shorter too, and the next twenty may seem like twenty weeks. We have all had exceptionally happy lives, I think, so far, and I hope our years will grow only pleasanter and pleasanter, and I do not see why they shouldn't for a long time to come, for the health of the whole family seems improving, and I trust we shall live together for many, many years.

I feel that we are together, though I am here and you there, because all our hearts are so together, and when that is the case, and *we can communicate*, there is no separation in its worst sense. These thoughts are apropos of the death of poor old Aunt Cilla, of "The Oaks," who died this morning after months of great suffering. . . .

We are in the midst of preparation for exhibition, and I have begun to teach "Pinafore,"* but oh! what an attempt! I am going to have "We Sail," and "I am the Captain," with the salutations before it,—"I am Monarch" and "Cousins and His Aunts"; also "Buttercup." This will fill out my time. Another of my exercises will be "Political Economy,"—just a little of what relates to capital, labor, and money,—the uses of rich and poor men; and that piece will wind up with Burns' "A man's a man for a' that."

Culmination of a Career

Sallie Holley

From John White Chadwick, *A Life for Liberty* (New York: G.P. Putnam's Sons, 1899).

Already fifty-six when she joined her lifelong friend Caroline Putnam at a freedmen's school in Virginia in 1870, Sallie

*Operetta by Gilbert and Sullivan.

*Holley (1818–1893) was "retiring" from more than two decades
of activism on behalf of the rights of black people and of
women. An Oberlin graduate (she entered at age twenty-
nine), she had toured the free states during the fifties and
sixties, advocating immediate emancipation and publishing
regularly in William Lloyd Garrison's Liberator.*

*Sallie Holley's letters, excerpted below, reveal a woman of
keen intelligence, confident and feisty in the fight to
maintain her beachhead in rebellious Virginia. Teaching year
after year, laboring on the land to make it yield, active in
local politics, Holley admitted in her correspondence that she
missed friends and cultural life in the North. On one of her
frequent visits to New York, she died, at age seventy-five.*

Lottsburgh, Oct. 13, 1874

We have two acres of land about us, but it was such poor,
worn-out soil that it 'aggravates my life near out of me,' to
get it all fertilised to grow my fruits and flowers. What I
especially plead with you to be sure to put into Maria's barrel, is
some root or vine from your garden that I can plant here. I should
like a young grape-vine and a rose-bush to keep the memory of
dear old times fresh and green even in this far-off country.

Miss Putnam and I have tugged and toiled, and striven and
struggled on through this summer, and though our new
schoolhouse is not entirely completed at this date, yet I rejoice
to write, the second coat of plaster is this day successfully going
on, and by November 1st our school will enter triumphantly.
These Virginia rebels are fairly confounded to see our schoolhouse spring up so magically, and our fortunes revive so elastic
from their hostile tread. Like the camomile bed, the more it is
trod upon, the more fragrant and lively it becomes. Our coloured
friends are cheered to the very marrow of their bones. Their faces
shine, as day after day they call on us to exult and crow. Still we
know the enemy ever sits with lance in rest to take advantage
as often as he can make a deadly thrust. These Virginia rebels are
no more reconstructed than those in Louisiana or Alabama.

It was so cool when I rose at 4.30 this morning that I put on
those nice, warm, grey stockings that Mrs. Porter knit with her

own fingers and sent down. As we are our own servants and cooks, for ourselves and our workmen, we are compelled to rise very early in order to run our daily race of duties.

To Mrs. Miller
Lottsburgh, Aug. 26, 1881

Miss Putnam has been in New England since early in April, but will return here next month. I am entirely alone with school, Post-office,* and house and garden. My health sweetens all life for me. The sea breezes always come and the heat is not oppressive. Did you know that Elizur Wright is writing the life of my father? He thinks his manuscript will be complete about the middle of September. It is most generous in him to take so much thought and toil and travel to accomplish this work. Those old abolitionists were a noble circle of men.

Lottsburgh, Oct. 12, 1885

Miss Putnam is still in office. But oh, what an excitement we have had! The coloured people have been intensely excited. They gathered night after night in the Democrat's little store to express their feelings against any removal of this post office. These Virgina Democrats are very unhappy and bitterly disappointed. The more liberal Democrats say they don't want the office removed. How much we are indebted to yourself and Col. Miller for all your large hearted interest in Miss Putnam's keeping the office! Without you we should have lost it.

New York, March 23, 1888

I *thank you for your generous thought about me. I have no ache, no pain; only 'nervous prostration,' as they call it. I weigh only one hundred pounds. I have no depression of spirits. To-day I am ordered to keep in bed. People advise me to take some 'tonic,' but I think only out-door air will restore me.*

---

*Miss Putnam was the postmaster of Lottsburgh, a position she held against the wishes of a number of whites.

March 28th. —Last Thursday afternoon I did not resist my great desire to attend the woman's suffrage convention here in Masonic Temple. The result was I became so deeply interested and deeply moved by the eloquent speakers that I was taken with a chill and had to leave before the meeting closed. Mrs. Dr. Miller and all the ladies in the house are very kind. Will you smile if I tell you something? Some time ago, one of the ladies, seeing that my appetite was rather dainty, went across the way to St. James Hotel, and brought me a cooked bird on toast and some French peas. Nothing ever tasted more delicious to me. But I dare not expatiate on the treat, for the lady is a working woman and a widow, and ought not to spend a cent on me. She is educating her only child,—a young lady,—and needs all she earns to do it.

To Robert Morville
Lottsburgh, Nov. 19, 1888

Twenty years ago this very month, out of pity, commiseration, and sorrow for the poverty and ignorance of these people, I came down to Virginia to lighten their burdens and kindle their souls to a better life. To-day I cannot but believe this school and its influences have accomplished a solid and enduring blessing, good for time and good for eternity. We have taught hundreds and hundreds to read and write and cipher, besides some knowledge of geography, history—especially that of the United States—the story of our own Government, the eloquent biography of its reformers and martyrs, saints, and apostles.

As ours is a free school,—no tuition exacted,—and we have no salary, it is only by such interested and large-hearted people as yourself, who donate the means to keep up our work, that we can continue this mission year after year.

Some of our old pupils are now teaching public coloured schools in this part of the state, earning, every month, twenty-five dollars. Many of our boys and girls are in service in Baltimore and New York. A few of the older scholars have married here and are now in homes of their own.

Not one of our coloured men failed to vote the Republican ticket on the sixth of November last.

This month our school counts seventy scholars and the

Sunday school adds a score or two more. Our mild November days favour many little young beginners coming, who for the first time have a slate and pencil to work out the profound mystery of writing their own names.

We now have two young ladies from Massachusetts, who are mobilising this little army of students after the pattern of Boston. It is touching to see these little dark faces light up with new thought as expressively as the pale-complexioned Saxon children's ever do. Again and again I thank you for your generous donation.

To Miss Tyler
Lottsburgh, Oct. 12, 1892

You kindly ask me what are my pleasures. I can count up a good many here on my little hill, surrounded with forest trees. I look up to the sky with never ceasing pleasure. I am up nearly every morning of the summer before Aurora mounts the chariot for her daily drive, and the summer dawn is exquisitely lovely. The broad, blue sky with its exalting influences is a very great pleasure to me, and the summer night is perpetually soothing and comforting. My garden, all summer, has abounded in fire-flies, 'piloting through airy seas frail barks of light.' My grounds are like cities of refuge to the birds of this country. The little wrens build nests in the school-house and rear their young. Bluebirds, mocking-birds, robins, cat-birds, brown thrashers—all like my garden and build their nests every summer in it.

My flowers now in bloom are nasturtiums, dahlias, roses, princess feathers, asters, and the lavender with its little greyish blue flowers and nice perfume.

My Sunday-school has been a great pleasure to me, but, also a great fatigue. I have the entire care of it three hours, from nine until twelve. The two oldest boys chose the story of David for our summer study. The eloquent and famous lament of David over the deaths of Saul and Jonathan, each girl and boy has committed to memory. I have a higher appreciation of the character of David than ever before. He was a most extraordinary man. The children and I have had a very interesting time.

Another of my 'pleasures' is the affectionate letters of my

friends. Aristotle said 'Without friends no one could choose to live, although he possessed all other blessings.' You, my dear friends, are a great 'pleasure' to me. I value your regard, your approval, your attentions, above all price, and forever and forever I thank you and your disinterested soul.

Books are an ever-flowing fountain of pleasure to me. This summer I have had hours of pleasure in reading the history of Greece. I have learned by heart two poems: Shelley's 'Arethusa,'' and Jean Ingelow's 'Persephone.'

Last month a friend wrote me asking if it would not be a pleasure to study and analyse one of Shakespeare's plays. So we are to take *Hamlet* as one of the 'pleasures' of autumn.

To Mrs. Miller
Lottsburgh, Nov. 27, 1892

Your letter to Miss Putnam was a great relief and comfort, as, since the election our Lottsburgh ex-slave-holders boast they will get the post-office in March. One of the most bitter told a white woman that 'The old Yankee,' meaning me, 'has ruined these Lottsburgh niggers, making them think they are as good as anybody.' An ex-slave-holding lady said to me, 'I am as great a rebel as I ever was.' I do not for a moment believe any Virginian has met with a change of heart. I am profoundly disappointed at the victory of the Southerners. They could not have won with a fair and honest count. Nobody of intelligence denies this fact. Grady [the Atlanta editor, since dead] admitted it in his banquet-speech in Boston, and insolently and impudently asked, 'Do you blame us? Wouldn't you do the same in our case? What are you going to do about it?' And he got applause and honours from *Boston* for it! He made the bold declaration that the South would effectually defy and resist the rule of the majority, and his reason was because he was 'opposed to nigger domination.' But George Bancroft wrote, 'We are indebted to the black race for the continuance of the Republic.'

I expect to arrive in New York the day before Christmas. O happy day! after nine months of this Virginia labour, 'joyfully onward and upward I go.' If my winter is as happy as the last two winters have proved, I will bow in gratitude to the great giver of every good and perfect gift. I have learned to love New York passionately. My friends there are inexpressibly dear to me. Your next letter must be addressed to me at Miller's Hotel, 39 W. 36th St., where I shall not have to draw water every day from a well fifty feet deep, nor lug in heavy oak-wood to keep fire in the house, nor be the servant of servants.

The March of Progress

Charles W. Chesnutt

From Charles W. Chesnutt, "The March of Progress," *The Century Illustrated Monthly Magazine*, Vol. 39 (11/1900-4/1901), pp. 422-428.

A fitting epilogue to the history of the Yankee schoolmarms, this short story by the black writer Charles W. Chesnutt (1858-1932) turns on the unexpected competition between a white Northern woman with fifteen years of freedmen's teaching to her credit and one of her former black pupils, returned home from college. The young black teacher, of course, represents the finest legacy of the freedmen's schools. At this point in his career, Chesnutt was writing openly about the sorrows of racial prejudice; thus the story's concluding protective view of Miss Noble is worth noting. Chesnutt is best known for The Wife of His Youth and Other Stories of Color *(1899),* The Conjur Woman *(1899), and* The Colonel's Dream *(1905).*

T he colored people of Patesville had at length gained the object they had for a long time been seeking—the appointment of a committee of themselves to manage the colored schools of the town. They had argued, with some show of reason, that they were most interested in the education of their own children, and in a position to know, better than any committee of white men could, what was best for their children's needs. The appointments had been made by the county commissioners during the latter part of the summer, and a week later a meeting was called for the purpose of electing a teacher to take charge of the grammar school at the beginning of the fall term.

The committee consisted of Frank Gillespie, or "Glaspy," a barber, who took an active part in local politics; Bob Cotten, a blacksmith, who owned several houses and was looked upon as a substantial citizen; and Abe Johnson, commonly called "Ole Abe" or "Uncle Abe," who had a large family, and drove a dray, and did odd jobs of hauling; he was also a class-leader in the Methodist church. The committee had been chosen from among a number of candidates—Gillespie on account of his political standing, Cotten as representing the solid element of the colored population, and Old Abe, with democratic impartiality, as likely to satisfy the humbler class of a humble people. While the choice had not pleased everybody,—for instance, some of the other applicants,—it was acquiesced in with general satisfaction. The first meeting of the new committee was of great public interest, partly by reason of its novelty, but chiefly because there were two candidates for the position of teacher of the grammar school.

The former teacher, Miss Henrietta Noble, had applied for the school. She had taught the colored children of Patesville for fifteen years. When the Freedmen's Bureau, after the military occupation of North Carolina, had called for volunteers to teach the children of the freedmen, Henrietta Noble had offered her services. Brought up in a New England household by parents who taught her to fear God and love her fellowmen, she had seen her father's body brought home from a Southern battle-field and laid to rest in the village cemetary; and a short six months later she had buried her mother by his side. Henrietta had no brothers or sisters, and her nearest relatives were cousins living in the far West. The only human being in whom she felt any special personal interest was a certain captain in her father's regiment, who had paid her some attention. She had loved this man deeply, in a maidenly, modest way; but he had gone away without speaking, and had not since written. He had escaped the fate of many others, and at the close of the war was alive and well, stationed in some Southern garrison.

When her mother died, Henrietta had found herself possessed only of the house where she lived and the furniture it contained, neither being of much value, and she was thrown upon her own resources for a livelihood. She had a fair education and had read many good books. It was not easy to find employment such as she desired. She wrote to her Western cousins, and they advised her to come to them, as they thought they could do something for her if she went there. She had almost decided to accept their offer, when the demand arose for teachers in the South. Whether impelled by some strain of adventurous blood from a Pilgrim ancestry, or by a sensitive pride that shrank from dependence, or by some dim and unacknowledged hope that she might sometime, somewhere, somehow meet Captain Carey—whether from one of these motives or a combination of them all, joined to something of the missionary spirit, she decided to go South, and wrote to her cousins declining their friendly offer.

She had come to Patesville when the children were mostly a mob of dirty little beggars. She had distributed among them the cast-off clothing that came from their friends in the North; she had taught them to wash their faces and to comb their hair; and patiently, year after year, she had labored to instruct them in the rudiments of learning and the first principles of religion and morality. And she had not wrought in vain. Other agencies, it is true, had in time cooperated with her efforts, but any one who had watched the current of events must have been compelled to admit that the very fair progress of the colored people of Patesville in the fifteen years following emancipation had been due chiefly to the unselfish labors of Henrietta Noble, and that her nature did not belie her name.

Fifteen years is a long time. Miss Noble had never met Captain Carey; and when she learned later that he had married a Southern girl in the neighborhood of his post, she had shed her tears in secret and banished his image from her heart. She had lived a lonely life. The white people of the town, though they learned in time to respect her and to value her work, had never recognized her existence by more than the mere external courtesy shown by any community to one who lives in the midst of it. The situation was at first, of course, so strained that she did not expect sympathy from the white people; and later when time had smoothed over some of the asperities of war, her work had so engaged her that she had not had time to pine over her social exclusion. Once or twice nature had asserted itself, and she had longed for her own kind, and had visited her New England home. But her circle of friends was broken up, and she did not find much pleasure in boarding-house life; and on her last visit to the North but one, she had felt so lonely that she had longed for the dark faces of her pupils, and had welcomed with pleasure the hour when her task should be resumed.

But for several reasons the school at Patesville was of more importance to Miss Noble at this particular time than it ever had been before. During the last few years her health had not been good. An affection of the heart similar to that from which her mother had died, while not interfering perceptibly with her work, had grown from bad to worse, aggravated by close application to her duties, until it had caused her grave alarm. She did not have perfect confidence in the skill of the Patesville physicians, and to obtain the best medical advice had gone to New York during the summer, remaining there a month under the treatment of an eminent specialist. This, of course, had been expensive and had absorbed the savings of years from a small salary; and when the time came for her to return to Patesville, she was reduced, after paying her traveling expenses, to her last ten-dollar note.

"It is very fortunate," the great man had said at her last visit, "that circumstances permit you to live in the South, for I am afraid you could not endure a Northern winter. You are getting along very well now, and if you will take care of yourself and avoid excitement, you will be better." He said to himself as she went away: "It's only a matter of time, but that is true about us all; and a wise physician does as much good by what he withholds as by what he tells."

Miss Noble had not anticipated any trouble about the school. When she went away the same committee of white men was in charge that had controlled the school since it had become part of the public-school system of the State on the withdrawal of support from the Freedmen's Bureau. While there had been no formal engagement made for the next year, when she had last seen the chairman before she went away, he had remarked that she was looking rather fagged out, had bidden her good-by, and had hoped to see her much improved when she returned. She had left her house in the care of the colored woman who lived with her and did her housework, assuming, of course, that she would take up her work again in autumn.

She was much surprised at first, and later alarmed, to find a rival for her position as teacher of the grammar school. Many of her friends and pupils had called on her since her return, and she had met a number of the people at the colored Methodist church, where she taught in the Sunday-school. She had many friends and supporters, but she soon found out that her opponent had considerable strength. There had been a time when she would have withdrawn and left him a clear field, but at the present moment it was almost a matter of life and death to her—cetainly the matter of earning a living—to secure the appointment.

The other candidate was a young man who in former years had been one of Miss Noble's brightest pupils. When he had finished his course in the grammar school, his parents, with considerable sacrifice, had sent him to a college for colored youth. He had studied diligently, had worked industriously during his vacations, sometimes at manual labor, sometimes teaching a country school, and in due time had been graduated from his college with honors. He had come home at the end of his school life, and was very naturally seeking the employment for which he had fitted himself. He was a "bright" mulatto, with straight hair, an intelligent face, and a well-set figure. He had acquired some of the marks of culture, wore a frock-coat and a high collar, parted his hair in the middle, and showed by his manner that he thought a good deal of himself. He was the popular candidate among the progressive element of his people, and rather confidently expected the appointment.

The meeting of the committee was held in the Methodist church, where, in fact, the grammar school was taught, for want of a separate school-house. After the preliminary steps to effect an organization, Mr. Gillespie, who had been elected chairman, took the floor.

"The principal business to be brought befo' the meet'n' this evenin'," he said, "is the selection of a teacher for our grammar school for the ensuin' year. Two candidates have filed applications, which, if there is no objection, I will read to the committee. The first is from Miss Noble, who has been the teacher ever since the grammar school was started."

He then read Miss Noble's letter, in which she called attention to her long years of service, to her need of the position, and to her affection for the pupils, and made formal application for the school for the next year. She did not, from motives of self-respect, make known the extremity of her need; nor did she mention the condition of her health, as it might have been used as an argument against her retention.

Mr. Gillespie then read the application of the other candidate, Andrew J. Williams. Mr. Williams set out in detail his qualifications for the position: his degree from Riddle University; his familiarity with the dead and living languages and the higher mathematics; his views of discipline; and a peroration in which he expressed the desire to devote himself to the elevation of his race and assist the march of progress through the medium of the Patesville grammar school. The letter was well written in a bold, round hand, with many flourishes, and looked very aggressive and overbearing as it lay on the table by the side of the sheet of small note-paper in Miss Noble's faint and somewhat cramped handwriting.

"You have heard the readin' of the applications," said the chairman. "Gentlemen, what is yo' pleasure?"

There being no immediate response, the chairman continued:

"As this is a matter of consid'able importance, involvin' not only the welfare of our schools, but the progress of our race, an' as our action is liable to be criticized, whatever we decide, perhaps we had better discuss the subjec' befo' we act. If nobody else has anything to obse've, I will make a few remarks."

Mr. Gillespie cleared his throat, and assuming an oratorical attitude, proceeded:

"The time has come in the history of our people when we should stand together. In this age of organization the march of progress requires that we help ourselves, or be left forever behind. Ever since the war we have been sendin' our child'n to school an' educatin' 'em; an' now the time has come when they are leavin' the schools an' colleges, an' are ready to go to work. An' what are they goin' to do? The white people won't hire 'em as clerks in their sto's an' factories an' mills, an' we have no sto's or factories or mills of our own. They can't be lawyers or doctors yet, because we haven't got the money to send 'em to medical colleges an' law schools. We can't elect many of 'em to office, for various reasons. There's just two things they can find to do—to preach in our own pulpits, an' teach in our own schools. If it wasn't for that, they'd have to go on forever waitin' on white folks, like their fo'fathers have done, because they couldn't help it. If we expect our race to progress, we must educate our young men an' women. If we want to encourage 'em to get education, we must find 'em employment when they are educated. We have now an opportunity to do this in the case of our young friend an' fellow-citizen, Mr. Williams, whose eloquent an' fine-lookin' letter ought to make us feel proud of him an' of our race.

"Of co'se there are two sides to the question. We have got to consider the claims of Miss Noble. She has been with us a long time an' has done much good for our people, an' we'll never forget her work an' friendship. But, after all, she has been paid for it; she has got her salary regularly an' for a long time, an' she has probably saved somethin', for we all know she hasn't lived high; an', for all we know, she may have had somethin' left by her parents. An' then again, she's white, an' has got her own people to look after her; they've got all the money an' all the offices an' all the everythin',—all that they've made an' all that we've made for fo' hundred years,—an' they sho'ly would look out for her. If she don't get this school, there's probably a dozen others she can get at the North. An' another thing: she is gettin' rather feeble, an it 'pears to me she's hardly able to stand teachin' so many child'n, an' a long rest might be the best thing in the world for her.

"Now, gentlemen, that's the situation. Shall we keep Miss Noble, or shall we stand by our own people? It seems to me there can hardly be but one answer. Self-preservation is the first law of nature. Are there any other remarks?"

Old Abe was moving restlessly in his seat. He did not say anything, however, and the chairman turned to the other member.

"Brother Cotten, what is yo' opinion of the question befo' the board?"

Mr. Cotten rose with the slowness and dignity becoming a substantial citizen, and observed:

"I think the remarks of the chairman have great weight. We all have nothin' but kind feelin's fer Miss Noble, an' I came here to-night somewhat undecided how to vote on this question. But after listenin' to the just an' forcible arguments of Brother Glaspy, it 'pears to me that, after all, the question befo' us is not a matter of feelin', but of business. As a business man, I am inclined to think Brother Glaspy is right. If we don't help ourselves when we get a chance, who is goin' to help us?"

"That bein' the case," said the chairman, "shall we proceed to a vote? All who favor the election of Brother Williams—"

At this point Old Abe, with much preliminary shuffling, stood up in his place and interrupted the speaker.

"Mr. Chuhman," he said, "I s'pose I has a right ter speak in dis meet'n? I *s'pose* I is a member er dis committee?"

"Certainly, Brother Johnson, certainly; we shall be glad to hear from you."

"I s'pose I's got a right ter speak my min', ef I is po' an' black, an' don' weah as good clo's as some other members er de committee?"

"Most assuredly, Brother Johnson," answered the chairman, with a barber's suavity, "you have as much right to be heard as any one else. There was no intention of cuttin' you off."

"I s'pose," continued Abe, "dat a man wid fo'teen child'n kin be 'lowed ter hab somethin' ter say 'bout de schools er dis town?"

"I am sorry, Brother Johnson, that you should feel slighted, but there was no intention to igno' yo' rights. The committee will be please' to have you ventilate yo' views."

"Ef it's all be'n an' done reco'nized an' 'cided dat I's got de right ter be heared in dis meet'n, I'll say w'at I has ter say, an' it won't take me long ter say it. Ef I should try ter tell all de things dat Miss Noble has done fer de niggers er dis town, it'd take me till ter-morrer mawnin'. Fer fifteen long yeahs I has watched her incomin's an' her outgoin's. Her daddy was a Yankee kunnel, who died fighting fer ou' freedom. She come heah when we—yas, Mr. Chuhman, when you an' Br'er Cotten—was jest sot free, an' when none er us did n' have a rag ter ou' backs. She come heah, an' she

tuk yo' child'n an' my child'n, an' she teached 'em sense an'
manners an' religion an' book-l'arnin'. When she come heah we
did n'hab no chu'ch. Who writ up No'th an' got a preacher sent to
us, an' de fun's ter buil' dis same chu'ch-house we're settin' in ter-
night? Who got de money f'm de Bureau to s'port de school? An'
when dat was stop', who got de money f'm de Peabody Fun'? Talk
about Miss Noble gittin' a sal'ry! Who paid dat sal'ry up to five
years ago? Not one dollah of it come outer ou' pockets!

"An' den, w'at did she git fer de yuther things she done? Who
paid fer teachin' de Sunday-school? Who paid her fer de gals she
kep' f'm thrown' deyse'ves away? Who paid fer de boys she kep'
outer jail? I had a son dat seemed to hab made up his min' ter go
straight ter hell. I made him go ter Sunday-school, an' somethin'
dat woman said teched his heart, an' he behaved hisse'f, an' I ain'
got no reason fer ter be 'shame' er 'im. An' I can 'member, Br'er
Cotten, when you did n'own fo' houses an' a fahm. An' when yo'
fus wife was sick, who sot by her bedside an' read de Good Book
ter'er, w'en dey wuz n'nobody else knowed how ter read it, an'
comforted her on her way across de col', dahk ribber? An' dat ain'
all I kin 'member, Mr. Chuhman! When yo' gal Fanny was a baby,
an' sick, an' nobody knowed what was de matter wid'er, who sent
fer a doctor, an' paid 'im fer comin', an' who he'ped nuss dat chile,
an' tol' yo' wife w'at ter do, an' save' dat chile's life, jes as sho' as de
Lawd had save' my soul?

"An' now, aftuh fifteen yeahs o' slavin' fer us, who ain't got no
claim on her, aftuh fifteen yeahs dat she has libbed 'mongs' us an'
made herse'f one of us, an' endyoed havin' her own people look
down on her, aftuh she has growed ole an' gray wukkin' fer us an'
our child'en, we talk erbout turnin' 'er out like a' ole hoss ter die!
It 'pears ter me some folks has po' mem'ries! Whar would we 'a'
be'n ef her folks at de No'th had n' 'membered us no bettuh? An'
we had n' done nothin', fer dem to 'member us fer. De man dat kin
fergit w'at Miss Noble has done fer dis town is unworthy de name
er nigger! He oughter die an' make room fer some 'spectacle dog!

"Br'er Glaspy says we got a' educated young man, an' we mus'
gib him sump'n' ter do. Let him wait; ef I reads de signs right he
won't hab ter wait long fer dis job. Let him teach in de primary
schools, er in de country; an' ef he can't do dat, let 'im work
awhile. It don't hahm a' educated man ter work a little; his

fo'fathers has worked fer hund'eds of years, an' we's worked, an'
we're heah yet, an' we're free, an' we's gettin' ou' own houses an'
lots an' hosses an' cows—an' ou' educated young men. But don't
let de fus thing we do as a committee be somethin' we ought ter
be 'shamed of as long as we lib. I votes fer Miss Noble, fus, las', an'
all de time!"

When Old Abe sat down the chairman's face bore a troubled
look. He remembered how his baby girl, the first of his children
that he could really call his own, that no master could hold a
prior claim upon, lay dying in the arms of his distracted young
wife, and how the thin, homely, and short-sighted white teacher
had come like an angel into his cabin, and had brought back the
little one from the verge of the grave. The child was a young
woman now, and Gillespie had well-founded hopes of securing
the superior young Williams for a son-in-law; and he realized
with something of shame that this later ambition had so dazzled
his eyes for a moment as to obscure the memory of earlier days.

Mr. Cotten, too, had not been unmoved, and there were tears in
his eyes as he recalled how his first wife, Nancy, who had borne
with him the privations of slavery, had passed away, with the
teacher's hand in hers, before she had been able to enjoy the
fruits of liberty. For they had loved one another much, and her
death had been to them both a hard and bitter thing. And, as Old
Abe spoke, he could remember, as distinctly as though they had
been spoken but an hour before, the words of comfort that the
teacher had whispered to Nancy in her dying hour and to him in
his bereavement.

"On consideration, Mr. Chairman," he said, with an effort to
hide a suspicious tremor in his voice and to speak with the
dignity consistent with his character as a substantial citizen, "I
wish to record my vote fer Miss Noble."

"The chair," said Gillespie, yielding gracefully to the majority,
and greatly relieved that the responsibility of his candidate's
defeat lay elsewhere, "will make the vote unanimous, and will
appoint Brother Cotten and Brother Johnson a committee to step
round the corner to Miss Noble's and notify her of her election."

The two committeemen put on their hats, and, accompanied
by several people who had been waiting at the door to hear the

result of the meeting, went around the corner to Miss Noble's house, a distance of a block or two away. The house was lighted, so they knew she had not gone to bed. They went in at the gate, and Cotten knocked at the door.

The colored maid opened it.

"Is Miss Noble home?" said Cotten.

"Yes; come in. She's waitin' ter hear from the committee."

The woman showed them into the parlor. Miss Noble rose from her seat by the table, where she had been reading, and came forward to meet them. They did not for a moment observe, as she took a step toward them, that her footsteps wavered. In her agitation she was scarcely aware of it herself.

"Miss Noble," announced Cotten, "we have come to let you know that you have be'n 'lected teacher of the grammar school fer the next year."

"Thank you; oh, thank you so much!" she said. "I am very glad. Mary"—she put her hand to her side suddenly and tottered—"Mary, will you—"

A spasm of pain contracted her face and cut short her speech. She would have fallen had Old Abe not caught her and, with Mary's help, laid her on a couch.

The remedies applied by Mary, and by the physician who was hastily summoned, proved unavailing. The teacher did not regain consciousness.

If it be given to those whose eyes have closed in death to linger regretfully for a while about their earthly tenement, or from some higher vantage-ground to look down upon it, then Henrietta Noble's tolerant spirit must have felt, mingling with its regret, a compensating thrill of pleasure; for not only those for whom she had labored sorrowed for her, but the people of her own race, many of whom, in the blindness of their pride, would not admit during her life that she served them also, saw so much clearer now that they took charge of her poor clay, and did it gentle reverence, and laid it tenderly away amid the dust of their own loved and honored dead.

Two weeks after Miss Noble's funeral the other candidate took charge of the grammar school, which went on without any further obstacles to the march of progress.

THREE: Teaching in the Big City

Women Staff the Education Factories

"EXCEPT FOR PROBLEMS in simple arithmetic, how to read and how to write...I have forgotten everything the schools ever taught me," wrote Catherine Brody of her New York childhood. "But the glamour of the lady teachers, shining on the East Side World, I shall never forget. I see them now, all fused and molded into one

symbolic figure, in dresses that seemed always delicate and gracefully silhouetted, in great puffed sleeves, with a neck that always seemed long and arched, with a pompadour that always seemed to make the forehead lofty and noble. The symbol sits enthroned on the dais-platform before a desk.... I see her with the record book, stumbling over the syllables of awkward foreign names, repeated over and over for her benefit by suffering, red-faced little girls."[1]

"But even more than the music of the hurdy-gurdy was the inspiring sight of the *teacher* as she passed the street," wrote Anzia Yezierska in her novel, *Bread Givers.* "How thrilled I felt if I could brush by Teacher's skirt and look up into her face as she

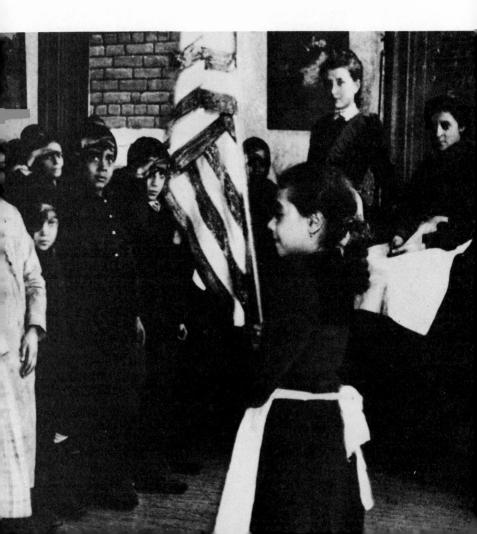

passed me. If I was lucky enough to win a glance or a smile from that superior creature, how happy I felt for the rest of the day! I had it ingrained in me from my father, this exalted reverence for the teacher."[2]

The teacher sat enthroned on the classroom platform; she stood out on the ghetto street. This was the typical image of the teacher of immigrant children, who touched and transformed the lives of individual children by her personal care and instruction. She was the link between the old world and the new, the intermediary who interpreted to the children the language and culture of their adoptive country. The teacher was the symbol of hope—that the young would escape their parents' destiny: the bent backs, "the swollen veins in our legs, on our work-stained hands" from the sweatshop, the factory, and domestic labor.[3] A guide to the realization of America's promise, the teacher, most immigrants believed, had in her keeping responsibility for the worldly prosperity of the next generation.

Like her sister teachers of nineteenth-century rural New England, the teacher of immigrants was expected to shape character and impart the rudiments of good citizenship, but her job differed in one significant regard from all previous teaching in the United States. Her students did not speak English, many could not read or write in their native languages, and most came from cultures of which the teacher herself was ignorant. In the absence of a sophisticated science of teaching English as a second language—no such normal school courses existed—the teacher forged ahead in English, with a prescribed curriculum derived from the work of the New England schoolmen.* Her students' first English words were her words; their first American ideas, her interpretation of American morals, manners, and culture. Thus, the teacher's personal power had an enhanced significance and was of a more intense quality than that she had exercised in earlier days.

The power the teacher exercised over the children "beneath" her was more than matched by the power of professional school

---

*Although there were some special classes for over-age, and non-English speaking children, most children simply entered grade one, no matter what their age, if they could not speak English. Today, there are still few practical courses to help teachers understand and solve the language problems of non-English speaking children.

administrators over the teacher herself. In relation to the men above them, teachers might as well have been children. Rather than encouraging the teacher to break away from the traditional behavior of daughter, sister, mother, or wife in becoming a member of the work force, the newly bureaucratized schools institutionalized this behavior in ways that many women found familiar and acceptable, and men advantageous. In 1841, the Boston School Committee had *commended* women teachers because they were unambitious, and "less intent on scheming for future honors or emoluments,"[4] and that attitude about women employees held on into the twentieth century. They were ideal for the newly centralized schools, which were structured on the heirarchical model of the factory, with levels of male managers and a female work force. Like the manager of the cotton mill, the school superintendent could regulate the performance of the "hands" (or teachers) and keep the "product" (educated children) of good quality. Lost to the city teacher were the freedom and independence that were hers for the taking in the ungraded rural school.

This section explores the teacher's personal relationship to and impact on the children she was to Americanize—her power; it explores her powerlessness as well, the extent to which she tolerated a hierarchy which rewarded not initiative and creativity, but obedience to authority. And finally, it defines the limits of her tolerance, the point at which she began to organize on her own behalf rather than remain ambiguously positioned in a strange environment of simultaneous strength and weakness.[5] Much of the material describes teaching in metropolitan New York, but the experience of teachers of immigrants in the East Coast cities, and as far west as Chicago, was similar. In so far as the chapter describes the building of big city school systems, the New York case can be taken as roughly representative.

The writing in this section includes sketches, fiction, journalism and essay, but unfortunately few diaries or letters by teachers about experience in the turn of the century urban classroom. One among an army of teachers numbering nearly 15,000 in New York City, for example (1910), and often still living with her family in the city of her birth, the urban teacher must have felt her work too commonplace to record, or, if she recorded it, too prosaic to publish or preserve. Luckily, her students memorialized her—for her love, for her ability to humiliate, and in remembrance of the youthful triumph conferred by her approval. Journalists judged her ability and criticized her. And today, more than three quarters of a century after she began to teach, the oral historian can recapture those experiences that live on in memory.

The Teacher's Power:
Thrall to "God's delegates on earth"[6]

"It was quarter past nine and Miss Bailey was calling the roll, an undertaking which, after months of daily practice, was still formidable. Beginning with Abraham Abrahamowski and continuing throughout the alphabet to Solomon Zaracheck, the roll call of the first Reader class was full of stumbling blocks and pitfalls." So wrote Myra Kelly, a New York school teacher in a 1904 volume called *Little Citizens*,[7] excerpted in this section. Although Miss Bailey spoke humorously of her navigation through the roll call, she did not obscure the most striking challenge to the big city school system—assimilating immigrants. Between the Eastern European Jewish names beginning with "A" and "Z" were surely others that reflected their Italian, Spanish, German, Russian, Irish, or Scotch origins. New York school superintendent William Maxwell reported, "There are more Jews in New York than in Palestine, more Italians than in Rome, and enough foreigners of other nationalities to make a city as big as St. Louis. Of the 75,000 new pupils who enter the New York schools every year, probably two-thirds cannot speak a word of English. In one school I counted children of twenty-nine different nationalities who spoke twenty-nine different languages or dialects."[8] By the turn of the century in New York City, native born Americans had become a minority of the population.

From the 1820's on, Irish immigrants, escaping from political persecution and repeated famine, had flooded East Coast seaport cities. There they settled into crowded tenements, the best they could manage on the wages of unskilled work on roads, as carters, teamsters, as drivers, laundresses, cooks, and maids. By

1900, they controlled local politics in Boston, New York, and Philadelphia, and had given pause to the old leadership of the city. But nothing compared in its power to transform urban life and institutions to the wave of immigration from the Mediterranean world and Eastern Europe at the turn of the century. In 1900, 449,000 arrived; then over 850,000 three years later. In 1907, immigration reached a peak with 1,285,000 entries recorded.[9] Those patricians who had grown rich on immigrant labor now saw the proliferation of social problems so devastating that they feared that their way of life and their children's would be utterly changed. "The dangerous classes," as they were called, were alleged to have brought with them or developed in their over-crowded ghettos a long list of vices: their family structure was weak, their women and children immoral, their men drunks; they carried smallpox, tuberculosis, vermin; they ignored the health and safety ordinances of the city, and worst of all, many clung to "the old ways."

Even those Americans who appreciated as "immigrant gifts" the new arrivals' culture agreed in one respect with those who saw them only as deplorably "un-American": that the immigrants must be thoroughly and quickly assimilated into American society, "melted" into decent facsimiles of Anglo-Saxon Protestants. There was general agreement, too, that the American public school was the institution destined to carry out the task. The "cornerstone of democracy" had a legal claim on immigrant youth: the law obliged them to attend school. School could substitute for family, church, and cultural center by teaching malleable children (and through them, their parents) American history and values, the legacy of the country's founders.[10] Thus, the cities would gradually be restored to a comfortable homogeneity.

In an address to the National Education Association, Julia Richman, herself a prospering Jewish immigrant and school administrator, made the classic statement about the function of the school, so common in the literature of the period:

Ours is a nation of immigrants. The citizen voter of today was yesterday an immigrant child. Tomorrow he may be a political leader. Between the alien of today and the citizen of tomorrow stands the school, and upon the influence exerted by the school depends the kind of citizen the immigrant will become.[11]

Oddly, neither the old line citizens nor the immigrants themselves questioned the power of the school to shape values, even when the claim was as excessive as that of a New York high school principal: "Education will solve every problem of our national life, even that of assimilating our foreign element.... Ignorance is the mother of anarchy, poverty, and crime. The nation has a right to demand intelligence and virtue of every citizen, and to obtain these by force if necessary."[12]

The burden of solving most social problems fell on the teacher, who, even under the best of conditions, had a hopeless charge. Eight hours a day in a dark, uncomfortable classroom with sixty or seventy children, some hungry and ill, she was not only to teach school subjects, but, as the journalist Adele Marie Shaw observed in an article excerpted below, "make self-supporting men of probable paupers, good men and women of probable criminals, and good American citizens of thousands and thousands of children whose parents speak no English, and learn loyalty to government only by seeing what it does for their offspring."[13] Then, after hours, for her meagre $650 a year,[14] she was to "go into the children's homes to teach the mothers," said Julia Richman, and "bring together in affection and mutual sympathy the foreign parents and the Americanized child.... The wives and mothers who nurture children [and] influence men [have] the destiny of the nation in their keeping." The day had passed, Richman thought, "when ability to teach the studies of the school course is regarded as the whole service required of the ideal teacher."[15]

When this lofty charge was reduced to actual practice, evidence suggests that miraculously many teachers did perform according to Julia Richman's ideal. Fiction, memoir, and oral reminiscence repeat two telling themes: the loving and disciplined passing on of language, and the honor of home visits—a mode of signalling the "specialness," or promise of a child. In language instruction, imitation was the style of instruction. "I would hang on his lips, striving to memorize every English word I could catch and watching intently, not only his enunciation, but also his gestures, manners, and mannerisms," wrote a man of his evening school teacher.[16] The fictional teacher Sara Smolinsky, heroine of *The Bread Givers*, explicitly linked the attainment of professional status with perfect English. Her brightest eleven year old ended "almost every sentence with 'ain't it.' " After having written "isn't it" one hundred times, he declared, " 'I got it all right now, Teacher! Ain't it?' " Sara Smolinsky replied, " 'Oh, Aby!'...'And you want to be a lawyer! Don't you know the judges will laugh you out of court if you plead your case with 'ain't it?' "[17]

In his memoir, *A Walker in the City*, written in 1952, the writer Alfred Kazin has a less benign memory of learning language by imitation. It meant "reproducing [the teacher's] painfully exact enunciation.... This English was peculiarly the ladder of advancement. Every young lawyer was known by it." It meant also that "we were somehow to be a little ashamed of what we were.[18]

Teaching writing presented a further challenge in breaking the silence of the foreign born. Mary Antin's beloved teacher Miss Dillingham, her "first American friend," as she characterizes her in the selection that follows, helped the young girl gather new words as if she were "gathering a posy blossom by blossom." Miss Dillingham succeeded in having Mary's composition, "Snow," published in an educational journal. Her introductory letter modestly but unmistakably attributed Mary's progress to the lessons of her classroom. "This is the uncorrected paper of a Russian child twelve years old, who had studied English only four months. She had never, until September, been to school even in her own country, and has heard English spoken *only* at school."[19] At the opposite end of the spectrum, but as powerful, is the image conjured up by Mary Agnes Dwyer, ninety-three years old when I conducted with her the interview printed in this section. Seventy years after she had taught her first class, she described returning to school at night to teach when she was only twenty-one. There she would hold the adults' hands to teach them to write. The physical contact seems symbolic of the passing on of language skills needed for the new world literally *through* the teacher. Of the immigrants she taught in a suburb near New York City, she said, "They are the people I still love and remember, because *they believed in us*.

We had a great deal to give and they needed it, but we needed them as well. They were going to be the future of our city, and they *were*, and they *are*, even now."[20]

There was, of course, another facet to the teacher's power—her power to humiliate and cow her students. Here the muck-raking journalists of the period were quick to open fire. Adele Shaw visited twenty-five New York public schools in 1903, and found that in a number "there exists a rigidity that is like *rigor mortis.*" Here teachers snapped and sneered at children. "In one class the very way in which the teacher intoned 'You—are—not—still' gave me a sensation of quick fright that brought back the awful moment of my childhood when I saw a boy arrested.... 'Somebody—foot!' the same teacher shouted suddenly, and my circulation stopped. My own foot, I felt sure, had moved." From schools like these, Shaw felt, would be graduated "brutal truck-drivers," and "amateur criminals," so simple was her view of the impact of schooling. To their credit, however, the journalists recognized that "under unwise management, a trained teacher may be reduced to the level of one who has had no training." "The wrong kind of teaching," as Shaw saw it, took place where "the subordinate must be forever on the jump to accomplish the set end of her day's labor...to carry out [the principal's] conscientiously relentless will."[21]

Pleasing the Authorities:
The Teacher's Proper Place

If, in a characteristic vignette of the teacher *outside* her classroom, the ghetto poor clear the sidewalk before her, and men raise their caps as she passes, a characteristic vignette *inside* the classroom portrays the young female teacher trembling under the scrutiny of a supervisor or inspector. And well she might. Ward bosses, superintendents or their delegated authorities visited every classroom, and held public examinations of the pupils. Graded secretly, these examinations determined the teacher's status—her pay, her promotion, or demotion.

In Myra Kelly's *Little Citizens*, the teachers so feared the surprise arrival of Timothy O'Shea, the associate superintendent for the area, that they devised a system of interclassroom communication to warn one another that he was in the building. Older teachers holding permanent licenses protected their younger sisters from "gum shoe Tim," then ministered to those women left either faint or hysterical from his criticisms. Tim is imagined as a man in love with power, animated by catching the teacher-off guard and crushing her spirits. An observer of the New York City Schools, writing in the same year as Kelly, portrayed supervisors as men who go about "from schoolroom to schoolroom, notebook and pencil in hand, sitting for a while in each room like malignant sphinxes, eyeing the frightened teacher, who in his terror does everything wrong, and then marking *him**[22] in a doomsday book."

Even in an enlightened public school, the Hancock School for Girls in Boston's North End, the "genial" principal forced a model teacher to become aware of how much she was "subservient to a higher authority." Marian Dogherty's first brush with Mr. Dutton was harmless. He merely opened the door to display her class to some visiting ladies, and heard her, teaching the music lesson she hated, yell "shut up" at "the wretches" who were openly enjoying "the racket they were making." Later in the year, however, he came to hear the girls read. Her girls held their books properly—"in their right hands, with the toes pointing at an angle of forty-five degrees, the head held straight and high, the eyes looking directly ahead," but they forgot to announce page and chapter. Mr. Dutton criticized; the teacher's heart sank, and she determined "that this sort of thing should never, never happen again."[23]

Throughout her description of "The First Class," reprinted in this section, Dogherty uses language and imagery which show her acceptance of the school hierarchy with its clearly delineated chain of command. Children obeyed the teacher. In stepping *up* to her high platform, she confirmed that she was above them. When the children forgot to say page and chapter, *she* had failed to perform her "duty" to the satisfaction of her "superior officer."

That teachers obediently carried out instruction from "above"

---

*Italics mine. The teacher was, of course, most likely to be female, despite the writer's use of the masculine pronoun.

should not be surprising. In the large urban school systems, women rarely held administrative positions above principal, and even these were few. The teacher was not taken seriously as a worker; simultaneously, her status as a woman-obliged-to-work made her socially suspect among the educated classes. And Victorian ideology encouraged her to think of teaching as an extension of her life as a daughter, and as preparation for her true work—motherhood.

From the earliest days of the development of urban school systems, women teachers were being given lessons in subservience. In Boston, New York, Philadelphia, and smaller cities, the schools were the fiefdom of local ward politicians who gave out jobs as rewards to loyal voters and to "buy" new ones. Teachers from many cities reported that positions were awarded by a system of "pulls." Acquaintance with the state superintendent (a political appointee) and some principals, a male teacher "confessed" in an *Atlantic Monthly* article of 1896, " 'pulled' me into a vacancy worth $1,650 a year."[24] Party members' daughters, it was also asserted, no matter what their qualifications, were given jobs, while well-trained but poorly connected teachers remained unemployed, unless they were willing to produce a bribe. In her "confession," also published in the *Atlantic,* Miss Amelia Allison described the pressure she came under because, in her perception, her father belong to the wrong party, the party *with* an issue (or platform).

"The party without an issue" thought that they saw a chance to win. As our district was likely to have a close contest, it was suggested that my father be "whipped into line." The only lash that he could be made to feel, they thought, was a threat to remove me. They s ent their candidate for school trustee to our home, and he knocked timidly at the back door....[25]

Although she refused to be bribed, she did manage to keep her job through a succession of party changes. Her strategy was typical of the dedicated teacher who eschewed politics—shut the classroom door; teach so well that parents demand you for their children; hide your independence from your superiors.

New York was the first of the big cities in which a campaign was launched to "take the schools out of politics." Dubbed "the great school war,"* and characterized as a school reform movement by its proponents, this struggle for political power pitted Protestant upper-class city leaders against Irish and German neighborhood politicians. At stake was the ownership of the city; and the reformers—professional people, exectives fresh from the boardrooms of powerful corporations, anxious to impart their morals to the immigrants—won the day. Although the reformers justly objected to a school system run by partisan ward committees, their theory that a small group of successful men should hire professional managers to direct the schools from a central office substituted one kind of politics for another.

The reformers did not regard the schools as a democracy, nor care that centralization would undermine the neighborhood's engagement with its schools. With their children safe in private seminaries and academies, these men and some of their wives made the schools their "project." Graduates of prestigious colleges, members of social and philanthropic organizations, ninety-two of the hundred and four new school board members were lawyers, eighteen bankers, and others writers, professors, philanthropists, university administrators, and doctors.[26]

If previously the teacher feared a capricious and arbitrary politician who cared more for votes than education, now her destiny was in the hands of trained administrators hired by and in agreement with the school board. These men knew exactly the kind of educational system they wanted—ordered, disciplined, with decision-making following the model of the business corporation. Thus the reformers elevated the superintendency to a position of great prestige, and spoke of the new system of education as "scientific." One supporter, the president of the University of Chicago, introduced the New York superintendent William Maxwell to a convocation saying, "I am convinced that next in difficulty and in importance to the work of the President of the United States stands that of the superintendent of schools of our great cities."[27] So the work of deciding a course of study, selecting books, hiring and supervis-

---

*Nicholas Murray Butler, President of Columbia Teachers' College, and ardent school reformer, coined this phrase.

ing teachers, and creating a new "learned profession" took on dimensions of national significance.*

A new and increasingly powerful interest group had been born. The school reformers had no intention of granting teachers a voice. They were the laborers in the system. John Dewey was not the only one to point out the "obvious discrepancy" between the teacher's obligation to *give* lessons about democracy, *and* her obligation to *take* orders and remain silent at her workplace. Ultimately, teachers did organize labor unions and confront the authority which ruled them, but that is getting ahead of the story.

The irony of the woman teacher's position was revealed by the census of 1900. While female teachers were present in great numbers—nearly 82% of urban teachers were women—they had almost no power over working conditions, school governance, or program. The pattern of women teachers' participation in the labor force and the social sanctions against working women combined to counteract the strength they might have found collectively.

Who was the typical female teacher in 1900? She was unmarried, twenty-six or younger, and would work for about five years before marriage.[28] In the general perception, motherhood was still her ultimate career, and teaching an apprenticeship. She could nuture other people's children while awaiting the man who would father her own. Thus she could not be counted on to give her most serious attention to working conditions which she would endure only temporarily—not as a male would, for three or four decades of his life. In addition, her sex and her youth were against her. Father and male school administrator saw it as appropriate to protect her—she had not a husband and, even if free of their patronage, working only during her late teen years and early twenties, she could hardly experience the pleasure and satisfaction of exercising mature authority in the workplace. School men even said that her youth and temporary status fit her particularly well for the urban graded school. They assumed that

---

*The new school reformers formed a national community with similar political strategies. New York began centralization in 1896, followed by St. Louis (1897), Baltimore (1898), Philadelphia (1905), Boston (1906), Chicago (1917), and San Francisco (1920).

she would happily teach a prescribed curriculum, preferring not to be taxed by work that required "intellectual range or versatility," since she had no ambition. As if to reinforce her second rate status, she was usually paid one third of the wage of a man.[29]

If the city system required obedience from the teacher, society did not encourage her to think herself worthy of independence and leadership, either, nor did it confer status upon her. Beyond school, she occupied an ambiguous social position. In choosing teaching over secretarial work—the only other genteel profession open to her—she had signalled her desire for acceptance in a social class above her own; however, she was far from finding a place among the city's social elite. Often a success in her own eyes and those of the family to whose support she contributed, she was not considered the match of upper-class graduates of schools like Vassar, Smith, and Wellesley.*

One teacher expressed her bitterness at being excluded from her city's "very energetic women's clubs. They certainly have not considered what they might give to the teacher, nor what the teacher could give to them, for they hold their meetings at an hour when teachers are at work."[30] From a survey of teachers asking what they felt their own "position" to be came the following two opinions. A teacher told the story of attending a party given by a society woman for teachers the night following one for her own "set." On a tray, the young women noticed a small cake with a bite taken out of it, obviously left over from the previous night. "At this revelation there were indignant looks, but the teacher's inviolable safeguard, the sense of humor, came to the rescue, and the holder of the telltale wafer lifted it up and proposed, sotto voce: 'Here's health to us: the rag-tag and bobtail of the learned professions: beloved by children, tolerated by youth; forgotten by maturity; considered municipally, financially and socially as good enough for what is left.'" But the sense of humor apparently was not always an adequate defense. Wrote another woman, "The office girl or the typewriter is more of a social success because her evenings are free and her spirit is

---

*The upper class women often chose philanthropic work—in settlement houses or in school improvement groups. They dominated the new fields of sociology and social work, and often viewed the teacher as a misguided public servant.

less fatigued; not because she has a mind or disposition equal to that of a teacher."[31]

Particularly poignant was the situation of the teacher who was a recent immigrant herself.* Not just routinely obedient in her work, she actively sought from the school the social approval others looked for elsewhere. The school had taught her to be American, and now it had become a substitute for the family which frequently represented to her the shame and ignorance of her past. With affecting intensity, a Cleveland teacher spoke at a National Education Association Convention: "I am an immigrant, a stranger in a strange land.... Please notice me, take hold of me, lead me.... Try to protect me from my own inexperiences. Take me in as a member of your great and glorious family. I want to belong."[32] Behind her plea was perhaps harsh generational and cultural conflict similar to that portrayed in Anzia Yezierska's story, "Children of Loneliness" (see selection, p. 273). One week home from college, Rachel Ravinsky, the new "teacherin" precipitated a bitter shouting match with her parents by asking her mother to eat with a fork. "*Pfui* on all your American colleges! *Pfui* on the morals of America! No respect for old age. No fear for God," shouted her father. "Aren't you dragging me by the hair to the darkness of past ages," Rachel screamed back before running from the house into the "crushing daze of loneliness."[33]

"Woman Labor" Organizes: The Beginning of Teachers' Unions

"The teacher [is] an automaton, a mere factory hand, whose duty it is to carry out mechanically and unquestioningly the ideas and orders of those clothed with the authority of position.... The individuality of the teacher and her power of initiative are thus destroyed, and the result is courses of study, regulations, and equipment which the teachers have had no voice in selecting, which often have no relation to the children's needs,

---

*The Immigration Commission found that in 1908, 43% of teachers were second generation immigrants. Magazines, such as *School*, reveal in their lists of appointments and retirements, many new Jewish teachers and retiring Irish ones around 1905.

and which prove a hindrance instead of a help in teaching,"
declared Margaret Haley to the 1904 General Session of the
National Education Association.[34]

Haley's address, "Why Teachers Should Organize," reprinted in
this section, was not a puff of theory intended to stimulate
debate on the working conditions of teachers. She stood before
the NEA as business agent of the Chicago Teacher's Federation, a
seven year old organization of elementary school teachers, and
as president of the new National Federation of Teachers. To the
credit of this "lady labor slugger" and her sister unionists were
impressive victories. "Maggie" Haley had been teaching for
twenty years in Chicago when, in 1900, she and Catherine
Goggin, Teacher's Federation president, forced the state supreme
court to wrest unpaid taxes from five public utility companies—
money, they argued, which should have gone for teachers' raises.
Subsequently, they took the Board of Education to court and
won, after it earmarked the back taxes for school maintenance,
not salaries. Haley also won a tenure law, a pension plan, and a
system of teachers' councils with some powers over curriculum
and discipline. Astute politically and tireless in seeking
alliances to promote the cause of teachers, Haley also engineered a successful campaign to affiliate her union with the
Chicago Federation of Labor. Although women had not yet won
the right to vote, Haley's voteless female constituents cam-
paigned *through* and with male workers for candidates who
supported a range of progressive issues: child labor laws, woman
suffrage, direct primaries, and equal wages for men and women.

The Chicago example inspired other women teachers to
organize. Particularly impressive was the "one issue" New York
City group, the Interborough Association of Women Teachers.
With "equal pay for equal work" as its slogan, it appealed to the
proletariat of the profession—elementary school teachers, who
were the lowest paid women in the system. Their salaries,
declared Grace Strachan, the union president, in her 1910 book,
Equal Pay for Equal Work, (see selection, p. 295), were exactly
"$11.53 a week. A woman in charge of one of the stations in the
city gets more."

The Irish leadership of the IAWT, schooled in the rough-and-
tumble of ward politics, argued their case in the mass media, and
sought allies among local politicians and in women's clubs. From

1907 on, backed by a teaching force which grew to 14,000 in 1910, district superintendent Strachan began to make her case in the state legislature. Delegations of teacher lobbyists traveled to Albany, absenting themselves without pay from their schools, and causing the city Board of Education to bellow its disapproval of women taking political positions, especially when they contradicted the Board's. In 1911, despite attempts to "gag" Strachan, and accuse her of neglecting her supervisory duties— she had written as the *official* report of her absences: "Work in a cause destined to uplift the moral standards of the school system, and hence the community, the State, the nation, and the world—the establishment of justice for the women workers in our public schools"—the legislature passed a law granting these voteless women their equal pay.[35]

These women's organizations marked the first wide recognition that teachers' issues were best analyzed as women's issues. For example, both the Chicago Teacher's Federation and the Interborough Association disposed of the genteel myth that women do not work. While it persisted, Boards argued that the young woman awaiting marriage hardly required the benefits of a worker—a decent wage, security, regular promotion, tenure, and pension. In *Equal Pay for Equal Work*, Grace Strachan argued that women had the same right to economic independence as men. Family responsibility had no place in fixing salary:

I hold that salary is for service, and should be measured by the service rendered, irrespective of the size, weight, color, complexion, race, previous condition of servitude, height, length of nose, location of ear, character of costume, religion, size of shoe, height of heel worn, hair or lack of hair on the face or head, number of children, nephews, nieces, aunts, grandfathers, parents.... I'm sure if a man comes to sweep off the snow from your front stoop, you do not ask him if he is married and how many children he has, in order to fix the price for his work.

In addition, she pointed out, the unmarried woman teacher supported elderly relatives who would not assist her in her old age while the married man had children as "an endowment policy" for his.[36]

Haley framed the issue differently. In limiting the CTF to elementary school teachers, she deliberately made it a women's organization, then argued not for women's wages, but for living wages and benefits, the rights of any working person. In her view, teachers shared the plight of other exploited workers, and only in organizing unions would the power of the bosses be tempered. Unlike Strachan, Haley worried little about teachers' respectability, and much about their freedom to think and express their opinions.

These women's organizations persisted with substantial power for a decade or two, swept along on the first wave of feminism that culminated in woman suffrage in 1920. And with the suffrage movement, they shared the energy and optimism of newly released woman power. Acting together, they tried to protect women teachers from intimidation and exploitation by sly supervisors, autocratic superintendents, or patrician boards. "The women teachers of New York City...have formed themselves into a great united body whose voice is being heard 'round the world,' " wrote Grace Strachan. "There are so many of us—fifteen thousand more—that the very strength of numbers has given us courage; and the timid, scattered cries of individuals have swelled into one great grand choral.... The Interborough Association of Women Teachers...sends greetings to all its sisters, and promises that the degradation and belittling will disappear 'as mists of the morning.' The recognition of women is but in its morning."[37]

The True Character of the New York Public Schools

Adele Marie Shaw

From Adele Marie Shaw, "The True Character of the New York Public Schools," *The World's Work*, Vol. 7, no. 2 (December 1903), pp. 4204–4221.

During 1903–1904, Adele Marie Shaw (1865?–1941), a New York writer and teacher, wrote a series of six "first hand studies of American public schools." The first of these investigative pieces, "The True Character of the New York Public Schools," presented a largely dismal portrait:

*overcrowded buildings, lack of sanitation, mindless
authoritarianism from some teachers, despotism from
administrators, and disrespect for immigrant children. But
Shaw saw rays of sunlight as well, sparks of creativity in
extraordinary classrooms and schools.*

*Shaw's third article, however, on another big city school
system—Philadelphia's—portrayed corruption of education at
the hands of politicians. There, she asserted, jobs were
bought and sold, women paid the lowest salaries of any city
of the Union's forty-three largest, and the only lesson for
"every growing boy and girl [is] that pull is stronger than
merit." The headnote to this article quotes a letter of a
Philadelphia teacher to her New York friend: "From the
political thraldom of Philadelphia, I look upon New York as a
pedagogical paradise."*

*Shaw, a Smith College graduate, had served as head of the
English department at Newtown (Queens) High School. A
journalist, novelist, and lyric verse writer, she enjoyed a
substantial career writing for Scribner's, Century, McClure's,
and other national magazines.*

*How are we to credit Shaw's portrait? Evidence from other
sources supports its accuracy, despite the occasional
sensational tone. The series of which the following article
was a part attracted considerable attention; in addition to the
systems already mentioned, it investigated schools near New
York City, the "ideal" schools of Menomonie, Wisconsin, and
vacation play schools. All of the articles appeared in* The
World's Work, *in the years 1903 and 1904.*

**Twenty-three Million Dollars This Year Well Spent But
Wholly Insufficient—Good Work of the Present
Board—But Unspeakably Unsanitary Conditions in
Some of the Schools—How Physical Examinations Are
Conducted by Doctors and Nurses—Bad Methods and
Bad Manners—The Improvements under Way—The
Problem Presented by Immigration**

T he future of this country is more than ever in the hands of the
public schools." We hear the statement often and are not
startled. Now and then we rally (in our newspapers) to shout

"Hands off!" to the sectarian and to the politician, and "Three cheers!" or "Down with fads!" to the reformer, but, unless some boy or girl in our own household raises the cry of injustice, we bother ourselves very little about the schoolroom influences that are making or spoiling American children.

What citizen or parent, for instance, who has no official connection with the public schools, has within a year been inside a schoolroom? or knows whether the work done in the public school nearest him is good or bad?

The Problem in New York City

I chose New York City as the starting point in a study of the public schools of the United States because New York's problem is so difficult that once solved it would shed a calcium light upon the problems of other places. No other municipality had ever to meet a problem so difficult, so peculiar, and at the same time so all-embracing. With eighty-five per cent of its population foreign or of foreign parentage; its salvation dependent upon the conversion of a daily arriving cityful of Russians, Turks, Austro-Hungarians, Sicilians, Greeks, Arabs, into good Americans; its average citizen ignorant or indifferent concerning educational ideals; its present effort weighted with the ignorance and corruption of the past, the city has a problem of popular education that is staggering. . . .

Can Any Amount of Work or Money
Really Solve the Problem?

There were enrolled in the public schools last year 588,614 pupils. This year there is an increase in the day schools of 40,408 (enrolled pupils). September 30th there were 89,316 children in part-time classes. When we consider that 73,226 of these should have been provided for during the Tammany administration, and that the new buildings when completed will furnish 21,447 more sittings than are now needed, we can guess in some fashion at the stupendous energy, skill, and determination of the present Board of Education. In the history of the world I doubt if money was ever more wisely expended than the $23,000,000 used in 1901–2 by the present managers of the public schools of this city. How many parents have any knowledge of the enormous gain of the past two years? How many, comparing poor conditions with the best, are ready to say, "Make it all good, *no matter what it costs.*"

And it will cost. For the first time in our history all children of school age are registered and cared for, all truants are followed up, all recreant parents coerced. This alone adds an army to the school registers. Under this administration more children live and fewer die. This, as well as immigration, crowds the schools. And all the time, back of this growth by avulsion and by restoration, are the natural accretion and expansion of a great and attractive city whose normal increase is almost forgotten behind the descending avalanche of aliens.

What in the face of growth like this are 20,000 or 200,000 sittings? Unless Tammany returns forever to power (and that is not possible), East Side babies will go on improving; fewer tiny coffins will be. needed, and more schoolroom chairs. Unless legislation dams the encroaching flood, more babies will be brought here and more babies will be born here than ever before. And unless New York ceases to draw like the magnet it is, its population will be swelled by contributions from the North and the East and the South and the West of our own country.

No one denies that New York's growth is abnormally large, its adoption of aliens abnormally confiding. If it hopes to Americanize a school population chiefly of foreign parentage it must use abnormal means. Last year one school had free baths; 1,000 baths were taken in that school in one week. Every school in the thickly settled districts should have free baths. If you sniff at "frills" and say, "Give them the three R's; let them get clean at home," you forget that they will not get clean at home, and that if they stay unclean in school every child and every home is endangered.

To educate the children of our adoption we must at the same time educate their families, and in a measure the public school must be to them family as well as school. To do this and not to neglect, as we are now forced to neglect, the children who are here, needs not twenty-three million dollars in a year, but five times twenty-three millions. If we withhold it we surrender the city to crime and to disease.

Scenes from Primary School Rooms

In order to make a fair picture of the work, good and bad, that is done in New York public schools, since the beginning of the school year I have visited twenty-five of the schools where little New Yorkers are trained. These schools were very carefully selected, both for location and for such other considerations as should make them representative of the elementary system, so that the change from building to building has often been as great as the change from tropic to pole. Some children spend their entire school life under a *regime* that would make criminals of harmless mollusks, and some from kindergarten to graduation know only the influences that strengthen and establish.

In one of these primary schoolrooms an eager little girl is reciting,

Down in the meadow where the stream runs blue
Lived an old mother fish and her little fishes two.

You suspect something amiss with the natural history, but you know the atmosphere is gentleness and good-will. Across the corridor the woman whom the children call "a murder" is devoting herself to "discipline."

The lower-grade teachers bear the heaviest burden of the public school system. Their classes are too large, and the demands made upon them are exacting.

The Material the Schools Must Work On

In a Brooklyn school not far from the Bridge I visited a room where sixty-five very small children were packed into a space properly intended for twenty. A bright-faced young woman was steadying a sleeping baby upon his third-of-a-seat while she heard the remaining sixty-four recite. By the end of the hour she had the sleepy one at the blackboard delightedly making a figure.

"He and his brother here are little Cubans," she explained. "They speak no English, but the brother can already imitate anything the rest can do."

I saw the small class a few days later and the two were already

melted into the rank and file and were losing the distinctly
foreign look. Soon they will begin to be ashamed of their
beautiful Spanish name, and will revise its spelling in deference
to their friends' linguistic limitations. Esther Oberrhein in the
entering class changes to Esther O'Brien in the next grade. Down
in Marion Street a dark-eye son of Naples who came last spring as
Guiseppi Vagnotti appeared in September as Mike Jones.

The adaptability of childhood modifies more than the names.
Mr. Hewitt, in looking for "types" to photograph, remarked the
extraordinary homogeneousness of uppergrade children. Swedish,
Norwegian, Italian—all were *American.* With every "type" the
primary teacher must deal. With the cruel-fingered boy who
"fell from a window a year ago and isn't quite right," to the big girl
just landed guiltless of any tongue save her native Yiddish, the
same magic must be made to work; the fusing and amalgamating
force of interest kept at white heat. It is exhausting labor.

Did you ever try to teach sixty-five or even fifty-five little
children how to thread a worsted needle? Did you ever take care
of a mere dozen for a morning? If you did, you will admire and not
carp at the woman who keeps her temper, treats them like
human beings, and teaches them to speak English and tell
the *and* story, even if she does say, as I heard one, "Don't that
come in lovely," "somewheres," and "O my goodness."

The good primary teacher has the power of making you forget
your environment. It was in the cavernous dimness of a very
dreary room that I became so absorbed I overstayed my hour. It
was here that Garcia, Mendelssohn, and Joshua sat in the same
row and made well-proportioned pictures with yellow crayon,
and a nasturtium for model. Whether it was drawing or
arithmetic, there was apparently not a minute of the day when
pleased attention and earnest effort languished. The teacher was
a thin, delicate girl who gave her entire mind, and soul, and heart,
and strength to her task. Philanthropists who never taught, and
even superintendents who have, urge such teachers to spend the
remnant of their force *in visiting the homes of their pupils,*and
praise is accorded those who add to an already suicidal labor the
taking of their flocks upon excursions. The excursions are
admirable, a wonderful stimulus to the children who share them,

but why not appoint wise, wholesome, responsible men and women and give them a salary as "conductors." Let the teacher go as a guest. Otherwise we shall always have the unconscientious too much in evidence while the sensitive and magnetic are killed off.

On the fifth floor of "No. 20" (Rivington, Forsythe, and Eldridge Streets in Manhattan) are the reading-room, library, sewing-room, cooking-room, girls' gymnasium, boys' gymnasium, modeling-room, draughting-room, and carpentry room. The principal of No. 6 (Miss Clara Calkins) can make her children happy, busy, and self-controlled in a building bare of even common necessities! What would she not accomplish for body and spirit in a building light, sanitary, and well equipped? It was at No. 6 that the photographer, taking a picture of the old form of assembly room, made by sliding walls (with no corridors), exclaimed at the remarkable stillness of the six classes during a long exposure. "If this is public school training," he said, "then I wish the children that come to my studio could have it. It's *extraordinary.*"

Some Examples of Wonderful Work and Model School Buildings

At 141 and 110 in Brooklyn I found the ideal principal and the modern building together. In both, sunshine—warmth and light—pervaded the place and the work. If there is any place where a citizen may find hope for the solution of an apparently insoluble problem it is in the new schools of the lower East Side of Manhattan. Let him see the cheerful athletes on the roof playground of No. I (Henry and Oliver Streets); let him watch the boys and girls fresh from the shower baths of 147 (Gouverneur and Henry Streets); let him see the "little mothers" and the ambitious newsboys in the evening study rooms of the recreation centres; and let him visit that humane product of a real civilization, the ungraded class for the mentally handicapped at school No. I. Such schools are making self-supporting men of probable paupers, good men and women of probable criminals, and good American citizens of thousands and thousands of children whose parents speak no English, and learn loyalty to government only by seeing what it does for their offspring.

The mere physical gain in these improved schools is a constantly rising scale of inventive excellence. I have pored literally hours over the plans for the new 106, realizing in them dreams that have been often scoffed at as "impossible." Here, easily accessible from the street, is to be a vast auditorium, that with its toilet rooms and special approaches can be shut off from the upper building. Weary mothers that would never have climbed four flights of stairs will slip in here to free evening lectures and rest worn eyes on stereopticon views of lake and country, sometimes the valleys and mountains of their native land. A laboratory is not in itself beautiful. But a laboratory filled with youthful workers, learning the dignity of toil and the way to think, is more than beautiful. To the patriot it is hope and assurance.

If I were to attempt the guidance of a visitor to New York schools I should not let him escape till he had seen 159, visited 77 (whose former principal, Miss Richman, is now district superintendent), had a glimpse of 170 (east of Central Park at 111th Street), and seen at least the outside of 63 and 175 in the Bronx. These are mentioned almost at random, picked out from a long list of schools that would inspire the interest of any real American from Cape Nome to the Florida Keys.

The Medical Inspector and the Nurse

In these modern schools education begins as far as possible, with the production of sound physical conditions in the child. The common sense of this method is plain to the cultivated man, but ignorant parents are chronic objectors to time thrown away on the care of the body. "You must stop teach my Lizzie fisical torture she needs yet readin' and figors mit sums more as that, if I want her to do jumpin' I kin make her jump," was an exasperated mother's protest.

It is this dead weight of ignorance that fell at first upon the shoulders of the medical inspectors and the nurses....

As a rule, the doctor's toil is briefly over. The nurse's lasts all

day.... The nurse's tact, humanity, and firmness are phenomen-
al. Everywhere she soothes eyes that look like martyrdom when
the lids are drawn down, treats skin diseases of which ringworm
and a scabby eruption are the most common, and examines
heads.

The patients I saw were so little and so plucky I found my
circulation quickening in admiration. Not a child whined or
begged off, and not one cried out at the smart. The thing that goes
straight to one's heart is the satisfied and utter confidence with
which they settle back into the nurse's hands. They *like* to be
cared for.

"Did your big sister use the kerosene?" asked the nurse, parting
a mop of hair to peer carefully at the forest within.

"Yes, ma'am," replied the afflicted one.

"Tell her to put on more, so it will soak all through, and come
to me tomorrow," was the day's direction.

The vermin present is of many kinds. In old days, it seems,
those that hopped found undisturbed delight in varied exploration; those that crawled, abode and multipled. But the day of
the hopper and of the crawler alike is over—or would be over
if the city could afford to give the same care to all neglected
children that it gives to some....

The Dark Side of the Picture

New York children do not have equal chances, physically, in
the New York schools. Yet the custom of seating two children (and
in crowded classrooms I frequently saw *three*) at the same desk
cannot be done away with till money can be spared for new
furniture and space allowed for single desks. A New York
physician has said that ninety-nine out of a hundred girls are
deformed by the schoolroom postures before they reach the high
school; curvature of the spine is one of the commonest effects of
schoolroom chairs. Yet the new course of study, which insists
upon a sensible change of position, with calisthenics and deep
breathing at frequent intervals, is condemned by old-fashioned
teachers as "wasting time." At present the attention given in the
lower schools to keeping children straight and well developed
varies with the caprices of the individual instructor.

The conditions of public education should provide for the right growth of body, mind, and chararcter; and proper physical training demands good air, cleanliness, and freedom from degrading surroundings. Good air in the months of September and October is not hard to obtain, yet in nearly every classroom that I entered the atmosphere was foul. Sometimes even the assembly hall and the corridors were distinctly offensive. A room in which forty-six little girls live and work five hours in the day contained only one outside window. The miserably flickering gas over their heads consumed the oxygen needed by starved lungs, and yet on the three warm days during which I visited this class I did not once see the window opened more than a few inches. The scourge of New York is consumption; the preventive of consumption is fresh air; and these children say "Draught" as they might cry "Tiger!"

A Murderous Hole of Darkness

The darkness would be less oppressive in such cases if the gas that burns on cloudy days in certain rooms of half the schools I saw, and on all days in some, was good gas, but its feeble uncertainty adds a melancholy to the gloom. In one dim assembly hall I groped my way to a platform on either side of which was drawn a cloth curtain. Behind the curtains two classes went on in simultaneous confusion, and I talked with the principal in a kind of cloth-bound cave, with grammar on one side, arithmetic on the other, and a "bad boy" awaiting discipline down in front.

The gas jets that eked out the scanty daylight in the curtained recesses had in one instance been replaced by Welsbach burners, and as one of the teachers said, "They're always breaking, and then they're worse than nothing."

The windows of this building opened on two sides into tenement back yards, whose washings were strung within a few feet of the children's desks, and whose sheds and water-closets just below were close to the schoolhouse wall.

Because of the stench that had floated in the windows, complaint had been made of the yard closets, and I was told that they had been closed and the air purified. I was not conscious of any unpleasant odor, but the closets were not entirely out of use.

In this building both principal and teachers appeared to take great pains with ventilation, but the conditions of their labors were more than difficult. The playground space was a small dark basement divided so as to give the girls the larger share. Sunken between the tenements and the school building was a narrow court not so large as a good city back yard, where 500 boys "went out to play." On rainy days they are often crowded so close in the hopeless darkness of the basement that there is barely standing-room. The teacher in charge of the playground must stay in this cell, though to see what is going on is impossible, and although on winter days the place is miserably cold for her and for the boys....

The Wrong Kind of Teaching

Nor is there any greater equality in the conditions in which the New York public-school child develops mind and character.

The well-to-do, who furnish the principal support of the public schools, send their children elsewhere. Three-fourths of New York's elementary teachers could not get positions in private schools.

"Who told you to speak out?" "*You've* paid attention!" scolded or sneered at a boy who is struggling to express an independent thought, will not make him a ready user of the gifts with which he is endowed.

The tone of continual exasperation in which more than one class is addressed would blight the forthputting powers of a Macaulay. Truancy from some of these classes should be imputed to a child for righteousness. In one room, where a geography recitation was in lumbering progress, I volunteered the beaming comment: "These seem like nice boys." "I haven't found them so," answered the teacher sourly, and a sudden animation and general straightening lapsed into stodginess....

In one school in which I spent the better part of two days I did not once hear any child express a thought in his own words. Attention was perfect. No pupil could escape from any grade without knowing the questions and answers of that grade. Every child could add, subtract, multiply, and divide with accuracy; every child could and did pronounce his reading words with unusual distinctness. The chant in which recitations were delivered was as uniform as everything else. "*Wren: w* is silent. The only sound of *r;* the second sound of *e;* the only sound of *n,*" was as near the heavy accentuation as I can get. It was the best and the worst school I ever saw. The best, because no pains, no time, *nothing* had been spared to bring it up to the principal's ideal; and the effort had been crowned with entire success. The worst, because it ignored absolutely any individuality in the pupils and rewarded them for nothing more than a mechanical obedience to another's thinking....

No School Better Than This School

In this school there exists a rigidity that is like a *rigor mortis;* it forbids such a natural outgiving of the natural teacher as the syllabus suggests. Here the subordinate must be forever on the jump to accomplish the set end of her day's labor, and while the principal is calm, pleasant in manner, and God-fearing in her life, most of the teachers who carry out her conscientiously relentless will are harassed, visibly worn, harsh, and unkind.

The children are apparently callous and happy in their indifference toward their environments. I saw a small boy whose elbow was suddenly jerked and shaken sneak a little mischievous grin toward the back of the room.

In one class the very way in which the teacher intoned "You—are—not—still" gave me a sensation of quick fright that brought back the awful moment of my childhood when I saw a boy arrested and haled away by a policeman. "Somebody—foot!" the same teacher shouted suddenly, and my circulation stopped. My own foot, I felt sure, had moved.

No child in this school ever "raises his hand" above the level of the shoulder excepting during the arithmetic recitation, when pencils that are not in actual use are held in the clenched fingers of the right hand, the right elbow resting on the desk, the left hand laid flat on the other side.

"My answer is—" began an infant arithmetician.

"Don't say that in my class"...

"Don't stand in my class with pencil, pen, or book in hand," snapped the teacher.

"Indeed! But you'll please sit down," was the sneer that greeted a wrong answer.

Neither the principal nor her first assistant, who was both sweet and gentle, "snapped," but the manner of one of the younger teachers who seemed a "kind of right-hand man" gave me an overwhelming desire to rescue the class committed to her, and to do it, if necessary, by physical violence.

In this school, probably the only one of its kind in the world, there is at least no indirection, no flabbiness. The apparent cruelty that kept me "on edge" is not half so fatal as the actual cruelty of methods known elsewhere.

"You dirty little Russian Jew, what are you doing?" seems even more ruinous to a child's spirit and temper.

The school most unrelieved in badness had no principal in evidence. Opposite the name of the "head" in charge I wrote in my notebook: "Coarse, fat woman, sensual look, youngish, diamond earrings, talks dialect." This woman's methods are summary, but according to her lights. If a child gets in her way she throws him out, lifting him by any portion of his person that "comes handy." From such a school graduate the brutal truck-drivers, the amateur criminals who, having little better in their minds, devise much mischief.

That the imitative powers of childhood are startling; that the teacher's thoughts, feelings, aspirations even, transfer themselves on invisible wings to the members of her class, proves itself every instant of the day. Yet in a majority of the schools I was continually embarrassed by the discourtesy with which the children were addressed—or ignored. There is sentimentalism that forgets the teacher's difficulties and there is "plain good sense." It is not sentimentality to recognize rudeness as rudeness even when its object is a child. What possible end but a common misery is to be attained by pointing out the "bad boy" to a stranger? What sort of example is the taste that discusses quickeared children even in lowered tones when they are present? "Get on to those eyes!" brought me a glance quite uncomfortable but already self-conscious. "*He* is a degenerate!" procured a sullen look of blank defiance that changed to sullen watchfulness as the talk went on.

About School Boards and Examinations

The stupid discourtesy of a good deal of schoolroom behavior is a direct reflex of the treatment of the teacher or the would-be teacher by the Board, and its employees.... How deeply the teachers resent the very treatment they too frequently "pass on to the children" only they and their intimates know.

"I could have borne it better," said a much-tried soul, "but from the Superintendent down every man made me feel he was the sole owner and proprietor of the city schools and that I had intruded on his private business."

Not long ago a New York teacher had occasion to be examined, and after several written requests that elicited no information she was sent by her principal to the office of Mr. Z——. Mr. Z—— was the wrong man, but he directed her to Mr. Y——. It was not Mr. Y——'s day," so she returned at another time and waited long upon a desolate bench until the interview was secured. Mr. Y—— was also the wrong man, but he kindly conducted her to Mr. X——, to whom she was evidently *non grata.*

"I can't see you today," he snarled with the air of an angry plutocrat dismissing a persistent beggar.

The teacher went. As she retired, Mr. Y——, who seemed to have a vein of true humanity, instructed her that she must fill out a certain printed blank and present it to Mr. X—— before she left the building for the day.

She filled the paper and with trepidation reentered the presence of the summary X——. For an hour she sat waiting before him while others who came later were received and dismissed, till, time failing, she ventured to approach the desk.

"I told you I couldn't see you," raged the indignant authority.

She halted, and, explaining deprecatingly, dropped the document upon the nearest support and fled as incontinently as self-respect would permit.

It took six journeys from her remote borough by steam and trolley before this unfortunate teacher was able to get that examination.

All servants of the Board are not like this, all buildings are not old, all teachers are not faulty. Mr. Snyder is the architect and head of the building department, and, busy as he is, his courtesy never fails, nor is he the only one of the authorities who can be approached without revolt. Moreover, in old buildings no less than in new are to be found a great corps of gently bred, enlightened teachers spending and being spent in the service of the city. All this ungracious setting forth of the dark side of things is the necessary and unpleasing task of one who tries to show that the opportunities of New York children are not all alike and not all good.

The Pay of Teachers

The most rational of all the good salary bills...made advance in the pay of teachers dependent on merit as well as on length of service. At present, length of service alone governs the advance in salary.

There are certain injustices in the distribution of salaries. It is an injustice that a woman who is principal of a school of 2,500 children should receive $750 less a year than a man head of a high school department, and $150 less than a woman high school assistant. If the men now wailing in the newspapers about their inability to secure elementary school positions would equalize the salaries so these should no longer be like animals male and female, they would have their positions. Economy now keeps them out. Everywhere women teachers have to keep order for the men who are getting so many hundreds more for their virile authority! No influence effeminizes the schools so fast as the average man teacher. Men like Mr. Doty, who will rule in the beautiful 106, are not common in the public schools. Men's or women's, the New York salaries are generous and promptly paid. They should command the best service in the world. That they do not is chiefly because our energy is increasingly absorbed in providing for immigration.

General Conclusions

Four conclusions stand out in my mind as the result of these weeks of visiting New York public schools and of study of the huge problem.

1. New York City has the most difficult educational problem in the country. It stands in a class by itself and has difficulties that no other city presents.

2. Under the present school administration it is doing wonderful work toward solving that problem.

3. But conditions still exist that put the complete solution of the problem beyond the reach of any normal effort and expense.

4. The only remedies for such conditions are the restriction of immigration and a vast increase in expenditure—larger than has yet been dreamed of.

My Mother's Principal and Mine

Nancy Hoffman

From a transcript of a personal interview with Mary Agnes Dwyer, October 3, 1977.

Mary Agnes Dwyer (1885–1979) was ninety-three years old when I interviewed her in an industrial city near New York. Her name had been suggested to me in my conversations with my mother, my aunt, and their friends—women in their seventies who had met as school girls. They agreed that if I wanted to learn more about immigrants in the schools, Miss Dwyer was the person to question. She had been a principal for some years when my mother served under her as a substitute teacher in the thirties; my mother's friend Edith Kondell had been her secretary on into the fifties; and I had been a pupil at her school. A regal woman, her white hair piled into a chignon, she was eager to talk to me. "I should be delighted," she said, elegantly enunciating each word. I was only one among many educators who had sought her out

after her retirement. The richness of her reminiscenses
suggests the potentiality of a fertile oral history among
teachers.

T he problem of schooling children today isn't anything as it
was to teach the immigrant in 1906. I began at twenty one,
in 1906. And it was only a matter of the children being trained
and particularly taught the English language. The parents were
vitally involved. They came to the school as students. We used
to have them from 7:30 to 9:30 in the same classrooms. Unpaid,
we went back to teach them after a day's work. They are the
people I still love and remember, because they believed in us. We
had a great deal to give and they needed it, but we needed them
because they were going to be the future of our city—and they
were, and they *are*, even now.

When I look back at the Doctors Ehrenfeld, Reshnevs, Starks,
Meyer Rothwax as a little boy, and his parents, the Cinnamons,
Pashmans, I find people who are still close to me in friendship
and remembrance. I was very young and I had a lot to learn. I was
eager to accept what these people were bringing to all of us—
their culture, their intellectual integrity, their desire to have
their children have the best. They trusted us and loved us, and
we did the same. Now, that was Number 2 school...

We did not need the PTA. There were always families that had
emergencies, as during the woolen strike, and in happier days,
too. The woolen industry strike went on for thirteen weeks. The
teachers carried kerosene lamps into their homes. They bought
the oil. People who had never touched those types of lamps
before learned how to use them, because the parents hadn't the
money just then, and everybody was in dire distress. Of course,
we had to keep the children in school, and we did all we could.
That was when Mrs. Barry of the Barry manufacturers, she and
her associates, lovely women, came down into our school, put
aprons on, and made warm soup, a regular soup kitchen.

I went up into the homes and saw how those people lived, and I
loved the experience. I'd never seen anything like it before.

The immigrants who were not able to speak English were
willing to come and study. We labored, holding their hands to

teach them to write. They never were tired, always eager and ambitious for success. They never thought in terms of money, but they thought in terms of what there was to do in this great big place they had just come to, and they promised us that they would speak as much English as possible to the children in their homes. So it was a learning experience for the children and an exercise by the parents.

I think that period in Passaic was the highest peak we ever reached in the schools. We had 100% cooperation from every organization—Red Cross, Salvation Army, and all of the fraternal organizations as well. They were never too busy to stop and listen to us. And they got things done we didn't seem to count in those days. One little incident makes me very happy when I remember it. Many of those children came to school with their shoes practically off their feet. There was a cobbler on the corner—we called him a shoemaker, but he was really a cobbler. He would mend the children's shoes, polish the shoes; the children would be in their stocking feet in the school. In the late afternoon, one of us, a teacher or maybe one of the secretaries, would go around to pay for the shoes. They were in excellent condition, and he never charged any of us five cents. Then there were occasions when accidents would happen and we would have to find the parents before the child could be taken care of. We had several marvelous doctors who would come in at our personal call, and who could get anything done. No red tape. Today teachers aren't really able to allow their own initiative to come out to solve something. You have to go to this agency and that agency and see three or four people, or five people, before you can get anything done.

I was the middle child in a family of six brothers, three sisters, and an adopted sister. I always wanted to teach dolls—even all the empty chairs were pupils. We had access to many wonderful books. My father was an avid reader and he wanted to read with us and instruct us. He was particular about what we read. The boys were away in boarding schools as they came along, and I reached the point that I was interested in going, too. My mother never wanted me to go to boarding school. We were shielded in our home. I insisted, because I knew what I wanted to do, and I couldn't do it unless I went away from home and boarded at a teacher's college. There was then a normal school in Trenton and in connection with it, there was a model school. You would go to the model school and take all your examinations. There were opportunities there, but things grew to be a little slow for me; I wanted to do it all in hurry, because I knew that I was the middle one in the family, and there were other ones to come along—I had a strong sense of responsibility, which is good. I had it all my life. I took six periods a day excepting Saturday, when we had a limited course. I did it so that I could get out, and get home again, and get to work.

I went to Trenton in 1901. I would have been sixteen. I had had a tutor. We were living in Garfield at the time, for one year. A Mrs. Rossi taught me trigonometry, Latin, which we needed, geometry, which was easy for me, and German. Those were the subjects we had to take in order to receive the entrance examinations. In the model school, I then completed the tests. Every test that you were exposed to, you had to receive at least 85%. Then you were permitted to take the pedagogy for that subject which was necessary for the license in that subject. So it was three and a half years—in Trenton, the model school, and the teachers college. I was able to get my license and my degree.

During all those years we had the opportunity of talking with people like Booker T. Washington, about Tuskegee and the situation with the blacks at that time. He had great faith in them, and I have lived to see some of his dream come true. I really have. I sat one afternoon with him and I listened and I learned. But I was so young, I was not yet 21. I taught my first class in 1906, in September, in Number Two school. I was twenty one and I didn't know anything about the foreign people at all, but it was the greatest experience of my lifetime to have been privileged to work on the east side of Passaic. The mills came—the Botany, Forseman, and the others—and the people came. It was as a magnet, pulling them because of the industry, and to me as I look back on it, it was the richest time we ever had in the city.

Many of the children came in the steerage. Their parents had huge bags with tags on them in which they had their belongings. When they stepped off the train at the Erie station, such far distant friends and relatives who had come previously were

(text continued on page 238)

Educating the New Masses

1: New York school children registering, 1913. To immigrants, the teacher was an exalted figure in a bewildering new world.

2: Immigrant children with teacher at Hancock School for Girls, Boston, 1909. Scene of Marian Dogherty's "The First Class," Hancock was considered a "model" school. The photograph by Lewis W. Hine is one of hundreds he made for the National Child Labor Committee.

3: New York school children making a garden.

4: "Playground in Poverty Gap," photograph by Jacob Riis, early 1890s. Teacher-journalist Adele Marie Shaw protested conditions of the kind pictured here. Some ghetto school "play" spaces described by Shaw were even worse, located in dank, airless basements.

1

4

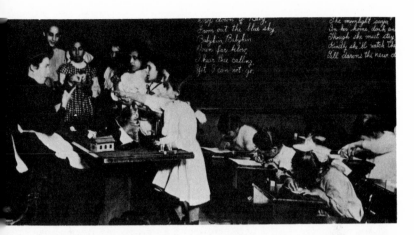

there to greet them. Then they were never alone and never lost. They soon found out that they could go to the drug store. Anyone would interpret and help. There was Mr. Wijak who ran the steamship agency. He was magnificent. There were firemen, the old Dundee 2. They would come in physically, or to help us interpret.

The immigrants had warm hand-made sweaters, underclothes, stockings, and pretty good shoes. They weren't the pasteboard shoes that some people had in those times. They had good substantial food. Their body structure was good. They were proud. We tried to teach them posture, cleanliness. They lived in cold water flats. There is nothing like them in the world. They did marvelously, and I was privileged to go to many of those homes.

I was invited to one place, and I walked into the tenement building. I had never seen a place like this in my life before. It was a maze of a place, great halls. A fireman came up to me and said, "What are you doing over here, Miss Dwyer," and I said, "I need your help right now." He brought me up to the person I was seeking. I opened that door to a darling little woman, laboring with her English. I wish you could have seen that home. Everything was pure white, starched white, beautiful table cloth, and over here a bed with feather quilts on it. I wish my dresser in my bedroom looked as well. She gave us all of the courtesies, even if we didn't understand. Two of us visited her together, two or three times. (It had been advised that we not go exploring too much alone. We were ignorant people).

The boys wore these woolen sweaters. The mothers made them—dark-toned, brown, or black or gray. And this mother would laugh and say when the front got dirty, then she'd turn the sweater inside out. It was just a good story, and not true. We had the services of a physician and a visiting nurse who went to the homes at any time of the day or night, as you called her, or on her own, according to lists that she received from her offices. The teachers were not permitted to expose themselves to disease. If there was an epidemic, we were told to keep out. We were teachers, not professional nurses.

Parents sent us disciplined children. We had forty, and they were different sizes. If it hadn't been for the home and the respect that the teacher had from the parents, we wouldn't have been able to do it, any more than teachers are doing it now.

The biggest problem that the teachers had, especially the young ones, was their idealism. I like it that way, but they have to temper their judgment. If they're very young, it's hard.

I remember the teachers. There was Minny Demarest, a kindergarten teacher, a wonderful woman. I have a picture of her. She was the wife of Doctor Demarest. There was Miss Hees, Miss Phelps from upper New York State, Oswego Normal School. There was a darling elderly woman, and she was such a teacher— Elizabeth Carnover was her name. She knew everything about every child. We also had some very wonderful superintendents.

At that time, most of the principals were women. Number 1 had a woman principal; Number 2 had a woman principal; Number 3 had a woman principal; Number 4 was Joe Constantine; Number 5 was Elsie Crawford; Number 6, the Sullivans were there, and then Miss Cane. (They're all dead, these people.) Number 7, Emma Gifford; she was there for years. Number 8, Dr. Reynold's sister; Number 9, Helen Spear; Number 10, Mr. Millar; and I went in as vice principal with him. How few men we had.

Each term there was some new thing. We had to go to college to keep learning. I remember when the work-study-play system came in—the Gary System. At Number 10, and in other schools where there were seventh and eighth grades, the children were in school half a day, and working at one of the mills the other half, a real mill.

The teachers worked as hard as the students. The teachers didn't have much money—I got $450 a year. That meant that we taught all day, every day; we visited homes after hours; and we assisted various organizations, where we could, in order to keep "in" with organizations that could help the schools.

The only restirctions on teachers were that they be on time and be decent. They were trusted, they weren't bound in. Many of the teachers lived in this building, and in other apartments; some lived in private homes. The girls went into New York a lot to the opera. They had season's tickets. Then the teachers' association became a very strong organization, and through the association, the musical agencies in New York arranged for us to have the finest speakers and lecturers. As an officer of the association, I once introduced Zimbalist, and held his Stradivarius.

I was fifteen years a teacher, and all this time I was studying at Columbia and Fordham and NYU to get my administrative credits. I hadn't thought I'd move from Number 2 school, but then there was a vacancy at Number 10. I went to Number 10 in the twenties, and I worked very hard because it was all so new. They had introduced the work-study-play system at Number 10 at that time, and it was a heavy thing, because we had all the contination school people. We had half a day in the factory, half a day in school, and I was getting interested in that sort of thing. Then a vacancy opened up for assistant principal, and Alma Smith pushed like fury, and kept at me. She said, "You're just wasting your time. Why don't you advance? The salary's better." I wasn't sure I was going to be happy away from the children. You never are, really. When you're with the children, you're living it all. The minute you go on, you're not. And then you're an authority, and some of the things that were close between you and your associates are no longer there. It's very hard.

There were people in that building who really wanted the promotion. They were "in." They knew everything. I was a Johnny-come-lately, and I had to learn. But Edith Kondell's lovely uncle, Mr. Brezlawski, was on the board, and Mr. Sylvester. They both approached me, and asked me to write and ask for the job as assistant principal. I said to them, "Well, if the board wants me.... " Eventually I had to do it, because Alma Smith wanted me in there. She was very good at pushing what she wanted. She was loyal, and she was a magnificent person. We all have our own faults....

Mr. Millar, the principal, hadn't been feeling well. He was in the school, though, on a Friday afternoon...and he dropped dead Saturday morning. The pressure began. The girls wanted me to be principal. There were a couple of men trying to get in, but the girls wanted me. So Mr. Brezlawski came to call on me. Edith was with me, then. He really insisted that I have Edith type a letter, which she did do, right there. He presented it, and that was the beginning.... It was a good life.

I learned much more about teachers. I remember one young girl. She brought a boy in. The boy was in a dreadful temper. She had caught him by the hair. She threw him into my office and said, "I don't like the way he looks at me." I looked at her, waited, moved a few things on my desk, and said: "Won't you sit down a minute." She did, and I said to the boy, "You go out and wait in the other office, and I'll send for you in a minute."

She sat down, and I said, "What could he do but look at you? He couldn't touch you, he couldn't answer you back, he couldn't throw anything."

She said, "I know, but he was angry."

I said, "You were too, dear."

She eventually gave up teaching, because she was quick-tempered, and she didn't have a something that has to be within you if you're going to try to form character and teach essentials.

It's a God-given something, and you never get away from that, never.

An Immigrant Student and Her Teacher

Mary Antin

From Mary Antin, *The Promised Land* (Boston: Houghton Mifflin Co., 1912).

The following chapter from The Promised Land, *the autobiography of Mary Antin (1881–1949), is the single selection here written from the pupil's perspective. A Russian Jewish immigrant whose love of writing blossomed by virtue of her teacher's patience, Antin's account is a classic playing out of the dream that the public schools would transform children into patriotic Americans. A model student, Antin strove to conform to Miss Dillingham's ideal, pronouncing English perfectly, and reading Longfellow's poetry. At a young age, she wrote about American opportunity and compared it to the deprivation of Russia, a theme of* The Promised Land. *For the teacher, evidently, such a pupil was a joy. She was a*

*confirmation of the personal power the teacher wielded by
her calling.*

*In 1901, Antin married a Lutheran scientist in Boston and
moved to New York, where she associated with a group of
Jews influenced by Ralph Waldo Emerson's transcendental-
ism. The Promised Land, published there in 1912, was greeted
enthusiastically, particularly by reviewers who considered it
an antidote to growing fears that the new wave of
immigrants, many living in poverty, would turn against
America. Until a nervous collapse suffered when she was
thirty-seven, Antin moved in literary circles, lecturing for
woman suffrage and against the restriction of immigration.
On the eve of World War II, Antin reclaimed her solidarity
with persecuted Jews in "House of One Father" (Common
Ground, Spring, 1941), an essay pleading for social justice.*

Initiation

It is not worth while to refer to voluminous school statistics to
see just how many "green" pupils entered school last September,
not knowing the days of the week in English, who next February
will be declaiming patriotic verses in honor of George
Washington and Abraham Lincoln, with a foreign accent,
indeed, but with plenty of enthusiasm. It is enough to know that
this hundred-fold miracle is common to the schools in every part
of the United States where immigrants are received. And if I was
one of Chelsea's hundred in 1894, it was only to be expected,
since I was one of the older of the "green" children, and had had a
start in my irregular schooling in Russia, and was carried along
by a tremendous desire to learn, and had my family to cheer me
on.

I was not a bit too large for my little chair and desk in the baby
class, but my mind, of course, was too mature by six or seven
years for the work. So as soon as I could understand what the
teacher said in class, I was advanced to the second grade. This
was within a week after Miss Nixon took me in hand. But I do not
mean to give my dear teacher all the credit for my rapid progress,
nor even half the credit. I shall divide it with her on behalf of my
race and my family. I was Jew enough to have an aptitude for
language in general, and to bend my mind earnestly to my task; I

was Antin enough to read each lesson with my heart, which gave me an inkling of what was coming next, and so carried me along by leaps and bounds. As for the teacher, she could best explain what theory she followed in teaching us foreigners to read. I can only describe the method, which was so simple that I wish holiness could be taught in the same way.

There were about half a dozen of us beginners in English, in age from six to fifteen. Miss Nixon made a special class of us, and aided us so skilfully and earnestly in our endeavors to "see-a-cat," and "hear-a-dog-bark," and "look-at-the-hen," that we turned over page after page of the ravishing history, eager to find out how the common world looked, smelled, and tasted in the strange speech. The teacher knew just when to let us help each other out with a word in our own tongue,—it happened that we were all Jews,—and so, working all together, we actually covered more ground in a lesson than the native classes, composed entirely of the little tots.

But we stuck—stuck fast—at the definite article; and sometimes the lesson resolved itself into a species of lingual gymnastics, in which we all looked as if we meant to bite our tongues off. Miss Nixon was pretty, and she must have looked well with her white teeth showing in the act; but at the same time I was too solemnly occupied to admire her looks. I did take great pleasure in her smile of approval, whenever I pronounced well; and her patience and perserverance in struggling with us over that thick little word are becoming to her even now, after fifteen years. It is not her fault if any of us to-day give a buzzing sound to the dreadful English *th*.

I shall never have a better opportunity to make public declaration of my love for the English language. I am glad that American history runs, chapter for chapter, the way it does; for thus America came to be the country I love so dearly. I am glad, most of all, that the Americans began by being Englishmen, for thus did I come to inherit this beautiful language in which I think. It seems to me that in any other language happiness is not so sweet, logic is not so clear. I am not sure that I could believe in my neighbors as I do if I thought about them in un-English words. I could almost say that my conviction of immortality is bound up with the English of its promise. And as I am attached to my prejudices, I must love the English language!

Whenever the teachers did anything special to help me over my private difficulties, my gratitude went out to them, silently. It meant so much to me that they halted the lesson to give me a lift, that I needs must love them for it. Dear Miss Carrol, of the second grade, would be amazed to hear what small things I remember, all because I was so impressed at the time with her readiness and sweetness in taking notice of my difficulties.

Says Miss Carrol, looking straight at me:—

"If Johnnie has three marbles, and Charlie has twice as many, how many marbles has Charlie?"

I raised my hand for permission to speak.

"Teacher, I don't know vhat is tvice."

Teacher beckons me to her, and whispers to me the meaning of the strange word, and I am able to write the sum correctly. It's all in the day's work her; with me, it is a special act of kindness and efficiency.

She whom I found in the next grade became so dear a friend that I can hardly name her with the rest, though I mention none of them lightly. Her approval was always dear to me, first because she was "Teacher," and afterwards, as long as she lived, because she was my Miss Dillingham. Great was my grief, therefore, when, shortly after my admission to her class, I incurred discipline, the first, and next to the last, time in my school career.

The class was repeating in chorus the Lord's Prayer, heads bowed on desks. I was doing my best to keep up by the sound; my mind could not go beyond the word "hallowed," for which I had not found the meaning. In the middle of the prayer a Jewish boy across the aisle trod on my foot to get my attention. "You must not say that," he admonished in a solemn whisper; "it's Christian." I whispered back that it wasn't, and went on to the "Amen." I did not know but what he was right, but the name of Christ was not in the prayer, and I was bound to do everything that the class did. If I had any Jewish scruples, they were lagging away behind my interest in school affairs. How American this was: two pupils side by side in the schoolroom, each holding to his own opinion, but both submitting to the common law; for the boy at least bowed his head as the teacher ordered.

But all Miss Dillingham knew of it was that two of her pupils whispered during morning prayer, and she must discipline them.

So I was degraded from the honor row to the lowest row, and it was many a day before I forgave that young missionary; it was not enough for my vengeance that he suffered punishment with me. Teacher, of course, heard us both defend ourselves, but there was a time and a place for religious arguments; and she meant to help us remember that point.

I remember to this day what a struggle we had over the word "water," Miss Dillingham and I. It seemed as if I could not give the sound of w; I said "vater" every time. Patiently my teacher worked with me, inventing mouth exercises for me, to get my stubborn lips to produce that w; and when at last I could say "village" and "water" in rapid alternation, without misplacing the two initials, that memorable word was sweet on my lips. For we had conquered, and Teacher was pleased.

Getting a language in this way, word by word, has a charm that may be set against the disadvantages. It is like gathering a posy blossom by blossom. Bring the bouquet into your chamber, and these nasturtiums stand for the whole flaming carnival of them tumbling over the fence out there; these yellow pansies recall the velvet crescent of color glowing under the bay window; this spray of honeysuckle smells like the wind-tossed masses of it on the porch, ripe and bee-laden; the whole garden in a glass tumbler. So it is with one who gathers words, loving them. Particular words remain associated with important occasions in the learner's mind. I could thus write a history of my English vocabulary that should be at the same time an account of my comings and goings, my mistakes and my triumphs, during the years of my initiation.

If I was eager and diligent, my teachers did not sleep. As fast as my knowledge of English allowed, they advanced me from grade to grade, without reference to the usual schedule of promotions. My father was right, when he often said, in discussing my prospects, that ability would be promptly recognized in the public schools. Rapid as was my progress, on account of the advantages with which I started, some of the other "green" pupils were not far behind me; within a grade or two, by the end of the year. My brother, whose childhood had been one hideous nightmare, what with the stupid rebbe,* the cruel whip, and the

*Teacher.

general repression of life in the Pale, surprised my father by the progress he made under intelligent, sympathetic guidance. Indeed, he soon had a reputation in the school that the American boys envied; and all through the school course he more than held his own with pupils of his age. So much for the right and wrong way of doing things.

There is a record of my early progress in English much better than my recollections, however accurate and definite these may be. I have several reasons for introducing it here. First, it shows what the Russian Jew can do with an adopted language; next, it proves that vigilance of our public-school teachers of which I spoke; and last, I am proud of it! That is an unnecessary confession, but I could not be satisfied to insert the record here, with my vanity unavowed.

This is the document, copied from an educational journal, a tattered copy of which lies in my lap as I write—treasured for fifteen years, you see, by my vanity.

Editor *Primary Education:*—

This is the uncorrected paper of a Russian child twelve years old, who had studied English only four months. She had never, until September, been to school even in her own country and has heard English spoken *only* at school. I shall be glad if the paper of my pupil and the above explanation may appear in your paper.

M.S. Dillingham
Chelsea, Mass.

SNOW

Snow is frozen moisture which comes from the clouds.

Now the snow is coming down in feather-flakes, which makes nice snow-balls. But there is still one kind of snow more. This kind of snow is called snow-crystals, for it comes down in little curly balls. These snow-crystals aren't quiet as good for snow-balls as feather-flakes, for they (the snow-crystals) are dry; so they can't keep together as feather-flakes do.

The snow is dear to some children for they like sleighing.

As I said at the top—the snow comes from the clouds.

Now the trees are bare, and no flowers are to see in the fields and gardens, (we all know why) and the whole world seems like asleep without the happy birds songs which left us till spring. But the snow which drove away all these pretty and happy things, try, (as I think) not to make us at all unhappy; they covered up the branches of the trees, the fields, the gardens and houses, and the whole world looks like dressed in a beautiful white—instead of green—dress, with the sky looking down on it with a pale face.

And so the people can find some joy in it, too, without the happy summer.

Mary Antin

And now that it stands there, with *her* name over it, I am ashamed of my flippant talk about vanity. More to me than all the praise I could hope to win by the conquest of fifty languages is the association of this dear friend with my earliest efforts at writing; and it pleases me to remember that to her I owe my very first appearance in print. Vanity is the least part of it, when I remember how she called me to her desk, one day after school was out, and showed me my composition—my own words, that I had written out of my own head—printed out, clear black and white, with my name at the end! Nothing so wonderful had ever happened to me before. My whole consciousness was suddenly transformed. I suppose that was the moment when I became a writer. I always loved to write,—I wrote letters whenever I had an excuse,—yet it had never occurred to me to sit down and write my thoughts for no person in particular, merely to put the word on paper. But now, as I read my own words, in a delicious confusion, the idea was born. I stared at my name: *Mary Antin*. Was that really I? The printed characters composing it seemed strange to me all of a sudden. If that was my name, and those were the words out of my own head, what relation did it all have to *me*, who was alone there with Miss Dillingham, and the printed page between us? Why, it meant that I could write again, and see my writing printed for people to read! I could write many, many things: I could write a book! The idea was so huge, so bewildering, that my mind scarcely could accommodate it.

I do not know what my teacher said to me; probably very little. It was her way to say only a little, and look at me, and trust me to understand. Once she had occasion to lecture me about living a shut-up life; she wanted me to go outdoors. I had been repeatedly scolded and reproved on that score by other people, but I had only laughed, saying that I was too happy to change my ways. But when Miss Dillingham spoke to me, I saw that it was a serious matter; and yet she only said a few words, and looked at me with that smile of hers that was only half a smile, and the rest a meaning....

What...was my joy, when Miss Dillingham, just before locking up her desk one evening, presented me with a volume of Longfellow's poems! It was a thin volume of selections, but to me it was a bottomless treasure. I had never owned a book before. The sense of possession alone was a source of bliss, and this book I already knew and loved. And so Miss Dillingham, who was my first American friend, and who first put my name in print, was also the one to start my library. Deep is my regret when I consider that she was gone before I had given much account of all her gifts of love and service to me.

About the middle of the year I was promoted to the grammar school. Then it was that I walked on air. For I said to myself that I was a *student* now, in earnest, not merely a school-girl learning to spell and cipher. I was going to learn out-of-the-way things, things that had nothing to do with ordinary life—things to *know*. When I walked home afternoons, with the great big geography book under my arm, it seemed to me that the earth was conscious of my step. Sometimes I carried home half the books in my desk, not because I should need them, but because I loved to hold them; and also because I loved to be seen carrying books. It was a badge of scholarship, and I was proud of it. I remembered the days in Vitebsk when I used to watch my cousin Hirshel start for school in the morning, every thread of his student's uniform, every worn copybook in his satchel, glorified in my envious eyes. And now I was myself as he: aye, greater than he; for I knew English, and I could write poetry.

If my head was not turned at this time it was because I was so busy from morning till night. My father did his best to make me vain and silly. He made much of me to every chance caller, boasting of my progress at school, and of my exalted friends, the teachers. For a school-teacher was no ordinary mortal in his eyes; she was a superior being, set above the common run of men by her erudition and devotion to higher things. That a schoolteacher could be shallow or petty, or greedy for pay, was a thing that he could not have been brought to believe, at this time. And he was right, if he could only have stuck to it in later years, when a new-born pessimism, fathered by his perception that in America, too, some things needed mending, threw him to the opposite extreme of opinion, crying that nothing in the American scheme of society or government was worth tinkering.

He surely was right in his first appraisal of the teacher. The mean sort of teachers are not teachers at all; they are self-seekers who take up teaching as a business, to support themselves and keep their hands white. These same persons, did they keep store or drive a milk wagon or wash babies for a living, would be respectable. As trespassers on a noble profession, they are worth no more than the books and slates and desks over which they preside; so much furniture, to be had by the gross. They do not love their work. They contribute nothing to the higher development of their pupils. They busy themselves, not with research into the science of teaching, but with organizing political demonstrations to advance the cause of selfish candidates for public office, who promise them rewards. The true teachers are of another strain. Apostles all of an ideal, they go to their work in a spirit of love and inquiry, seeking not comfort, not position, not old-age pensions, but truth that is the soul of wisdom, the joy of big-eyed children, the food of hungry youth.

The Inquisition of the Teacher, or, "Gum Shoe Tim" on the War-path

Myra Kelly

From Myra Kelly, *Little Citizens* (New York: McClure, Phillips & Co., 1904).

Excerpted from Myra Kelly's book Little Citizens, *published in 1904, this piece illuminates the typical structure of power in the urban public school of the era. The associate*

superintendent, accompanied by the intimidated principal,
inspects each classroom. A man beyond the teachers in years,
the superintendent enjoys the power he can wield over
young, attractive—and nervous—women. The teacher has no
opportunity to speak on her own behalf. Kelly's writing in
general reflects the common prejudices about foreign ethnic
groups, and illustrates, as well, a tone of condescension and
"cuteness" often found in writings by and about teachers.
Kelly's Miss Bailey makes light of the children's tattered
dress, and she herself is portrayed more as a housekeeper
than as an educator.

Myra Kelly (1876–1910) was born in Dublin and
immigrated to New York as a child with her father, a
physician. A teacher in a Lower East Side school, she was also
the author of several books of sketches and stories. S.S.
McClure, the editor who published her first work in his
magazine, said of her in his introduction to Little Citizens,
"She loved her little people, and in depicting them made an
imperishable classic."

O n the first day of school, after the Christmas holidays, Teacher found herself surrounded by a howling mob of little savages in which she had much difficulty in recognizing her cherished First-Reader Class. Isidore Belchatosky's face was so wreathed in smiles and foreign matter as to be beyond identification; Nathan Spiderwitz had placed all his trust in a solitary suspender and two unstable buttons; Eva Kidansky had entirely freed herself from restraining hooks and eyes; Isidore Applebaum had discarded shoe-laces; and Abie Ashnewsky had bartered his only necktie for a yard of "shoe-string" licorice.

Miss Bailey was greatly disheartened by this reversion to the original type. She delivered daily lectures on nail-brushes, hair-ribbons, shoe polish, pins, buttons, elastic, and other means to grace. Her talks on soap and water became almost personal in tone, and her insistence on a close union between such garments as were meant to be united, led to a lively traffic in twisted and disreputable safety-pins. And yet the First-Reader Class, in all other branches of learning so receptive and responsive, made but halting and uncertain progress towards that state of virtue which is next to godliness.

Early in January came the report that "Gum Shoe Tim" was on the war-path and might be expected at any time. Miss Bailey heard the tidings in calm ignorance until Miss Blake, who ruled over the adjoining kingdom, interpreted the warning. A license to teach in the public schools of New York is good for only one year. Its renewal depends upon the reports of the Principal in charge of the school and of the Associate Superintendent in whose district the school chances to be. After three such renewals the license becomes permanent, but Miss Bailey was, as a teacher, barely four months old. The Associate Superintendent for her vicinity was the Honourable Timothy O'Shea, known and dreaded as "Gum Shoe Tim," owing to his engaging way of creeping softly up back stairs and appearing, all unheralded and unwelcome, upon the threshold of his intended victim.

This, Miss Blake explained, was in defiance of all the rules of etiquette governing such visits of inspection. The proper procedure had been that of Mr. O'Shea's predecessor, who had always given timely notice of his coming and a hint as to the subjects in which he intended to examine the children. Some days later he would amble from room to room, accompanied by the amiable Principal, and followed by the gratitude of smiling and unruffled teachers.

This kind old gentleman was now retired and had been succeeded by Mr. O'Shea, who, in addition to his unexpectedness, was adorned by an abominable temper, an overbearing manner, and a sense of cruel humour. He had almost finished his examinations at the nearest school where, during a brisk campaign of eight days, he had caused five dismissals, nine cases of nervous exhaustion, and an epidemic of hysteria.

Day by day nerves grew more tense, tempers more unsure, sleep and appetite more fugitive. Experienced teachers went stolidly on with the ordinary routine while beginners devoted time and energy to the more spectacular portions of the curriculum. But no one knew the Honourable Timothy's pet subjects and so no one could specialize to any great extent.

Miss Bailey was one of the beginners, and Room 18 was made to shine as the sun. Morris Mogilewsky, Monitor of the Gold-

Fish Bowl, wrought busily until his charges glowed redly against the water plants in their shining bowl. Creepers crept, plants grew, and ferns waved under the care of Nathan Spiderwitz, Monitor of the Window Boxes. There was such a martial swing and strut in Patrick Brennan's leadership of the line that it informed even the timid heart of Isidore Wishnewsky with a war-like glow and his feet with a spasmodic but well-meant tramp. Sadie Gonorowsky and Eva, her cousin, sat closely side by side, no longer "mad on theirselves," but "mit kind feelings." The work of the preceeding term was laid in neat and docketed piles upon the low book case. The children were enjoined to keep clean and entire. And Teacher, a nervous and unsmiling Teacher, waited dully.

A week passed thus, and then the good-hearted and experienced Miss Blake hurried ponderously across the hall to put Teacher on her guard.

"I've just had a note from one of the grammar teachers," she panted. " 'Gum Shoe Tim' is up in Miss Greene's room. He'll take this floor next. Now, see here, child, don't look so frightened. The Principal is with Tim. Of course you're nervous, but try not to show it. And you'll be all right, his lay is discipline and reading. Well, good luck to you!"

Miss Bailey took heart of grace. The children read suprisingly well, were absolutely good, and the enemy under convoy of the friendly Principal would be much less terrifying than the enemy at large and alone. It was, therefore, with a manner almost serene that she turned to greet the kindly concerned Principal and the dreaded "Gum Shoe Tim." The latter she found less ominous of aspect than she had been led to fear, and the Principal's charming little speech of introduction made her flush with quick pleasure. And the anxious eyes of Sadie Gonorowsky, noting the flush, grew calm as Sadie whispered to Eva, her close cousin:

"Say, Teacher has a glad. She's red on the face. It could be her papa."

"No. It's comp'ny," answered Eva sagely. "It ain't her papa. It's comp'ny the whiles Teacher takes him by the hand."

The children were not in the least disconcerted by the presence of the large man. They always enjoyed visitors and they liked the heavy gold chain which festooned the wide white waistcoat of this guest; and, as they watched him, the Associate Superintendent began to superintend.

He looked at the children all in their clean and smiling rows: he looked at the flowers and the gold fish; at the pictures and the plaster casts: he looked at the work of the last term and he looked at Teacher. As he looked he swayed gently on his rubber heels and decided that he was going to enjoy the coming quarter of an hour. Teacher pleased him from the first. She was neither old nor ill-favoured, and she was most evidently nervous. The combination appealed both to his love of power and his peculiar sense of humour. Settling deliberately in the chair of state, he began:

"Can the children sing, Miss Bailey?"

They could sing very prettily and they did.

"Very nice, indeed," said the voice of visiting authority. "Very nice. Their music is exceptionally good. And are they drilled? Children, will you march for me?"

Again they could and did. Patrick marshaled his line in time and triumph up and down the aisles to the evident interest and approval of the "comp'ny," and then Teacher led the class through some very energetic Swedish movements. While arms and bodies were bending and straightening at Teacher's command and example, the door opened and a breathless boy rushed in. He bore an unfolded note and, as Teacher had no hand to spare, the boy placed the paper on the desk under the softening eyes of the Honourable Timothy, who glanced down idly and then pounced upon the note and read its every word.

"For you, Miss Bailey," he said in the voice before which even the school janitor had been know to quail. "Your friend was thoughtful, though a little late." And poor palpitating Miss Bailey read.

"Watch out! 'Gum Shoe Tim' is in the building. The Principal caught him on the back stairs and they're going round together. He's as cross as a bear. Greene in dead faint in dressing-room. Says he's going to fire her. Watch out for him, and send the news on. His lay is reading and discipline."

Miss Bailey grew cold with sick and unreasoning fear. As she gazed wide-eyed at the living confirmation of the statement that "Gum Shoe Tim" was "as cross as a bear," the gentle-hearted Principal took the paper from her nerveless grasp.

"It's all right," he assured her. "Mr. O'Shea understands that you had no part in this. It's *all* right. You are not responsible."

But Teacher had no ears for his soothing. She could only watch with fascinated eyes as the Honourable Timothy reclaimed the note and wrote across its damning face: "Miss Greene may come to. She is not fired. —T.O'S."

"Here, boy," he called; "take this to your teacher." The puzzled messenger turned to obey, and the Associate Superintendent saw that though his dignity had suffered his power had increased. To the list of those whom he might, if so disposed, devour, he had now added the name of the Principal, who was quick to understand that an unpleasant investigation lay before him. If Miss Bailey could not be held responsible for this system of inter-classroom communication, it was clear that the Principal could.

Every trace of interest had left Mr. O'Shea's voice as he asked: "Can they read?"

"Oh, yes, they read," responded Teacher, but her spirit was crushed and the children reflected her depression. Still, they were marvellously good and that blundering note had said, "Discipline is his lay." Well, here he had it.

Schoolteacher's Nightmare

Mary Abigail Dodge

From Mary Abigail Dodge, *Our Common Schools* (Boston: Estes & Lauriat, 1880).

An amusing verification of the growth of school bureaucracies in the East Coast cities, this poem portrays the woman teacher at work on a weekend night with her record book. The poem appeared in 1880 in Our Common Schools *by Mary Abigail Dodge (1833–1896) with the note: "It must have been one of these overworked teachers, gifted with a sense of humor, that produced the following."*

A former teacher devoted to the education of working girls,
a feminist and a journalist, in her book Dodge attacked the
school system for degrading women teachers by forcing them
to undergo "petty and minute supervision," among other
humiliations. She believed that trained women teachers
should control the schools. Dodge was instrumental in the
founding of Teacher's College of Columbia University,
directed by Nicholas Murray Butler.

Twas Saturday night, and a teacher sat
    Alone, her task pursuing:
She averaged this and she averaged that
    Of all her class were doing.
She reckoned percentage, so many boys,
    And so many girls all counted,
And marked all the tardy and absentees,
    And to what all the absence amounted.

Names and residence wrote in full,
    Over many columns and pages;
Yankee, Teutonic, African, Celt,
    And averaged all their ages,
The date of admission of every one,
    And cases of flagellation,
And prepared a list of the graduates
    For the coming examination.

Her weary head sank low on her book,
    And her weary heart still lower,
For some of her pupils had little brain,
    And she could not furnish more.
She slept, she dreamed; it seemed she died,
    And her spirit went to Hades,
And they met her there with a question fair,
    "State what the per cent of your grade is."

Ages had slowly rolled away,
    Leaving but partial traces,

And the teacher's spirit walked one day
    In the old familiar places.
A mound of fossilized school reports
    Attracted her observation,
As high as the State House Dome, and as wide
    As Boston since annexation.*

She came to the spot where they buried her bones,
    And the ground was well built over,
But laborers digging threw out a skull
    Once planted beneath the clover.
A disciple of Galen wandering by,
    Paused to look at the diggers,
And plucking the skull up, looked through the eye,
    And saw it was lined with figures.

"Just as I thought," said the young M.D.,
    "How easy it is to kill 'em—"
Statistics ossified every fold
    Of cerebrum and cerebellum.
"It's a great curiosity, sure," said Pat,†
    "By the bones can you tell the creature?"
"Oh, nothing strange," said the doctor, "that
    Was a nineteenth century teacher."

The First Class

Marian Dogherty

From Marian Dogherty, *Scusa Me Teacher* (Francestown, N.H.: Marshall Jones, 1943).

"I can no more forget that first class than a man forgets his first love or a warrior his first battle," says Marian Dogherty

---

*In the 1870s, Boston incorporated several large suburbs previously separate villages.
†*Pat,* or *Paddy* were detractory or slang names for the Irish immigrant.

unforgettably in 'Scusa Me Teacher, an 1889 account of
teaching in Boston's model public school for immigrants, the
Hancock School for Girls. A writer who chose her images
with care, Dogherty's comparison suggests that for her,
teaching was both profundly emotional and challenging—a
test of her strengths. Like other teachers of immigrants,
Dogherty gave lessons on the virtues of soap and water (most
tenements had no indoor plumbing; bathing was an ordeal),
and bemoaned her students' unkempt appearance. But
Dogherty was also genuinely appreciative of "the interesting
traditions of European life," the cultural diversity that could
lead one child to spirited rebellion, another to fiery bursts of
temper.

Dogherty was the author of another book, about teaching
literature, but research yields little else about her life. She
apparently taught in Boston for many years.

The odd thing about the first class is that while other classes
may fade more or less from the memory, that first group
given to the young green girl in a September of long ago, emerges
strong and clear, with the distinction of a well cut cameo. I
remember that first day of school, though it is more than forty
years ago, better than I remember yesterday; I recall its events, its
emotions, more vividly than this morning's. It was a pleasant
time to be alive. The whole world though it may have been a
smoldering volcano, was apparently at peace. There was
positively not a thing to worry about except to acquit oneself
with credit in a happily chosen profession. Of course the pay was
small or so it seems today. But at that time it seemed to me
ridiculously large: thirty-eight dollars a month was the handsome
beginning, and one looked forward to an increase of four dollars
each month after the first year. I wondered how I could spend it
all! My happiness was complete and I felt such a feverish urge to
start that I left home at half past seven though school began at
nine and though it was a short half hour's ride. It was good to be
in the open car, to breathe in the fresh September morning air, to
ride through shaded quiet streets not yet awake, to see the
gardens of petunias and asters, to feel the chill from the river as
we went over the old bridge from Cambridge to Boston and
finally to become a part of the turbulent city.

When I reached the master's office and told him it was hard to wait for the school term to begin, he shook with ill-suppressed laughter. That puzzled me. What was funny? Did he not feel that way, too?

Then he ushered me to the room that was to be mine. It had fifty-six desks besides extra movable ones, in case the class should be larger. School rooms were hospitable in those days. There was always room for one more Fifty-six and sixty were average classes. There was a high platform where the teacher sat. This was her throne and helped to fix her above the rest of the world in the minds of the children. If they desired converse with her, they had to step *up*; when they returned to their own quarters, they must step *down*. Now, the platform is no more. As an institution, it is gone, and with it went a little of that reverence for the teacher, so wholesome for the child, so pleasant for her,—that reverence which like mercy is twice blessed, blessing him that gives as well as him that takes.

At quarter of nine on that first day, the children came eagerly in, stiffly starched, and shining from recent scrubbing. They were radiantly happy. It was the fourth grade and they had left forever the ignominy of a primary school. Report had it that they were to have "geographies" and "rithmatic" books. No longer would they be slightingly referred to as "in the third reader." Such books were forever past. They would now hold in their hands a story-book, and read real stories and "pomes." Rumor whispered that they would carry these books home and prepare lessons by the evening lamp, but rumor was a fickle lady, and not to be believed too trustingly. Still all things were possible and it might be that books would no longer be regarded as too sacred for transportation to the home fireside, now that they were entering the august grammar department. Thus, encumbered by a large, flat volume of marvelous redness, easily recognized as a "jography", they could stick their tongues out merrily at those miserable little ignoramuses that still wallowed in the multiplication table. So, there was reason for their elation. Moreover, there was to be a new teacher. The one who had occupied that room was now too old to teach and had got married (she had reached the decrepitude of thirty-three). Would the new one be young or old, nice or cross?

I can no more forget that first class than a man forgets his first love or a warrior his first battle. Others might be better, but they would be without that mystic something that the first always has. They were chiefly Jews and Italians, with an Irish girl here and there like the plums in a pudding. Little embryo American citizens with interesting traditions of European life and a background of European oppression behind them. Some were dreamy and indolent; others promisingly alert; some with plain evidence of intellect in their small faces; others heavy with stupidity. Yet, all were peculiarly respectful. Depraved indeed is the child who exhibits his naughty propensities on the first day! The good are too happy and the bad do not *dare* lest they be banished to the class just left. Even the janitor seemed to them a celestial being, for when he shuffled in and banged the furniture about, an awe rested on their innocent faces, because he was a part of that great system that held them in its benign but awful hand.

There were many fascinating people in that first class: little Maria Ragucci, for instance. If only Sir Joshua might have seen Maria before painting his "Angels' Heads"! Then there was Sarah Bloominsky, Russian, and even at that tender age, darkly tinged with anarchy; big, brow-beating Sarah who matched her mulishness with mine, and generally came out ahead. And Immaculata! It took me some time to understand just why she had been so called. It certainly did not relate to the externals of face or of raiment, for Immaculata's acquaintance with soap and water was openly superficial. Rather had her mother with prophetic wisdom thus named her for the purity of spirit which successfully shone through the various layers of dirt. Immaculata had two accomplishments. When she was not chewing her tongue, she was begging permission to wash her hands. She was our Lady Macbeth; moreover she seemed no more successful than the tragic queen in removing the stains. This mania of hers developed after I had delivered a series of talks on the beauty of water and the efficacy of soap. I had told them in confidence that in certain high classes of society, daily immerson is not unknown; at this point, looks partly horrified, wholly incredulous were exchanged. "If you expect anything like that, you will be bitterly disappointed" the looks emphatically stated. Such things, I admitted, were wholly unreasonable, but would it not be a capital way to begin each new week, at least, with a scouring, an "altogether" as the vulgar termed it?

These talks had their effect, for Immaculata presented herself one morning, and with the shining eyes of the conqueror, exclaimed excitedly, "Oh, teacher, teacher, like that I had *two* baths, one here!" as she whacked her chest, "and one here!" indicating with a red and clean hand her entire face.

"That's fine, Immaculata, perhaps the next time you will have three!"

Rome was not built in a day and Immaculata had made a beginning. When she no longer felt that paralyzing distrust of water that held so many of her fellows in its grip, I deemed the time ripe to speak on behalf of the comb. Immaculata had soft brown hair that fell into curls as easily as the water falls into spray. These curls clung fetchingly to her smooth neck and untroubled brow; that is to say they so clung on Monday; the rest of the week they went, like the wicked in Isaiah "every one to his own way" until on Friday, complete lawlessness reigned. As the transforming effects of a daily combing were portrayed, Immaculata's eyes sparkled with pleasure, and soon she kept in her desk a little pocket comb which she took out at all sorts of unseemly times, flourishing it ostentatiously. In executive session I explained that there was a time and season for all things, but still, Immaculata would forget. Then, for five consecutive mornings, I read solemnly from the third chapter of Ecclesiastes: "To everything there is a season and a time to every purpose under the heaven: a time to be born; a time to die; a time to plant and a time to pluck up that which is planted."

The rhythms sank into Immaculata's ear, and on the third day their import penetrated her cerebrum, for while reading, I caught her eye, wherein was an understanding twinkle which said more plainly than her tongue could have done, "I get you, teacher, it's all right from now on;" and it was, for though Immaculata's curls continued to be irreproachable, the comb was never seen again.

Francesca, too, was of that first class,—Francesca, who could be so amiable, but who chose to be so disagreeable much of the time. Thin of lip and with eyes that smouldered constantly, Francesca was the product of generations of unleashed temper.

Hers would flame up with no provocation, and the conflagration would nearly consume the child who was almost as thin as a skeleton. After the fire had spent itself, Francesca would become a limp and tearful wreck. Each teacher struggled with her and helped her to overcome somewhat this beast within her. After six years in the school, she had conquered it enough to hold it in curb in public. Still her thin lips would be drawn together in a single line; still her eye would glitter omniously, but Francesca, herself, no longer disintegrated before our eyes.

Margharita was scarcely bigger than a gallon jug but every inch was one of kindness. She kept school for every teacher who had the good fortune to inherit her. If I rose to close a window, Margharita was there first. If a knock was heard, Margharita had opened the door before the stranger's hand was withdrawn. She cleaned the blackboards, swept the corners that the brooding janitor never saw, kept orderly the desk of her disorderly teacher, opened windows if we needed them open, shut them if we needed them shut, and all with perfect grace and modesty on her part. Nor was Margharita a creeper for the favor of teacher. She was never officious, but possessed a genious for making life comfortable for others by interposing her small body between those she loved and any hardship or difficulty. One wonders how long such a blithe spirit has survived in a none too gentle world.

Even now, I cannot think of Mary Morton without a smile; Mary, sallow and thin and plain, but radiant with intellect and spirit. Mary belonged peculiarly to the sisterhood of saints, a limited order in the public schools. She had her human side, however, and on rare occasions displayed it.

It was the physiology lesson, and in those days we were required to acquaint those tender innocents with certain of their interior organs, the more picturesque ones, so to speak, like the heart and stomach and the intestines. It was hard to work up any real interest in such things,—to convey to an indifferent little girl, for instance, the appalling length of her small intestine. To announce, statistically, that this portion of her digestive tract measured fifteen to eighteen feet would have been the work of a dullard and would have been received with unsuppressed yawns. To present figures is not the fine art of teaching. But to picture the thing with vividness, to make them *see* this wonderful creation so adroitly folded in their little insides, that was teaching! To this end, I explained that were we to behold this particular portion of the alimentary canal of only *one* of them placed lengthwise in a straight line, it would reach from end to end of the school room. At this, there issued from a remote corner a prodigious whistle: a whistle that expressed many things, amazement, consternation, horror, unbelief. A roar of laughter went up from the class, which was possessed of a healthy sense of humor. Mary's crimson cheeks betrayed her. So she was human after all, and quite capable of challenging the teacher when she became too theatrical.

At the same time that Mary's whistle broke the silence, little Margharita exclaimed reverently, "Oh, my God!" Do not mistake this for profanity. It was merely the human spirit's salutation to its Creator as the awfulness of his work dawned upon her understanding.

I had meant to be graphic, and had succeeded in being grotesque.

Somehow, I never could mention the small intestine again, and if those girls who came after the illustrious first class went through life never suspecting that they were the happy possessors of such an organ, I hope it did them no real harm.

That year we had with us Katie Colori. Are you still enlivening this planet, Katie, with your look of the slums and your heart of gold? How you shuffled across the floor, in those sadly worn shoes of yours, revealing the soiled and naked feet! Your hair was matted with innumerable snarls, but the sunlight of your smile so dazzled the eye as to blind it to these imperfections. Do you remember the day of my disgrace, Katie? Do you recall after all these years, just where you sat, in the first seat of the last row, beside the eastern window where the sun came in each morning and played about your unkempt hair and pretty eyes? I dare say that you do not remember that terrible morning. I dare say that you never even suspected that your teacher *was* disgraced.

It was Monday morning and on Monday morning came the music period. If there was a time in the week when my spirit rebelled it was in that half hour given over to sweet melody. Throughout the week for the most part, I could maintain an equable temperature, but in the music time, the thermometer rose as with a fever. Music was the skeleton in our closet. The children knew it, and the teacher knew it, and on Monday he rattled his bones frightfully.

In order that other classes might not be entertained by the bellowing of the musicians or the awful yet restrained tones of the teacher during these periods, I always took the precaution to close the door, or rather, Margharita, whose knowledge bordered on the uncanny, did so.

Now, on this particular morning, we were practicing "How can I leave thee, how can I from thee part?" The notes came with a desperate slowness; the altos rumbled in dreary monotones while the sopranos screeched in discord. The teacher was beside herself, the more so that the wretches so openly enjoyed the racket they were making. So, as usual, she lost her temper. She brought down her baton, and said with ominous control, that if the next attempt proved no better, the music books would be closed and *remain so for one entire week.* Now such a threat would not in itself have depressed them, for though they did love to roar discordantly, they knew very well that I was temperamentally unfitted to teach music and sure to give evidence of that unfitness. What depressed them was the manner of delivering it for with children the manner is everything.

With a chastened demeanor, and a more earnest effort at accuracy, they resumed their singing, and the result was a little less painful, a shade nearer the printed score. I accepted it because I knew I had to, and we closed our books feeling that all was well.

As I left the side of the room and came in view of the door, I noticed that it was slightly ajar. Now, every teacher has *tête-à-tête* talks with her class, little private reckonings of the sort that every family enjoys, and she is no more willing to admit the public than the family is. So, naturally, as we had a family row, I felt disturbed to see the door open. Betraying, however, none of the anxiety I felt, I asked, "Has the door been open throughout the lesson?" and they shouted, "No, ma'am!" Then Katie spoke up, "Teacher, like that, the boss come in wid some ladies, yes ma'am."

So that was it! The genial master had entered innocently to

show off a nice little class and had suddenly changed his mind. "About when did Mr. Dutton and these ladies come?" I asked, for I was determined to know the worst. I got it, too, for Katie yelled with inaccuracy but force, "Teacher, like that, they come in wen you said shut-up." Katie never suspected the pain, and the mortification her free translation of my English wrought. "Thou stickest a dagger in me," I exclaimed, but she thought I was only talking to myself.

Then there was Cecilia: little Cecilia with the face of an angel and the movements of a dove; Cecilia, lover of poetry and music and every beautiful thing. One day when the children were assembled in the hall, Cecilia recited Longfellow's "Children's Hour." The lines that run,

"Do you think O blue eyed banditti, because you have scaled the wall,
Such an old moustache as I am is not a match for you all?"

Cecilia spoke as follows:

"Do you think, O blue eyed banditti, because yous have skated the wall,
Such an old moustache as I am is not a mash for yous all?"

Funnier than Cecilia's mangling of the lines was the fact that no child in the audience suspected a joke, but applauded solemnly and generously. I am sure that the verse was as intelligible to them that way as any other.

Once little Cecilia invited me to her home: four small rooms meagerly fitted but scrupulously clean. Cecilia's mother was tall and gaunt, worn thin by ill health and hard work, yet happy and living completely in her children. She took from the bare wooden dresser the needlework brought from Italy,—the counterpane that her mother had made; the yards upon yards of fine lace that her own busy fingers had snatched time to make, that her children might own real Italian needlework in the years to come. Then papa brought out his best Italian cordial, and with little almond cakes and honeyed confections made across the sea, they completed their hospitality....

It was with that first class that I became aware that a teacher was subservient to a higher authority. I became increasingly aware of this subservience to an ever growing number of authorities with each succeeding year, until there is danger today of becoming aware of little else. A young teacher, however, eager to accomplish, forgets happily all the machinery of organization until it is forced upon her attention. It was unmistakably borne in upon me a few months after I had begun to teach. The genial principal came in one day to see how things were going with the new teacher. He took his seat on the platform beside me, thus temporarily sharing the throne, and announced that he would hear the little girls read.

The children were delighted to have any visitor, but especially a man, for the feminine influence preponderates in the public school. So, everything started pleasantly enough until one child, the first to read, failed to state the page on which the new chapter began. Our principal was a stickler for the proprieties, and the proper way to read in the public school in the year 1899 was to say, "Page 35, Chapter 4," and holding the book in the right hand, with the toes pointing at an angle of forty-five degrees, the head held straight and high, the eyes looking directly ahead, the pupil would lift up his voice and struggle in loud, unnatural tones. Now, I had attended to the position of the toes, the right arm, and the nose, but had failed to enforce the mentioning of page and chapter, for two reasons.

In the first place figures seemed to me a cold douche on the interest of a story and in the second place, I never could master Roman numerals myself and the chapters were always printed in those detestable x's and v's and l's. This grave omission at the very outset irritated the good man and he said in his most professional tone, "Perhaps, tomorrow, your teacher will tell you about Roman numerals." That was the first blow. I had failed to perform my duty and my superior officer had hinted as much with the additional suggestion that on the morrow I mend my ways. My heart sank. Would the children suspect? I watched them carefully. No, they were unconscious of everything excepting that they were having what in those days was termed a "perfectly bully" time.

Whenever the master would ask them a question, they would answer hastily, "Yes, ma'am."

"Say 'yes, *sir*' when you are talking to a gentleman," he said very
sternly, and they replied cheerfully, "Yes, ma'am." This annoyed
him doubly. Not only there was their lack of good taste, but what
seemed like disobedience as well.

The word "spice" then occurring in the reading matter, the
examiner propounded the question, "What is spice, who can tell
me that?" Hands were raised everywhere. Cheerfully would they
give of their store, be it knowledge, or be it darkest ignorance.
"Carrots" exclaimed one. "No, ma'am, it ain't, it's bananas," said
another. "No ma'am, teacher, spiders," ventured a third. When
vegetables and fruits had failed, they tried bugs. Never had they
seemed more pleased with themselves or with the world in
general. An unnatural calm became apparent in the master's
manner. "Put down your hands, children," he said quietly, "and
tomorrow your teacher will tell you about spices." "Yes ma'am"
they shouted joyously, as though he had made them a gift.

This was a signal for closing the visit. It had been painful to
him and painful to me, but they had enjoyed it thoroughly. Mr.
Dutton was a large man and he rose from the chair with all his
natural dignity. Then, deciding to let bygones be bygones, he
said kindly, "Good afternoon, little girls," and they spake as one
voice, "Good afternoon, Mr. Dogherty."

The door closed with a bang!

As for me, only centuries of the civilization process kept me
safe. I had followed my primitive instincts—but it is no matter!
Meanwhile, the wretches looked up pleasantly at me, as if
wondering what entertainment came next on this diverting
program. Determined that this sort of thing should never, never
happen again, I made them say, "Good-night, Mr. Dutton" and
"Good-morning, Mr. Dutton" over and over and over, until the
walls reverberated with the name. Then I impersonated him,
imitating his mode of approach, talking to them as he was wont,
making it all as realistic as possible letting them practice saying,
"yes, sir," and "no, sir," and "thank you, sir." I finally dismissed
them, long after the closing hour in the twilight of day and a
midnight of interest. According to custom I said, "Good night,
Girls." In chastened but absent manner, they answered sleepily,
"Good night, Mrs. Dutton."

Public Schools "Owned" by Politicians

Amelia Allison

From "Confessions of Public School Teachers," *Atlantic Monthly* (July 1896), pp. 107–08.

In 1896, Atlantic Monthly *ran a series of articles designed to "get the schools out of politics." In "confessions" like the one below, teachers wrote anonymously of the widespread system of using "pulls" or personal influence to get jobs, and of being passed over on account of one's politics. To protect themselves from the capriciousness of politicians, teachers supported a tenure system, and school reformers fought to put professional educators into supervisory positions.*

During the period of my preliminary service as teacher in the public schools, my name was reported for a permanent place, and was "on the slate" when it left the teachers' committee. My father was at that time a voter with the party in power; but the teacher who was number five on the list had a kinsman on the board, who saw that unless she was appointed during his term she might never be. One of the trustees, therefore, brought in a charge of "cruelty to a boy" against me, and, without an investigation, my name was taken off, and number five was elected. To fail of appointment when it was my right was astonishing; but to have any one believe that I pulled a boy's ears till he could not put his head on a pillow hurt me deeply. I began an investigation on my own account, and I discovered that number five's sister was the guilty teacher. The boy's father appeared before the board and explained. The teacher was not even censured; but I had lost the permanent position.

For a year I went from one school to another, teaching for six weeks in the high school. When not busy in a schoolroom, I was visiting, studying, or reading. I attended the teachers' meetings,
(text continued on page 270)

A Teacher's Album

1: Margaret Haley, "lady labor slugger," fought for the advancement of teachers. She became business agent of the Chicago Teachers' Federation in 1901 and was one of the first presidents of the National Federation of Teachers.
2: Ella Flagg Young (1845–1918), close associate of Haley and a leader in progressive education. Beginning her career as a grade school teacher, she became a professor of pedagogy at the University of Chicago and, in 1909, Superintendent of Chicago Public Schools.
3: Mary Dwyer, recalled by the author as "my mother's principal and mine," served in New Jersey schools, 1906–1951.
4: Malvina Rosenberg Hoffman as a student at Newark State Normal School, 1925. She later taught under Miss Dwyer.

269

and was surprised to find so many who had no opinion to express on important subjects. When the year had passed, I was put on the permanent list. I was assigned to a first-year school of fifty-four scholars. Most of them were beginners, and some "left-overs." I felt ready for my work. But my greatest trial was when Superintendent Goodenough selected my room as his place to doze, or really to sleep, while my little people were doing their work. He was never known to praise a teacher's work while she was in service. The only consolation was that he praised teachers who died, or regretted that it was always the "bright teachers who married." I might never marry, and therefore I could with confidence look forward to his praise only at my funeral.

A change in the political control of the city took place, and the party long in power was defeated. The other party decided to do without a supervisor for a year. Superintendent Goodenough, therefore, was dropped. It was a monotonous year. But I had now a chance to throw away the old and to use the new. I made all kinds of word and number games; I bought new readers for my supplementary work; I learned new songs, and I looked up kindergarten games.

˙The next August the board elected a superintendent, and there was no politics in this election. But there was much anxiety as to what kind of man he would turn out to be. Superintendent Quincy, a live New Englander, came, and he brought a breeze. At first he said little. He asked me what I had read. The next time he brought Mr. Michael Brannigan, chairman of the teachers' committee. He said, "Miss Allison is doing the kind of work I want. Has she your permission to carry it on?" Mr. Michael Brannigan was kind enough to abstain from any action that affected me. Superintendent Quincy rid us of many harmful practices. He held grade meetings; he required the schoolrooms to be empty fifteen minutes after the close of school; and no corporal punishment could be inflicted and not reported.

My scholars liked to come to school, and now they numbered eighty-seven. They sat on the edge of the platform, and even on the floor against the wall. I suggested that some come in the morning, and the others in the afternoon. This was done, and one little girl said, "Miss Allison is the best teacher, for we have to go only a half day, and we learn as much as they learn all day at the other schools." I found the work easier, and just as many were promoted to the next class as before.

This year I obtained my state certificate, and I felt that I could now be called a teacher. But a great misfortune threatened me just as I began to feel secure. My father had left the "party without an issue," and had become a member of the "party with a principle." Election time came, and the "party without an issue" thought that they saw a chance to win. As our district was likely to have a close contest, it was suggested that my father be "whipped into line." The only lash that he could be made to feel, they thought, was a threat to remove me. They sent their candidate for school trustee to our home, and he knocked timidly at the back door and made known his errand. In a very few minutes he walked rapidly away. His party was defeated,—luckily for me, no doubt, for a local politician was asked how a teacher whose work was good could be dismissed without "charges." He replied, "We always have charges when we need them." This is the only time that I ever heard of danger to a teacher in our city because of her father's political faith. The rule has been, once a teacher, always a fixture, even when glaring deficiencies could not be hidden, and complaints were "too numerous to mention."

But Superintendent Quincy was too progressive, and his church was on the wrong street. Perhaps he might have been kept if one of the teachers had not wanted the salary. This teacher always reminded us of the line of a hymn,

I can tarry, I can tarry but a term.

He never sat down; but he stood by the door with his coat and hat in his hands, as if something were urging him on.

About this time there was a vacancy in the grammar school, and the superintendent asked me if I would take the place. I liked my work, and declined the empty honor. It meant longer hours for no greater salary; for we are paid according to length of service, and there is no strife for promotion. Of course principals of the higher schools get more pay, but not principals of buildings, unless there are grammar schools in them.

In the middle of the year the superintendent left to study a profession, and a man who had "taught his way through" one of our best normal schools became his successor. At last this superintendent fell a victim to church influences, and he gave place to a young teacher whose church was right, but whose political party was wrong. "He had no principles to hinder," as one of our legislators said, so he turned his back on the party which claimed his first vote, and the position was his. He was younger than most of the teachers, but see how wise he was! He would come into the classroom and say, "Go to page 73 this month." He delivered extempore speeches at the teachers' meetings, and we wondered what it had all been about. In the three years that he was in service he never listened to one recitation in my room. He generally came to gather statistics or to dole out pages of textbooks. I did what I could to keep pace with the other schools, but I felt that there was nothing done thoroughly. At last came his turn to be decapitated, and his successor, who now holds the office, is the best of the long succession of superintendents. They say that he may not be here next year. It is time for a change.

For two years I have had a real grievance. Miss Wellpaid has a school of the same grade as mine, but mine requires more personal work. Yet Miss Wellpaid receives $260 a year more than I am paid, and my salary is the same as that of her assistants, who have no responsibility. Every one admits the justice of my claim, and the board promises to equalize the salary. Children who, by school district lines, ought to attend Miss Wellpaid's school ask six months ahead if I will save them seats if there be room for outsiders. I will not take one of these pupils, even when they bring a demand from two trustees. Once, however, I was obliged to take two of them. They had an order from the president of the board, and a doctor's certificate which said, "It is bad for the health of these girls to attend Miss Wellpaid's school." I must be a "natural healer" of the woes of school life.

Is there nothing to make up that missing $260? Yes, many things. The ambition of every child in the building is "to go to school to Miss Amelia Allison." Ask a kindergarten child who will be his next teacher, and he will generally say, "Miss Allison." One of the ways of inciting good behavior and perfect lessons is to promise a visit to my school. Then I have once more my little people grown tall, sitting in my classes, glad to anticipate my desires about their work and play. Half of my present school have been in my first-year grades. When they argue that it is not late enough in the week to be Friday, one girl says, "We have only two days in our room, and they are Monday and Friday; nothing between." I have also notes of appreciation from parents, and I think with Whittier:—

And when the world shall link your names
    With gracious lives and manners fine,
The teacher shall assert her claims,
    And proudly whisper, "These were mine!"

Children of Loneliness

Anzia Yezierska

From Anzia Yezierska, "Children of Loneliness," *Children of Loneliness* (New York: Funk & Wagnalls Co., 1923).

Anzia Yezierska's short story "Children of Loneliness" from a collection of the same title depicts in bitter, almost brutal detail, the conflict between the Americanized "teacherin" and her old world, Jewish parents in the lower East Side ghetto of New York City. Rachel Ravinsky's private and lonely despair must have been shared by many who yearned for but could not attain ease in the culture they had assimilated. Set apart from her self-confident college classmates, Rachel wandered "between worlds that are at once too old and too new to live in." The complex and contradictory emotions with which this young teacher must have ruled her classroom may well be imagined.

An immigrant to New York City like the young heroine of this story, Yezierska (1885–1970) left home not to marry, but to earn money for college by working in East Side sweatshops and factories. She became not a teacher, but a writer. Her first collection of ghetto stories, Hungry Hearts *(1920) was so well received that on its reputation "the rags to riches girl," as she was called, went to Hollywood. But flight from the ghetto unsettled her, and she returned to New York to write* Bread Givers *(1925),* Children of Loneliness *(1923) and other short stories, and journalism.*

A "lost" woman writer for nearly fifty years, Yezierska has recently been rediscovered, and some of her work reprinted. Her contemporary appeal lies in the anger and raw emotion of her characters,—typically, young women escaping the domestic confinement of old world Jewish tradition.

I

Oh, Mother, can't you use a fork?" exclaimed Rachel as Mrs. Ravinsky took the shell of the baked potato in her fingers and raised it to her watering mouth.

"Here, *Teacherin* mine, you want to learn me in my old age how to put the bite in my mouth?" The mother dropped the potato back into her plate, too wounded to eat. Wiping her hands on her blue-checked apron, she turned her glance to her husband, at the opposite side of the table.

"Yankev," she said bitterly, "stick your bone on a fork. Our *teacherin* said you dassn't touch no eatings with the hands."

"All my teachers died already in the old country," retorted the old man. "I ain't going to learn nothing new no more from my American daughter." He continued to suck the marrow out of the bone with that noisy relish that was so exasperating to Rachel.

"It's no use," stormed the girl, jumping up from the table in disgust; "I'll never be able to stand it here with you people."

" 'You people?' What do you mean by 'you people?' " shouted the old man, lashed into fury by his daughter's words. "You think you got a different skin from us because you went to college?"

"It drives me wild to hear you crunching bones like savages. If you people won't change, I shall have to move and live by myself."

Yankev Ravinsky threw the half-gnawed bone upon the table with such vehemence that a plate broke into fragments.

"You witch you!" he cried in a hoarse voice tense with rage. "Move by yourself! We lived without you while you was away in college, and we can get on without you further. God ain't going to turn his nose on us because we ain't got table manners from America. A hell she made from this house since she got home."

"*Shah!* Yankev *leben,*" pleaded the mother, "the nieghbors are opening the windows to listen to our hollering. Let us have a little quiet for a while till the eating is over."

But the accumulated hurts and insults that the old man had borne in the one week since his daughter's return from college had reached the breaking-point. His face was convulsed, his eyes flashed, and his lips were flecked with froth as he burst out in a volley of scorn:

"You think you can put our necks in a chain and learn us new tricks? You think you can make us over for Americans? We got through till fifty years of our lives eating in our own way—"

"Wo is me, Yankev *leben!*" entreated his wife. "Why can't we choke ourselves with our troubles? Why must the whole world know how we are tearing ourselves by the heads? In all Essex Street, in all New York, there ain't such fights like by us."

Her pleadings were in vain. There was no stopping Yankev Ravinsky once his wrath was roused. His daughter's insistence upon the use of a knife and fork spelled apostasy, Anti-Semitism, and the aping of the Gentiles.

Like a prophet of old condemning unrighteousness, he ran the gamut of denunciation, rising to heights of fury that were sublime and godlike, and sinking from sheer exhaustion to abusive bitterness.

"*Pfui* on all your American colleges! *Pfui* on the morals of America! No respect for old age. No fear for God. Stepping with your feet on all the laws of the holy Torah. A fire should burn out the whole new generation. They should sink into the earth, like Korah."

"Look at him cursing and burning! Just because I insist on their changing their terrible table manners. One would think I was killing them."

"Do you got to use a gun to kill?" cried the old man, little red threads daring out of the whites of his eyes.

"Who is doing the killing? Aren't you choking the life out of me? Aren't you dragging me by the hair to the darkness of past ages every minute of the day? I'd die of shame if one of my college friends should open the door while you people are eating."

"You—you—"

The old man was on the point of striking his daughter when his wife seized the hand he raised.

"*Mincha!* Yankev, you forgot *Mincha!*"

This reminder was a flash of inspiration on Mrs. Ravinsky's part, the only thing that could have ended the quarreling instantly. *Mincha* was the prayer just before sunset of the orthodox Jews. This religious rite was so automatic with the old man that at his wife's mention of *Mincha* everything was immediately shut out, and Yankev Ravinsky rushed off to a corner of the room to pray.

"*Ashrai Yoishwai Waisahuh!*"

"Happy are they who dwell in Thy house. Ever shall I praise Thee. *Selah!* Great is the Lord, and exceedingly to be praised; and His greatness is unsearchable. On the majesty and glory of Thy splendor, and on Thy marvelous deeds, will I mediate."

The shelter from the storms of life that the artist finds in his art, Yankev Ravinsky found in his prescribed communion with God. All the despair caused by his daughter's apostasy, the insults and disappointments he suffered, were in his sobbing voice. But as he entered into the spirit of his prayer, he felt the man of flesh drop away in the outflow of God around him. His voice mellowed, the rigid wrinkles of his face softened, the hard glitter of anger and condemnation in his eyes was transmuted into the light of love as he went on:

"The Lord is gracious and merciful; slow to anger and of great loving-kindness. To all that call upon Him in truth He will hear their cry and save them."

Oblivious to the passing and repassing of his wife as she warmed anew the unfinished dinner, he continued:

"Put not your trust in princes, in the son of man in whom there is no help." Here Reb Ravinsky paused long enough to make a silent confession for the sin of having placed his hope on his daughter instead of on God. His whole body bowed with the sense of guilt. Then in a moment his humility was transfigured into exaltation. Sorrow for sin dissolved in joy as he became more deeply aware of God's unfailing protection.

"Happy is he who hath the God of Jacob for his help, whose hope is in the Lord his God. He healeth the broken in heart, and bindeth up their wounds."

A healing balm filled his soul as he returned to the table, where the steaming hot food awaited him. Rachel sat near the window pretending to read a book. Her mother did not urge her to join them at the table, fearing another outbreak, and the meal continued in silence.

The girl's thoughts surged hotly as she glanced from her father to her mother. A chasm of four centuries could not have separated her more completely from them than her four years at Cornell.

"To think that I was born of these creatures! It's an insult to my soul. What kinship have I with these two lumps of ignorance and superstition? They're ugly and gross and stupid. I'm all sensitive nerves. They want to wallow in dirt."

She closed her eyes to shut out the sight of her parents as they silently ate together, unmindful of the dirt and confusion.

"How is it possibly that I lived with them and like them only four years ago? What is it in me that so quickly gets accustomed to the best? Beauty and cleanliness are as natural to me as if I'd been born on Fifth Avenue instead of the dirt of Essex Street."

A vision of Frank Baker passed before her. Her last long talk with him out under the trees in college still lingered in her heart. She felt that she had only to be with him again to carry forward the beautiful friendship that had sprung up between them. He had promised to come shortly to New York. How could she possibly introduce such a born and bred American to her low, ignorant, dirty parents?

"I might as well tear the thought of Frank Baker out of my heart," she told herself. "If he just once sees the pigsty of a home I come from, if he just sees the table manners of my father and mother, he'll fly through the ceiling."

Timidly, Mrs. Ravinsky turned to her daughter.

"Ain't you going to give a taste the eating?"

No answer.

"I fried the *lotkes* special' for you—"

"I can't stand your fried, greasy stuff."

"Ain't even my cooking good no more either?" Her gnarled, hard-worked hands clutched at her breast. "God from the world, for what do I need yet any more my life? Nothing I do for my child is no use no more."

Her head sank; her whole body seemed to shrivel and grow old with the sense of her own futility.

"How I was hurrying to run by the butcher before everybody else, so as to pick out the grandest, fattest piece of *brust!*" she wailed, tears streaming down her face. "And I put my hand away from my heart and put a whole fresh egg into the *lotkes,* and I stuffed the stove full of coal like a millionaire so as to get the *lotkes* fried so nice and brown; and now you give a kick on everything I done—"

"Fool woman," shouted her husband, "stop laying yourself on the ground for your daughter to step on you! What more can you expect from a child raised up in America? What more can you expect but that she should spit in your face and make dirt from you?" His eyes, hot and dry under their lids, flashed from his wife to his daughter. "The old Jewish eating is poison to her; she must have *trefa* ham—only forbidden food."

Bitter laughter shook him.

"Woman, how you patted yourself with pride before all the neighbors, boasting of our great American daughter coming home from college! This is our daughter, our pride, our hope, our pillow for our old age that we were dreaming about! This is our American *teacherin!* A Jew-hater, an Anti-Semite we brought into the world, a betrayer of our race who hates her own father and mother like the Russian Czar once hated a Jew. She makes herself so refined, she can't stand it when we use the knife or fork the wrong way; but her heart is that of a brutal Cossack, and she spills her own father's and mother's blood like water."

Every word he uttered seared Rachel's soul like burning acid. She felt herself becoming a witch, a she-devil, under the spell of his accusations.

"You want me to love you yet?" She turned upon her father like an avenging fury. "If there's any evil hatred in my soul, you have roused it with your cursed preaching."

"*Oi-i-i!* Highest One! pity Yourself on us!" Mrs. Ravinsky wrung her hands. "Rachel, Yankev, let there be an end to this knife-stabbing! *Gottuniu!* my flesh is torn to pieces!"

Unheeding her mother's pleading, Rachel rushed to the closet where she kept her things.

"I was a crazy idiot to think that I could live with you people under one roof." She flung on her hat and coat and bolted for the door.

Mrs. Ravinsky seized Rachel's arm in passionate entreaty.

"My child, my heart, my life, what do you mean? Where are you going?

"I mean to get out of this hell of a home this very minute," she said, tearing loose from her mother's clutching hands.

"Wo is me! My child! We'll be to shame and to laughter by the whole world. What will people say?"

"Let them say! My life is my own; I'll live as I please." She slammed the door in her mother's face.

"They want me to love them yet," ran the mad thoughts in Rachel's brain as she hurried through the streets, not knowing where she was going, not caring. "Vampires, bloodsuckers fastened on my flesh! Black shadow blighting every ray of light that ever came my way! Other parents scheme and plan and wear themselves out to give their child a chance, but they put dead stones in front of every chance I made for myself."

With the cruelty of youth th everything not youth, Rachel reasoned:

"They have no rights, no claims over me like other parents who do things for their children. It was my own brains, my own courage, my own iron will that forced my way out of the sweatshop to my present position in the public schools. I owe them nothing, nothing, nothing."

II

Two weeks already away from home. Rachel looked about her room. It was spotlessly clean. She had often said to herself while at home with her parents: "All I want is an empty room, with a bed, a table, and a chair. As long as it is clean and away from them, I'll be happy." But was she happy?

A distant door closed, followed by the retreating sound of descending footsteps. Then all was still, the stifling stillness of a rooming-house. The white, empty walls pressed in upon her, suffocated her. She listened acutely for any stir of life, but the continued silence was unbroken save for the insistent ticking of her watch.

"I ran away from home burning for life," she mused, "and all I've found is the loneliness that's death." A wave of self-pity weakened her almost to the point of tears. "I'm alone! I'm alone!" she moaned, crumpling into a heap.

"Must it always be with me like this," her soul cried in terror, "either to live among those who drag me down or in the awful isolation of a hall bedroom? Oh, I'll die of loneliness among these frozen, each-shut-in-himself Americans! It's one thing to break away, but, oh, the strength to go on alone! How can I ever do it? The love instinct is so strong in me; I can not live without love, without people."

The thought of a letter from Frank Baker suddenly lightened her spirits. That very evening she was to meet him for dinner. Here was hope—more than hope. Just seeing him again would surely bring the certainty.

This new rush of light upon her dark horizon so softened her heart that she could almost tolerate her superfluous parents.

"If I could only have love and my own life, I could almost forgive them for bringing me into the world. I don't really hate them; I only hate them when they stand between me and the new America that I'm to conquer."

Answering her impulse, her feet led her to the familiar Ghetto streets. On the corner of the block where her parents lived she paused, torn between the desire to see her people and the fear of their nagging reproaches. The old Jewish proverb came to her mind: "The wolf is not afraid of the dog, but he hates his bark." "I'm not afraid of their black curses for sin. It's nothing to me if they accuse me of being an Anti-Semite or a murderer, and yet why does it hurt me so?"

Rachel had prepared herself to face the usual hail-storm of

reproaches and accusations, but as she entered the dark hallway of the tenement, she heard her father's voice chanting the old familiar Hebrew psalm of "The Race of Sorrows":

"Hear my prayer, O Lord, and let my cry come unto Thee.

"For my days are consumed like smoke, and my bones are burned as an hearth.

"I am like a pelican of the wilderness.

"I am like an owl of the desert.

"I have eaten ashes like bread and mingled my drink with weeping."

A faintness came over her. The sobbing strains of the lyric song melted into her veins like a magic sap, making her warm and human again. All her strength seemed to flow out of her in pity for her people. She longed to throw herself on the dirty, ill-smelling tenement stairs and weep: "Nothing is real but love—love. Nothing so false as ambition."

Since her early childhood she remembered often waking up in the middle of the night and hearing her father chant this age-old song of woe. There flashed before her a vivid picture of him, huddled in the corner beside the table piled high with Hebrew books, swaying to the rhythm of his Jeremiad, the sputtering light of the candle stuck in a bottle throwing uncanny shadows over his gaunt face. The skull cap, the side-locks, and the long gray beard made him seem like some mystic stranger from a far-off world and not a father. The father of the daylight who ate with a knife, spat on the floor, and who was forever denouncing America and Americans was different from this mystic spirit who could thrill with such impassioned rapture.

Thousands of years of exile, thousands of years of hunger, loneliness, and want swept over her as she listened to her father's voice. Something seemed to be crying out to her to run in and seize her father and mother in her arms and hold them close.

"Love, love—nothing is true between us but love," she thought.

But why couldn't she do what she longed to do? Why, with all her passionate sympathy for them, should any actual contact with her people seem so impossible? No, she couldn't go in just yet. Instead, she ran up on the roof, where she could be alone. She stationed herself at the air-shaft opposite their kitchen window, where for the first time since she had left in a rage she could see her old home.

Ach! what sickening disorder! In the sink were the dirty dishes stacked high, untouched, it looked, for days. The table still held the remains of the last meal. Clothes were strewn about the chairs. The bureau drawers were open, and their contents brimmed over in mad confusion.

"I couldn't endure it, this terrible dirt!" Her nails dug into her palms, shaking with the futility of her visit. "It would be worse than death to go back to them. It would mean giving up order, cleanliness, sanity, everything that I've striven all these years to attain. It would mean giving up the hope of my new world—the hope of Frank Baker."

The sound of the creaking door reached her where she crouched against the air-shaft. She looked again into the murky depths of the room. Her mother had entered. With arms full of paper bags of provisions, the old woman paused on the threshold, her eyes dwelling on the dim figure of her husband. A look of pathetic tenderness illumined her wrinkled features.

"I'll make something good to eat for you, yes?"

Reb Ravinsky only dropped his head on his breast. His eyes were red and dry, sandy with sorrow that could find no release in tears. Good God! never had Rachel seen such profound despair. For the first time she noticed the grooved tracings of withering age knotted on his face and the growing hump on her mother's back.

"Already the shadow of death hangs over them," she thought as she watched them. "They're already with one foot in the grave. Why can't I be human to them before they're dead? Why can't I?"

Rachel blotted away the picture of the sordid room with both hands over her eyes.

"To death with my soul! I wish I were a plain human being with a heart instead of a monster of selfishness with a soul."

But the pity she felt for her parents began now to be swept away in a wave of pity for herself.

"How every step in advance costs me my heart's blood! My greatest tragedy in life is that I always see the two opposite sides at the same time. What seems to me right one day seems all wrong the next. Not only that, but many things seem right and wrong at the same time. I feel I have a right to my own life, and yet I feel just as strongly that I owe my father and mother something. Even if I don't love them, I have no right to step over them. I'm drawn to them by something more compelling than love. It is the cry of their dumb, wasted lives."

Again Rachel looked into the dimly lighted room below. Her mother placed food upon the table. With a self-effacing stoop of humility, she entreated, "Eat only while it is hot yet."

With his eyes fixed almost unknowingly, Reb Ravinsky sat down. Her mother took the chair opposite him, but she only pretended to eat the slender portion of the food she had given herself.

Rachel's heart swelled. Yes, it had always been like that. Her mother had taken the smallest portion of everything for herself. Complaints, reproaches, upbraidings, abuse, yes, all these had been heaped by her upon her mother; but always the juiciest piece of meat was placed on her plate, the thickest slice of bread; the warmest covering was given to her, while her mother shivered through the night.

"Ah, I don't want to abandon them!" she thought; "I only want to get to the place where I belong. I only want to get to the mountain-tops and view the world from the heights, and then I'll give them everything I've achieved."

Her thoughts were sharply broken in upon by the loud sound of her father's eating. Bent over the table, he chewed with noisy gulps a piece of herring, his temples working to the motion of his jaws. With each audible swallow and smacking of the lips, Rachel's heart tightened with loathing.

"Their dirty ways turn all my pity into hate." She felt her toes and her fingers curl inward with disgust. "I'll never amount to anything if I'm not strong enough to break away from them once and for all." Hypnotizing herself into her line of self-defense, her thoughts raced on: "I'm only cruel to be kind. If I went back to them now, it would not be out of love, but because of weakness— because of doubt and unfaith in myself."

Rachel bluntly turned her back. Her head lifted. There was iron will in her jaws.

"If I haven't the strength to tear free from the old, I can never conquer the new. Every new step a man makes is tearing away from those clinging to him. I must get tight and hard as rock inside of me if I'm ever to do the things I set out to do. I must learn to suffer and suffer, walk through blood and fire, and not bend from my course."

For the last time she looked at her parents. The terrible loneliness of their abandoned old age, their sorrowful eyes, the wrung-dry weariness on their faces, the whole black picture of her ruined, desolate home, burned into her flesh. She knew all the pain of one unjustly condemned, and the guilt of one with the spilt blood of helpless lives upon his hands. Then came tears, blinding, wrenching tears that tore at her heart until it seemed that they would rend her body into shreds.

"God! God!" she sobbed as she turned her head away from them, "if all this suffering were at least for something worth while, for something outside myself. But to have to break them and crush them merely because I have a fastidious soul that can't stomach their table manners, merely because I can't strangle my aching ambitions to rise in the world!"

She could no longer sustain the conflict which raged within her higher and higher at every moment. With a sudden tension of all her nerves she pulled herself together and stumbled blindly down stairs and out of the house. And she felt as if she had torn away from the flesh and blood of her own body.

III

Out in the street she struggled to get hold of herself again. Despite the tumult and upheaval that racked her soul, an intoxicating lure still held her up—the hope of seeing Frank Baker that evening. She was indeed a storm-racked ship, but within sight of shore. She need but throw out the signal, and help was nigh. She need but confide to Frank Baker of her break with her people, and all the dormant sympathy between them would surge up. His understanding would widen and deepen because of her great need for his understanding. He would love her the more because of her great need for his love.

Forcing back her tears, stepping over her heart-break, she hurried to the hotel where she was to meet him. Her father's impassioned rapture when he chanted the Psalms of David lit up the visionary face of the young Jewess.

"After all, love is the beginning of the real life," she thought as Frank Baker's dark, handsome face flashed before her. "With him to hold on to, I'll begin my new world."

Borne higher and higher by the intoxicating illusion of her great destiny, she cried:

"A person all alone is but a futile cry in an unheeding wilderness. One alone is but a shadow, an echo of reality. It takes two together to create reality. Two together can pioneer a new world."

With a vision of herself and Frank Baker marching side by side to the conquest of her heart's desire, she added:

"No wonder a man's love means so little to the American woman. They belong to the world in which they are born. They belong to their fathers and mothers; they belong to their relatives and friends. They are human even without a man's love. I don't belong; I'm not human. Only a man's love can save me and make me human again."

It was the busy dinner-hour at the fashionable restaurant. Pausing at the doorway with searching eyes and lips eagerly parted, Rachel's swift glance circled the lobby. Those seated in the dining-room beyond who were not too absorbed in one another, noticed a slim, vivid figure of ardent youth; but with dark, age-old eyes that told of the restless seeking of her homeless race.

With nervous little movements of anxiety, Rachel sat down, got up, then started across the lobby. Half-way, she stopped, and her breath caught.

"Mr. Baker," she murmured, her hands fluttering toward him with famished eagerness. His smooth, athletic figure had a cock-sureness that to the girl's worshipping gaze seemed the perfection of male strength.

"You must be doing wonderful things," came from her admiringly, "you look so happy, so shining with life."

"Yes,"—he shook her hand vigorously,—"I've been living for the first time since I was a kid. I'm full of such interesting experiences. I'm actually working in an East Side settlement."

Dazed by his glamourous success, Rachel stammered soft phrases of congratulation as he led her to a table. But seated opposite him, the face of this untried youth, flushed with the health and happiness of another world than that of the poverty-crushed Gehtto, struck her almost as an insincerity.

"You in an East Side settlement?" she interrupted sharply. "What reality can there be in that work for you?"

"Oh," he cried, his shoulders squaring with the assurance of his master's degree in sociology, "it's great to get under the surface and see how the other half live. It's so picturesque! My conception of these people has greatly changed since I've been visiting their homes." He launched into a glowing account of the East Side as seen by a twenty-five-year-old college graduate.

"I thought them mostly immersed in hard labor, digging subways or slaving in sweatshops," he went on. "But think of the poetry which the immigrant is daily living!"

"But they're so sunk in the dirt of poverty, what poetry do you see there?"

"It's their beautiful home life, the poetic devotion between parents and children, the sacrifices they make for one another—"

"Beautiful home life? Sacrifices? Why, all I know of is the battle to the knife between parents and children. It's black tragedy that boils there, not the pretty sentiments that you imagine."

"My dear child,"—he waved aside her objection,—"you're too close to judge dispassionately. This very afternoon, on one of my friendly visits, I came upon a dear old man who peered up at me through horn-rimmed glasses behind his pile of Hebrew books. He was hardly able to speak English, but I found him a great scholar."

"Yes, a lazy old do-nothing, a bloodsucker on his wife and children."

Too shocked for remonstrance, Frank Baker stared at her.

"How else could he have time in the middle of the afternoon to pore over his books?" Rachel's voice was hard with bitterness. "Did you see his wife? I'll bet she was slaving for him in the kitchen. And his children slaving for him in the sweat-shop."

"Even so, think of the fine devotion that the women and children show in making the lives of your Hebrew scholars possible. It's a fine contribution to America, where our tendency is to forget idealism."

"Give me better a plain American man who supports his wife and children and I'll give you all those dreamers of the Talmud."

He smiled tolerantly at her vehemence.

"Nevertheless," he insisted, "I've found wonderful material for my new book in all this. I think I've got a new angle on the social types of your East Side."

An icy band tightened about her heart. "Social types," her lips formed. How could she possibly confide to this man of the terrible tragedy that she had been through that very day? Instead of the understanding and sympathy that she had hoped to find, there were only smooth platitudes, the sightseer's surface interest in curious "social types."

Frank Baker talked on. Rachel seemed to be listening, but her eyes had a far-off, abstracted look. She was quiet as a spinning-top is quiet, her thoughts and emotions revolving within her at high speed.

"That man in love with me? Why, he doesn't see me or feel me. I don't exist to him. He's only stuck on himself, blowing his own horn. Will he never stop with his 'I,' 'I,' 'I'? Why, I was a crazy lunatic to think that just because we took the same courses in college, he would understand me out in the real world."

All the fire suddenly went out of her eyes. She looked a thousand years old as she sank back wearily in her chair.

"Oh, but I'm boring you with all my heavy talk on sociology." Frank Baker's words seemed to come to her from afar. "I have tickets for a fine musical comedy that will cheer you up, Miss Ravinsky—"

"Thanks, thanks," she cut in hurriedly. Spend a whole evening sitting beside him in a theater when her heart was breaking? No. All she wanted was to get away—away where she could be alone. "I have work to do," she heard herself say. "I've got to get home."

Frank Baker murmured words of polite disappointment and escorted her back to her door. She watched the sure swing of his athletic figure as he strode away down the street, then she rushed up-stairs.

Back in her little room, stunned, bewildered, blinded with her disillusion, she sat staring at her four empty walls.

Hours passed, but she made no move, she uttered no sound. Doubled fists thrust between her knees, she sat there, staring blindly at her empty walls.

"I can't live with the old world, and I'm yet too green for the new. I don't belong to those who gave me birth or to those with whom I was educated."

Was this to be the end of all her struggles to rise in America, she asked herself, this crushing daze of loneliness? Her driving thirst for an education, her desperate battle for a little cleanliness, for a breath of beauty, the tearing away from her own flesh and blood to free herself from the yoke of her parents— what was it all worth now? Where did it lead to? Was loneliness to be the fruit of it all?

Night was melting away like a fog; through the open window the first lights of dawn were appearing. Rachel felt the sudden touch of the sun upon her face, which was bathed in tears. Overcome by her sorrow, she shuddered and put her hand over her eyes as tho to shut out the unwelcome contact. But the light shone through her fingers.

Despite her weariness, the renewing breath of the fresh morning entered her heart like a sunbeam. A mad longing for life filled her veins.

"I want to live," her youth cried. "I want to live, even at the worst."

Live how? Live for what? She did not know. She only felt she must struggle against her loneliness and weariness as she had once struggled against dirt, against the squalor and ugliness of her Ghetto home.

Turning from the window, she concentrated her mind, her poor tired mind, on one idea.

"I have broken away from the old world; I'm through with it. It's already behind me. I must face this loneliness till I get to the new world. Frank Baker can't help me; I must hope for no help from the outside. I'm alone; I'm alone till I get there.

"But am I really alone in my seeking? I'm one of the millions of immigrant children, children of loneliness, wandering between worlds that are at once too old and too new to live in."

Why Teachers Should Organize

Margaret Haley

From Margaret Haley, "Why Teachers Should Organize," *National Education Association Addresses and Proceedings* (St. Louis, 1904).

When "Maggie" Haley (1867–1939) stood before the National Education Association to make the case that teachers should organize, she had already established herself as a power in Chicago politics and within the teaching profession. The turn of the century had seen significant growth in labor unions in Chicago, with consequent strikes, disputes and unrest, as industry attempted to counter labor's power. Haley allied herself with the progressive wing of the union movement and, in a precedent-breaking move, engineered a formal alliance between organized labor and the Teachers' Federation. She saw in the union movement not only a chance to improve teachers' wages and working conditions, but an opportunity to exercise the democratic ideals she discusses in the speech that follows.

For Haley, democracy meant the empowerment of working people, among whom she counted "public school and industrial workers," or "manual and mental workers." In their alliance, she saw the defeat of commercialism—the end of the subordination of the worker to the machine. The work-place democracy she advocated, the attention to child labor, woman suffrage, municipal ownership of utilities, and security for workers in tenure and pension plans posed a powerful alternative to the single-issue campaigns which had previously brought teachers together.

Haley was born and educated near Joliet, Illinois. She taught in Chicago until 1901, when she became full-time business agent for the Chicago Teachers' Federation. Besides her activity on behalf of that union, Haley was active in the Women's Trade Union League, the Public Ownership League, and the Labor Party. A force for women's rights and the rights of grade school teachers within the National Education Association, Haley was the first woman to speak from the

floor at an NEA convention. Haley worked with other women
educators and advocates of teachers' rights—notably
Catherine Goggin, for a time president of the Chicago
Teachers' Federation, and Ella Flagg Young, superintendent of
schools in Chicago and first woman president of the NEA
(1910).

The responsibility for changing existing conditions so as to
make it possible for the public school to do its work rests
with the people, the whole people. Any attempt on the part of the
public to evade or shift this responsibility must result in
weakening the public sense of civic responsibility and the
capacity for civic duty, besides further isolating the public
school from the people, to the detriment of both.

The sense of responsibility for the duties of citizenship in a
democracy is necessarily weak in a people so lately freed from
monarchical rule as are the American people, and who still
retain in their educational, economic, and poltical systems so
much of their monarchical inheritance, with growing tendencies
for retaining and developing the essential weaknesses of that
inheritance instead of overcoming them.

Practical experience in meeting the responsibilities of citizenship directly, not in evading or shifting them, is the prime need
of the American people. However clever or cleverly disguised
the schemes for relieving the public of these responsibilities by
vicarious performance of them, or however appropriate those
schemes in a monarchy, they have no place in a government of
the people, by the people, and for the people, and such schemes
must result in defeating their object; for to the extent that they
obtain they destroy in a people the capacity for self-government.

If the American people cannot be made to realize and meet
their responsibility to the public school, no self-appointed
custodians of the public intelligence and conscience can do it for
them. Horace Mann, speaking of the dependence of the
prosperity of the schools on the public intelligence, said:

The people will sustain no better schools and have no better education
than they personally see the need of; and therefore the people are to be
informed and elevated as a preliminary step toward elevating the
schools.

Sometimes, in our impatience at the slowness with which the public moves in these matters, we are tempted to disregard this wise counsel.

The methods as well as the objects of teachers' organizations must be in harmony with the fundamental object of the public school in a democracy, to preserve and develop the democratic ideal. It is not enough that this ideal be realized in the administration of the schools and the methods of teaching; in all its relations to the public, the public school must conform to this ideal.

Nowhere in the United States today does the public school, as a branch of the public service, receive from the public either the moral or financial support needed to enable it properly to perform its important function in the social organism. The conditions which are militating most strongly against efficient teaching, and which existing organizations of the kind under discussion here are directing their energies toward changing briefly stated are the following:

1. Greatly increased cost of living, together with constant demands for higher standards of scholarship and professional attainments and culture, to be met with practically stationary and wholly inadequate teachers' salaries.

2. Insecurity of tenure of office and lack of provision for old age.

3. Overwork in overcrowded schoolrooms, exhausting both mind and body.

4. And, lastly, lack of recognition of the teacher as an educator in the school system, due to the increased tendency toward "factoryizing education," making the teacher an automaton, a mere factory hand, whose duty it is to carry out mechanically and unquestioningly the ideas and orders of those clothed with the authority of position, and who may or may not know the needs of the children or how to minister to them.

The individuality of the teacher and her power of initiative are thus destroyed, and the result is courses of study, regulations, and equipment which the teachers have had no voice in selecting, which often have no relation to the children's needs, and which prove a hindrance instead of a help in teaching.

Dr. John Dewey, of the University of Chicago, in the *Elementary School Teacher* for December, 1903, says:

As to the teacher: If there is a single public-school system in the United States where there is official and constitutional provision made for submitting questions of methods of discipline and teaching, and the questions of the curriculum, text-books, etc., to the discussion of those actually engaged in the work of teaching, that fact has escaped my notice. Indeed, the opposite situation is so common that it seems, as a rule, to be absolutely taken for granted as the normal and final condition of affairs. The number of persons to whom any other course has occurred as desirable, or even possible—to say nothing of necessary—is apparently very limited. But until the public-school system is organized in such a way that every teacher has some regular and representative way in which he or she can register judgment upon matters of educational importance, with the assurance that this judgment will somehow affect the school system, the assertion that the present system is not, from the internal standpoint, democratic seems to be justified. Either we come here upon some fixed and inherent limitation of the democratic principle, or else we find in this fact an obvious discrepancy between the conduct of the school and the conduct of social life—a discrepancy so great as to demand immediate and persistent effort at reform.

A few days ago Professor George F. James, dean of pedagogy of the State University of Minnesota, said to an audience of St. Paul teachers:

One hundred thousand teachers will this year quit an occupation which does not yield them a living wage. Scores and hundreds of schools are this day closed in the most prosperous sections of this country because the bare pittance offered will not attract teachers of any kind.

Professor James further maintained that school-teachers are not only underpaid, but that they are paid much less proportionately than they received eight years ago.

It is necessary that the public understand the effect which teaching under these conditions is having upon the education of the children.

A word, before closing, on the relations of the public-school teachers and the public schools to the labor unions. As the professional organization furnishes the motive and ideal which shall determine the character and methods of the organized effort of teachers to secure better conditions for teaching, so is it the province of the educational agencies in a democracy to furnish the motive and ideal which shall determine the character and methods of the organization of its members for self-protection.

There is no possible conflict between the good of society and the good of its members, of which the industrial workers are the vast majority. The organization of these workers for mutual aid has shortened the hours of labor, raised and equalized the wages of men and women, and taken the children from the factories and workshops. These humanitarian achievements of the labor unions—and many others which space forbids enumerating—in raising the standard of living of the poorest and weakest members of society, are a service to society which for its own welfare it must recognize. More than this, by intelligent comprehension of the limitations of the labor unions and the causes of these limitations, by just, judicious, and helpful criticism and co-operation, society must aid them to feel the inspiration of higher ideals, and to find the better means to realize these ideals.

If there is one institution on which the responsibility to perform this service rests most heavily, it is the public school. If there is one body of public servants of whom the public has a right to expect the mental and moral equipment to face the labor question, and other issues vitally affecting the welfare of society and urgently pressing for a rational and scientific solution, it is the public school teachers, whose special contribution to society is their own power to think, the moral courage to follow their convictions, and the training of citizens to think and to express thought in free and intelligent action.

The narrow conception of education which makes the mechanics of reading, and arithmetic, and other subjects, the end and aim of the schools, instead of a means to an end—which mistakes the accidental and incidental for the essential— produces the unthinking, mechanical mind in teacher and pupil, and prevents the public school as an institution, and the public-school teachers as a body, from becoming conscious of their relation to society and its problems, and from meeting their responsibilities. On the other hand, that teaching which is most scientific and rational gives the highest degree of power to think and to select the most intelligent means of expressing thought in every field of activity. The ideals and methods of the labor unions are in a measure a test of the efficiency of the schools and other educational agencies.

How shall the public school and the industrial workers, in their struggle to secure the rights of humanity thru a more just and equitable distribution of the products of their labor, meet their mutual responsibility to each other and to society?

Whether the work of co-ordinating these two great educational agencies, manual and mental labor, with each other and with the social organism, shall be accomplished thru the affliliation of the organizations of brain and manual workers is a mere matter of detail and method to be decided by the exigencies in each case. The essential thing is that the public-school teachers recognize the fact that their struggle to maintain the efficiency of the schools thru better conditions for themselves is a part of the same great struggle which the manual workers— often misunderstood and unaided—have been making for humanity thru their efforts to secure living conditions for themselves and their children; and that back of the unfavorable conditions of both is a common cause.

Two ideals are struggling for supremacy in American life today: one the industrial ideal, dominating thru the supremacy of commercialism, which subordinates the worker to the product and the machine; the other, the ideal of democracy, the ideal of the educators, which places humanity above all machines, and demands that all activity shall be the expression of life. If this ideal of the educators cannot be carried over into the industrial field, then the ideal of industrialism will be carried over into the school. Those two ideals can no more continue to exist in American life than our nation could have continued half slave and half free. If the school cannot bring joy to the work of the world, the joy must go out of its own life, and work in the school as in the factory will become drudgery.

Viewed in this light, the duty and responsibility of the educators in the solution of the industrial question is one which must thrill and fascinate while it awes, for the very depth of the significance of life is shut up in this question. But the first requisite is to put aside all prejudice, all preconceived notions, all misinformation and half-information, and to take to this question what the educators have long recognized must be taken to scientific investigation in other fields. There may have been justification for failure to do this in the past, but we cannot face the responsibility of continued failure and maintain our title as thinkers and educators. When men organize and go out to kill, they go surrounded by pomp, display, and pageantry, under the inspiration of music and with the admiration of the throng. Not so the army of industrial toilers who have been fighting humanity's battles, unhonored and unsung.

It will be well indeed if the teachers have the courage of their convictions and face all that the labor unions have faced with the same courage and perseverance.

Today, teachers of America, we stand at the parting of the ways: Democracy is not on trial, but America is.

Equal Pay for Equal Work

Grace C. Strachan

From Grace C. Strachan, *Equal Pay for Equal Work* (New York: B.F. Buck, 1910).

Inspired by the success of the Chicago Federation of Teachers, in 1906 Kate Hogan, a New York seventh grade teacher, organized the Interborough Association of Women Teachers (IAWT). The goal of this union—which reached a peak with a membership of 14,000 in 1910—was "equal pay for equal work." Grace Strachan, the enterprising school district superintendent who headed the union's executive committee from 1906 on, put women teachers in the news as she fought their battle in New York City and in the state capital at Albany. Outraged when male teachers proposed a raise in women's annual pay from $600 to $750, but still below their own, Strachan retorted publicly. Her response was *headlined in the* New York Times *of June 10, 1909: "Tell Men Teachers They Sha'n't Meddle. Women in the Schools Flatly Inform Them That Their Aid Isn't Wanted."*

The "single issue" approach of Strachan contrasts sharply with the broad political platform advocated by Chicago's Margaret Haley. Each contributed in her way, however, to strengthening the collective power of women teachers.

Preface

Salary—A periodical allowance made as compensation to a person for his official or professional services or for his regular work.—*Funk and Wagnalls.*

Notice the words, "a person." Here is no differentiation between male persons and female persons.

Yet the City of New York pays a "male" person for certain "professional services" $900, while paying a "female" person only $600 for the same "professional services." Stranger still, it pays for certain experience of a "male" person $105, while paying a "female" person only $40 for the identical experience. These are but samples of the "glaring inequalities" in the teachers' salary schedules.

Why is the male in the teaching profession differentiated from the male in every other calling, when his salary is concerned?

Why does the city differentiate the woman it hires to teach its children from the woman it hires to take stenographic notes, use a typewriter, follow up truants, inspect a tenement, or issue a license?

Why are not the appointees from the eligible lists established by the Department of Education, entitled to the same privileges and rights as appointees from Civil Service lists from other City and State Departments?

Some ask, "Shall the single woman, in teaching, be given the married woman's wage?" I do not know what they mean, But I say, "Why not the single woman in teaching just as much as the single woman in washing, in farming, in dressmaking, in nursing, in telephoning?"

Again, some ask, is there such a thing as "equal work" by two people?

Technically, no. No two people do exactly the same work in the same way. This is true of all professional and official work. Compare Mayor Gaynor's work with Mayor McClellan's. Will any one say their work as Mayor is "Equal Work"? And yet the pay is the same. Do all policemen do "Equal Work"? Yet they receive equal pay. So with firemen, school physicians, tenement house inspectors. The taxpayers, no doubt, believe that, judged by his work, Mayor Gaynor is worth a far higher salary than many of his predecessors. But a great corporation like the City of New York cannot attempt to pay each of its employees according to the work of that particular street cleaner or fireman or stenographer, and so must be content with classifying its positions, and fixing a salary for each. So should it do for its teachers. That is all we ask.

The Family-to-Support Argument

It is rather a sad commentary on our profession that its men members are the only men who object to women members of the same profession getting the same pay for the same work. Who ever heard of a man lawyer fighting a woman lawyer in this way? A man doctor arguing that another doctor should give her services for less pay simply because she happened to be a woman? And leaving the professions, what attitude do we find the men who form our "Labor Unions" taking on this question? They form a solid phalanx on the side of "Equal Pay." The most powerful of all unions in many respects—"Big Six"—has a By-Law making it a misdemeanor to pay a woman less than a man working at the same form. All Labor Unions fight "two prices on a job."

Is it not sad to see men, American men, shoving aside, trampling down, and snatching the life preservers from their sisters? I say life preservers seriously and mean it literally. For to the woman obliged to support herself, is not her wage earning ability truly a life preserver. How can any man except one whom she is legally privileged to assist, take from a woman any part of the wages she has earned and remain worthy even in his own eyes? The excuses he makes to himself and to others in the attempt to justify his act, tend to belittle him more and more.

And yet some men whose blood sisters have by teaching provided the money to enable them, their brothers, to become teachers, oppose those very sisters in their efforts to obtain "Equal Pay for Equal Work." Can one ask for stronger proof of the insidious danger to our manhood which lurks in unjust standards of salary for service rendered? The true man, the good man, ought to put the woman who earns a respectable living, on a pedestal, as a beacon of encouragement to other women to show them one who wanted clothes to wear, and food to eat, and a place to live, and who obtained them by honorable labor.

I am firmly convinced that while teaching is a natural vocation for most women, it is rarely the true vocation of a man. And that those who enter the profession without the love for it which overshadows even the pocket returns, invariably deteriorate. Their lives are spent largely among those whom they consider their subordinates—in position or in salary, if not in intellect—the children and the women teachers. They grow to have an inordinate opinion of themselves. No matter how ridiculous or absurd or unfair may be the attitudes they take and the things they say, there is no one to say, "Nonsense!" as would one of his peers in the outer world. The novelist David Graham Phillips in the following description of one of his characters expresses my opinion better than I can myself: "Peter was not to blame for his weakness. He had not had the chance to become otherwise. He had been deprived of that hand-to-hand strife with life which alone makes a man strong. Usually, however, the dangerous truth as to his weakness was well hidden by the fictitious seeming of strength which obstinacy, selfishness and the adulation of a swarm of sycophants and dependents combine to give a man of means and position."

Recently in one of our schools, a male assistant to the principal resigned. The vacancy thus caused was filled by a woman. This woman is doing the same work as the man did, but with greater satisfaction to the principal. But she is being paid $800 a year less than the man was.

In another school I know there was a woman assistant to principal. As a grade teacher she had married and resigned, expecting—as most girls do when they marry—that she wouldn't have to work outside the home any more. But her husband became a victim of tuberculosis, and they went to Colorado in search of health for him. Time passed, their funds were exhausted, the invalid was unable to work, and so they came back, and the wife—after certifying, as our by-laws require, that her husband was unable to support her and had been so for two years—was reappointed. Later she secured promotion to assistant to principal. During the day she labored in a large, progressive school, composed almost wholly of children born in Russia, or of Russian parentage. At night she taught a class of foreign men. Now, although she actually had a family to support, she was receiving $800 a year less than a man in her position would receive. A married man? Oh, no, not necessarily. He might be a millionaire bachelor, or the pet of a wealthy wife—it is only necessary for him to be a "male" assistant to principal. Possibly on account of her family responsibilities, probably because she was ambitious, she strove for a principalship. During the school year, she traveled to Columbia University and took post graduate courses after school and on Saturdays; during the summer, when she should have been resting, she was studying with Professor This and Professor That. Last September she took the examination for a principal's license: in October, she died— typhoid, the doctors said. The husband she had cheerfully and lovingly supported for years survived her but a few weeks.

Why have I dwelt on this? To show the absurdity of the "family wage" argument of the male teacher. . . . Under a system of equal pay, where services should be paid for irrespective of sex, some women who now marry would remain single. But there are some men to-day who remain single because of relative economic independence, which they desire to maintain. These men are, however, relatively few. Women are as instinctive and as normal as men are, and independence, which they feared to lose, would prevent very few from marrying when they could make marriages which were attractive to them. Independence of women would improve marriage, since fewer women would marry because of necessity. By the same means divorce would be decreased, and human happiness would have a boom.

Our Association early in 1908 gathered some statistics. They

showed 377 women—eleven of them married and six widows—
supporting 707 others besides themselves. These teachers are all
women, but the people depending wholly upon them or partly
upon them are their mothers or their fathers or both or a brother
or a sister or a niece or a nephew. These are actual figures
collated from written answers to our questionnaire. You see,
then, that here is an average of two people for every woman to
support besides herself. Now, what salary is offered to these
young women of twenty-one years of age, after they have spent
all these years in preparing for the position of teacher? What
salary is she being paid by the City of New York, the greatest city
in the world, with the greatest public school system in the world?
$11.53 a week. A woman in charge of one of the stations in the
city gets more than that. Does the latter have to spend as much
money on clothes? No. She can wear the same clothes from one
end of the year to the other if she wants to, and not be criticised.
But I know when I go into a classroom, among the things that I
notice is the teacher's dress—whether it is neat, whether it is
appropriate. She must be a model for her class. Besides, the
teacher must live in a respectable neighborhood and make a
good appearance at home and abroad, and she must continue her
studies in order to give satisfactory service.

Epilogue

THE HISTORIES IN *Woman's "True" Profession* end in the early part of the twentieth century. There is evidence, however, that until fairly recently, the woman who devoted a life to teaching did not differ much from women of the past. At least through˚the 1950s, teaching seemed a wise and creative choice for an ambitious, intelligent young woman. Reading the obituaries of any local or national newspaper reveals the story. Spare accounts like those of Millicent Cook Daly and Elsie Farnham, below, outline lives devoted to the work of education.

Millicent C. Daly, Ex-Teacher, Kin to D.C. Educators

Millicent Cook Daly, 57, who retired in 1977 after 33 years as a D.C. public schoolteacher, died of cancer Friday at the Mar-Salle Convalescent Center here.

Miss Daly, a Washington native, was born into a family of Washington educators. Her earliest ancestor here was Thomas Cook, who settled here in 1806 and operated a vegetable garden, known as Cook's Farm, site of the present day corner of 16th and K Streets NW.

Her great-great-grandfather, John F. Cook, was a militant Washington educator. His son, George F.T. Cook, a school superintendent, directed the public education of "children of freed colored people" at the Sumner School here from 1869 until 1900.

For 29 years, until Sumner's closing in 1972, Miss Daly taught her first-grade in the same room that her great-grandfather had used as his office.

After the school's closing, she taught at the Ross School in Washington.

A graduate of Dunbar High School, where her mother, the late Adelaide Cook Daly, taught Spanish for 30 years, Miss Daly earned a bachelor's degree from the old Miner Teachers College and a master's degree in education from New York University.

Survivors include her father, Victor Daly, a retired deputy director of the U.S. Employment Service, and her stepmother, Lenore B. Daly, both of Washington, and a sister, Peggy D. Waters of San Jose, Calif.*

*Washington Post, October 21, 1979.

301

Elsie Farnham;
Won teachers'
Right to marry

Mrs. Elsie M. Bremner Farnham, 79, of Wakefield, formerly of Stoneham, where she was a member of the School Committee for nine years, died suddenly yesterday in Grove Manor Hospital in Revere.

Mrs. Farnham was active in the women's rights movement in the 1920s and was a principal in a Massachusetts Supreme Judicial Court case during that period. She was a teacher in the Somerville school system and was fired after getting married. Carrying her case to the state's highest court, she won the right of married women to teach in Massachusetts schools.

Mrs. Farnham was graduated in 1918 from Jackson College, where she was a member of Phi Beta Kappa and Sigma Kappa sorority.

Her interest in education continued and she served on the state Board of Education during the 1950s. She leaves her husband, Bertram A. Farnham 2nd., and a son, Leonard Fiske of Ipswich. Services will be at 2 p.m. tomorrow in First Congregational Church in Stoneham.*

Each of these women represents a tradition. Millicent Daly came from a background of educators. She grew up in a family in which, for five generations, work had been the education of "freed colored people." A graduate of Washington's prestigious black academic high school, where her mother taught for thirty years, Daly probably had little doubt about her "calling," or vocation. For Elsie Farnham, teaching, the rights of women, and responsibility for the governance of education must have been linked. Just as she fought for the right of married women to teach, it is evident that she also fought to make her mark on local and state school policy.

Woman's "True" Profession is in press at a very different moment from the twenties and the forties when Farnham and Daly entered the profession. In significant numbers, women are training for, seeking, and entering jobs they never would have imagined possible in a previous era. And while more women than even before are in the work force, fewer, and less accomplished women are choosing to work at teaching—or so

*Boston Globe, December 1, 1976.

statistics would indicate. Recent statistics released by the Education Testing Service indicate that students of both sexes taking the graduate record examination in education have lower scores and lower college grades than any other group.* Given the ambivalent climate of support for public education, the well-publicized decline in enrollments, and the national despair about the basic skills of high school graduates, one might speculate that teaching today is attracting those with few other choices—or the foolhardy.

What will be the state of teaching, with respect to women, in the year 2000? No doubt there will be more women principals, and even superintendents, but will teaching remain a woman's profession? Perhaps not. The rapidity with which women have made other choices of work in the last decade confirms what women have long known: that teaching was woman's "true" profession, in part, because there was little else that a lively, well-educated young woman could do.

In spite of this reality, there continue to be women inspired to teaching by a private vision and a public challenge, as the youthful Millicent Daly and Elsie Farnham must have been. Yet if these two women were choosing careers today, we do not know how they would answer the question: "Shall I be a teacher?" Only unforseen, positive changes in education and the status of teaching seem likely to lead many more young women of their kind to an affirmative answer.

---

*A *New York Times* article of September 18, 1979 quoted Dr. Timothy Weaver, associate professor of education, Boston University, as reporting that the performance of education majors had "declined significantly" since 1970, more so than overall scores, and were "substantially lower than majors in eight other fields compared in 1975–1976."

About the Author

NANCY HOFFMAN is currently a program officer at the Fund for the Improvement of Post-secondary Education, Department of Education, Washington, D.C. She is on leave from the College of Public and Community Service, University of Massachusetts, Boston, where she is an associate professor of humanities. She has also taught at Massachusetts Institute of Technology, Portland State University, and at the University of California, Santa Barbara. She received the B.A. and the Ph.D. at the University of California, Berkeley. Hoffman is the author of *Spenser's Pastorals* and co-editor, with Florence Howe, of *Women Working: Stories and Poems;* she is also the author of articles on women's studies, education, and literature. Hoffman was among the civil rights workers who went South to teach in the "freedom schools" in the 1960s; she was active, as well, in Boston school reform and desegregation efforts. In the early 1970s she helped to found women's studies programs at the University of California, Santa Barbara, and at Portland State University; she has also chaired the Commission on the Status of Women of the Modern Language Association.

A Note on Language

IN EDITING BOOKS, The Feminist Press attempts to eliminate harmful sex and race bias inherent in the language. In order to retain the authenticity of historical and literary documents, however, our policy is to leave thier original language unaltered. We recognize that the task of changing language usage is extremely complex and that it will not be easily accomplished. The process is an ongoing one that we share with many others concerned with the relationship between a humane language and a more human world.

Notes

Introduction

1. From an unpublished "Utterance," or prose poem, spoken at the University of Massachusetts, Boston, 1977.

2. Among the most interesting historians writing about public school teachers currently are Geraldine Clifford, Barbara Finkelstein, Alison Prentice, David Tyack, and Myra Strober. For general reference, see the *History of Education Quarterly*.

3. *The Sociology of Teaching* (New York: Wiley, 1932).

4. Dan C. Lortie, *School Teacher* (Chicago: University of Chicago Press, 1975), pp. 10–12.

5. Frances Donovan, *The Schoolma'am* (1938; reprinted, New York: Arno, 1969), pp. 13, 21.

6. As quoted in the Diary of Mary Swift. *The First State Normal School in America: The Journals of Cyrus Peirce and Mary Swift,* edited by Arthur O. Norton (Cambridge: Harvard University Press, 1926).

7. These dual prohibitions (against marriage, against courtship), I believe, had fascinating and contradictory sources. While marriage and child bearing were woman's proper activities, the route to them—romance and sex— undermined the notion of her purity.

8. Catherine Beecher to Mary Dutton, 8 February, 1830, Collection of American Literature, quoted in Kathryn Sklar, *Catherine Beecher* (New Haven, Yale University Press, 1973), p. 97.

9. *Freedmen's Record,* New England Freedmen's Aid Society, Vol. I, 5 May 1865, pp. 70, 71.

10. *Notable American Women,* 1607–1950 (Cambridge: Harvard University Press, 1971), Vol. 2, p. 18–19.

11. For Forten, see section 2. For more information on Wells Barnett and Terrell, see Dorothy Sterling, *Black Foremothers: Three Lives* (Old Westbury, N.Y.: The Feminist Press, 1979).

12. Report of a Committee of the National Education Association on Teachers' Salaries and Cost of Living, Ann Arbor, National Education Association, 1913, pp. 240–241 as quoted in David Tyack, *The One Best System* (Cambridge: Harvard University Press, 1975), p. 259.

13. "Why Teachers Should Organize," *National Education Association Addresses and Proceedings* (St. Louis, 1904), p. 148.

14. Personal interview with Mary Ellen Smith, Boston, Massachusetts, 1972. For the story of the walk-out, see Phillip Sterling, *The Real Teachers* (New York: Random House, 1972), pp. 17–29.

15. *The Real Teachers,* pp. 305, 307.

Seminary for Social Power

1. *The Evils Suffered by American Women and American Children: The Causes and the Remedy* (New York: Harper & Bros., 1846), pp. 10, 11.

2. Minerva Leland Papers, Schlesinger Library, Cambridge, Massachusetts.

3. Minerva Leland Papers.

4. Quoted in Willie Lee Rose, *Rehearsal for Reconstruction* (New York: Oxford University Press 1964), p. 229

5. Quoted in Robert L. Reid, "The

Professionalization of Public School
Teachers: The Chicago Experience,
1895-1920" (Ph.D. dissertation,
Northwestern University, 1968) p.
12. note 30.

6. "The School Mistress," *Harper's
New Monthly Magazine*, Vol. 57
(September 1878), p. 608

7. Edith Abbott, *Women in
Industry* (New York: Appleton, 1910),
p.55, quoted in Mary P. Ryan,
Womanhood in America (New York:
Franklin Watts, 1975), p. 105.

8. Percy Wells Bidwell, "Popula-
tion Growth in Southern New
England, 1810-1860," *Quarterly Pub-
lications of the American Statistical
Association*, New Series, no. 120
(December 1917), p. 813.

9. Catherine Beecher, *The
Elements of Mental and Moral Philo-
sophy, Founded Upon Experience,
Reason and the Bible*, (Hartford,
Conn., 1831), p. 263, quoted in
Catherine Beecher p.87.

10. For exploration of statistics,
and formulation of the hypothesis
that rural and urban labor markets
for teachers made different demands,
and that rapid feminization accompanied the growth of urban graded
schools, designed "for" women teachers, see Myra Strober and David
Tyack, "Sexual Asymmetry in Educational Employment: Male Managers
and Female Teachers." Draft Report,
Institute for Research on Educational
Finance and Governance, Stanford
University, February 1979.

11. Catherine Beecher to Mary
Dutton, 8 February 1830, Collection
of American Literature, quoted in
Catherine Beecher, p. 97

12. *The Evils Suffered*, p. 11

13. *Common School Journal*,
12:236 (August 1850), quoted in
Michael B. Katz, *The Irony of Early
School Reform* (Cambridge: Harvard
University Press, 1968), p. 118; Boston
School Committee, 1857-58, pp. 10,
11, quoted in Katz, p. 120.

14. *The First State Normal
School, p. 83*.

15.Ibid., pp. 81, 87, 90, 91.

16. Ibid., p. 86.

17. Ibid., pp. 183, 184.

18. "Domestication" is the phrase
used by Paul Mattingly (*The Classless Profession* (New York: New York
University Press, 1975). He characterizes the attitudes of two generations of normal school leadership as
follows: 1830-1860, upper class, "au-
thoritarian and benevolent" with an
emphasis on "intellectual discipline,
spirituality, and self-possession"; and
1860-1890, lower middle class, with
an emphasis on skills and teaching
methods, and the assumption of
shared values. From 1890 on, he
argues that the superintendency
became the socializing force for
teachers. (For an example of the
superintendency's force, see section
3 of *Woman's "True" Profession*. For
detailed analysis of the decline of
the nineteenth century normal
school, see Mattingly, especially,
"From Inspiration to Domestication,"
pp. 134-168.)

19. Dan C. Lortie thus characterizes the "social ambiguity" that has
"stalked" teaching. He believes the
"real regard" shown teachers has
never matched the "professed regard."
Lortie attributes this ambiguity in
part to "the relative position of the
young and the female in the nineteenth century." *Schoolteacher* (Chicago: University of Chicago Press,
1975), pp. 10-12.

20. Helen W. Pierson, "Tom's
Education," *Harper's New Monthly
Magazine*, Vol. 30 (January 1865), p.
191.

21. Anna Fuller, "The Schoolmarm," *Pratt Portraits* (New York;
G.P. Putnam's, 1892),

22. Rev. A.D. Mayo, "The Kitchen
and the School-room," *The National
Teacher*, Vol. II, no. 5 (May 1872), p.
155.

A Noble Work Done Earnestly

1. To Elizabeth Cady Stanton, April [?], 1861, E.C. Stanton Papers, Library of Congress.

2. Estimates of the number of teachers in the South vary. Jacqueline Jones points out that 7,000 is a more reasonable estimate than 10,000, since many served more than one year. "The 'Great Opportunity': Northern Teachers and the Georgia Freedmen, 1865-1873" (Ph.D. dissertation, University of Wisconsin, 1975).

3. *Freedmen's Record* Vol. I, no. 5 (May 1865), pp. 70-71.

4. In this chapter, when I use the term "typical", I signal a conclusion I have drawn based on three years of reading primary materials—published memoirs and correspondence of teachers, some manuscripts, the publications and records of the various relief and missionary associatons, and unpublished correspondence. In addition, I have read all the secondary works on the subject. Among these, by far the most helpful and provocative are James McPherson's *The Struggle for Equality* (Princeton: Princeton University Press, 1964) and *The Abolitionist Legacy* (Princeton: Princeton University Press, 1975); Willie Lee Rose's specialized study of the Port Royal experiment, *Rehearsal for Reconstruction* (New York: Oxford University Press, 1964); and finally, a recent dissertation on the teachers themselves, Jacqueline Jone's "The 'Great Opportunity'," *op. cit.*

5. Ware was among the first teachers to go South. Her letters are published in *Letters from Port Royal (1862-1868)*, ed. Elizabeth Ware Pearson (New York: Arno Press and the New York Times, 1969).

6. *From a New England Woman's Diary in Dixie in 1865* (Springfield, Mass.: Plimpton Press, 1906), pp. 55, 125.

7. With this phrase, the Quaker teacher Lucy Chase began her letters home. Her correspondence and that of her sister Sarah is collected in *Dear Ones at Home*, ed. Henry L. Swint (Nashville, Tenn.: Vanderbilt University Press, 1966).

8. *Woman's Work for the Lowly*, American Missionary Society, 1874, quoted in *The Abolitionist Legacy*, *op. cit.*, p. 165.

9. *Letters and Diary of Laura M. Towne*, edited by Rupert Sargent Holland (1912; reprinted, New York: Negro Universities Press, 1969), p. 8.

10. *The Freedmen of the South*, edited by Linda Warfel Slaughter (Cincinnati: Elm St. Printing Co., 1869), p. 126.

11. "Life on the Sea Islands," *Atlantic Monthly*, May 1864, p. 74.

12. *Letters and Diary*, late April, 1862, p.19. See Chase selection, pp. 125-134, for an example of administrative spirit and manner during the first days of organizing large numbers of students into schools.

13. Elizabeth Hyde Botume, *First Days Amongst the Contrabands* (1893; reprinted, New York: Arno Press and the New York Times, 1968), p. 247.

14. *Letters and Diary*, May 29, 1870, p. 219.

15. *From a New England Woman's Diary*, pp. 88-89.

16. In Henry Swint, *The Northern Teacher in the South, 1862-1868* (1941; reprinted, New York: Octagon Press, 1967), p. 94.

17. *Dear Ones*, p. 21.

18. Letter from teacher Arthur Sumner to his cousin Nina, August 8, 1864, Penn School Papers, Southern Historical Collection, University of North Carolina.

19. *First Days*, p. 129.

20. *Letters and Diary*, p. 66

21. Typescript Diary, September 7, 1863, p. 150, Penn School Papers.

22. *Freedmen's Record,* Vol. III, no. 4 (April 1867), p.54.

23. *First Days,* pp. 62, 63.

24. *Freedmen's Bulletin,* Vol II, no. 7 (June 1866), p. 114.

25. Ednah D. Cheney, July 9, 1865, Cheney Papers, Boston Public Library, Boston.

26. "M.C.G.," *Freedmen's Record,* Vol. I, no. 6 (June 1865).

27. *The American Freedman* (New York Branch, December 1867), p. 361.

28. *Pennsylvania Freedmen's Bulletin,* December 1865. Cited in Rose, *Rehearsal for Reconstruction,* p. 150.

29. *The Journal of Charlotte L. Forten,* edited by Ray A. Billington (New York: Dryden Press, 1952).

30. *Dear Ones at Home,* p.236.

31. *First Days,* p. 107.

32. Maria Waterbury, *Seven Years Among the Freedmen* (Chicago: T.B. Arnold, 1891), frontispiece.

33. Details from an unpublished senior thesis by Judy Cohen (University of Massachusetts, 1977).

34. Amy Williams to D.E. Emerson, March 5, 1878, American Missionary Association archives. Quoted in James McPherson, *The Abolitionist Legacy,* p. 171.

35. Perhaps on account of their substantial *informal* authority, the teachers seemed to tolerate their own disenfranchisement and that of black women. Several, however, made comments to the effect that when women got the vote, the black men would have to give up their notions of "being higher than women generally." *First Days,* p. 233.

36. John Chadwick, *A Life for Liberty* (New York: G.P. Putnam's, 1899), pp. 215–16. Although Greeley represented "good government" and presented an alternative to Ulysses S. Grant's patronage policy, most abolitionists opposed him because they feared he would "forgive" the South and remove freed people from federal protection.

37. In correspondence (1876–1878) with Penn School benefactor Francis Cope of Philadelphia, Laura Towne expressed bitterness about the treatment of blacks at court, by vigilantes and politicians. Cope and his brothers cautioned moderation, called people of Miss Towne's opinion "impatient and impracticable critics. What can any of us do but watch and pray?" Penn School Papers.

38. *Letters and Diary,* August 19, 1877, p. 271.

39. *Letters and Diary,* p. 222.

40. *The Souls of Black Folk* (Greenwich, Conn.: Fawcett, 1961), pp. 31, 83.

Teaching in the Big City

1. Catherine Brody, "A New York Childhood," *The American Mercury,* Vol. XIV, no. 53 (May 1928), p. 62.

2. Anzia Yezierska, *Bread Givers* (1925; reprinted, New York: G. Braziller, 1975), p. 269.

3. Tillie Olsen, "Utterance" (unpublished).

4. William Elsbree, *The American Teacher* (New York: American Book, 1939), Ch. 17, quoted in David Tyack, *The One Best System* (Cambridge: Harvard University Press, 1975), p. 60.

5. This chapter could not have been written without the benefit of David Tyack's *The One Best System.* His book appeared just as I wrote the prospectus for *Woman's "True" Profession.* I had given up hope that any of the books that accounted for teachers' experience would mention that teachers are women. Tyack not only analyzed "Teachers and the Male Mystique," but attended throughout to the relation between teachers' femaleness and the growth

of school bureacracy. This section draws on Tyack's research and conceptual framework. Frequently, his sources were the only ones available to illustrate a point. Without them, teachers' voices would not be heard in this chapter.

6. So Alfred Kazin characterized the teacher of immigrants in *A Walker in the City* (New York: Harcourt Brace, 1951), p. 18.

7. Myra Kelly, *Little Citizens* (New York: McClure, Phillips & Co., 1904), p. 161.

8. William Maxwell, "The Personal Power of the Teacher in Public School Work," *National Education Association Addresses and Proceedings* (Annual Meeting, Cleveland, Ohio, 1908), p. 118.

9. *Historical Statistics of the United States, Colonial Times to 1970*, Bureau of the Census (Washington, DC, 1975), p. 115.

10. New York Superintendent Maxwell boasted of little Russians and Italians, six months after landing, "declaiming with tremendous fervor Patrick Henry's apostrophe to liberty or telling in their compositions about the day when their forefathers landed on Plymouth Rock." "The Personal Power of the Teacher," p. 119.

11. Julia Richman, "The Immigrant Child," *National Education Association Addresses and Proceedings* (Asbury Park, New Jersey, 1905), p. 113.

12. Quoted in Tyack, *The One Best System*, p. 232.

13. Adele Marie Shaw, "The True Character of the New York Public Schools," *The World's Work*, Vol. 7 (December 1903), p. 4207–4221.

14. This was an average wage of 86,730 city elementary school teachers in 1905. In all but four of forty-eight cities surveyed, unskilled municipal laborers and sewer workers earned more. Stenographers earned about the same amount. *Report of the Committee on Salaries, Tenure, and Pensions of Public School Teachers in the United States to the National Council of Education, July, 1905* (National Education Association, 1905), p. 54.

15. Richman, "The Immigrant Child," p. 121.

16. Abraham Cahan, *The Rise of David Levinsky* (New York: Harper & Bros., 1917, 1960), p. 129.

17. *Bread Givers*, pp. 272, 273.

18. *A Walker in the City*, pp. 18–21.

19. Mary Antin, *The Promised Land* (Boston: Houghton Mifflin, 1912), p. 211.

20. Mary Agnes Dwyer, personal interview. See selection, pp. 232.

21. "The True Character," pp. 4212, 4213. See also Joseph Mayer Rice, *The Public School System of the United States* (New York: Century, 1893), p. 39.

22. Charles B. Gilbert, *The School and Its Life* (New York: Silver, Burdett, 1906), p. 85, quoted in Tyack, *The One Best System*, p. 97.

23. Marian Dogherty, *'Scusa Me Teacher* (Francestown, N.H.: Marshall Jones, 1943), pp. 37, 38.

24. "Confessions of Public School Teachers," *Atlantic Monthly*, July 1896, p. 101.

25. *Ibid.*, 107 See selection, p. 267.

26. This story is told in detail by Diane Ravitch, *The Great School Wars* (New York: Basic Books, 1974); and in David Tyack, *The One Best System*.

27. William Rainey Harper as quoted in Robert L. McCaul, "Dewey's Chicago," *School Review*, Vol 67 (Autumn 1959), p. 265. My source for the quotation is Tyack, *The One Best System*, p. 135.

28. In 1960, the profile of the teacher had changed radically. Only

29% of teachers were unmarried; the average age was forty-four and typically, the teacher left teaching, raised children, and returned. (John Folger and Charles Nam, *Education of the American Populace*, 1960 Census Monograph [Washington, D.C.], pp. 80, 82.) This pattern however, also perpetuated the woman teacher's powerlessness. Today males dominate teachers' unions, and women make up 12.9% of administrators. (*Statistics of Public Elementary and Secondary Day Schools, 1977–78*, National Center for Education Statistics, Washington, D.C., pp. 18, 19.)

29. Lotus D. Coffman, "Social Composition of the Teaching Population," *Contributions to Education*, No. 41 (Teachers College, Columbia, 1911); Myra Strober and David Tyack, *Draft Report*, "Sexual Asymetry in Educational Employment," p. 17.

Seuxal division of labor shows up most pronouncedly in the cities. Here men had a chance at long-term professional careers as school administrators. Rural schools, with their teaching principals, could not confer a status at all comparable.

3C "Confessions," p. 104.

31. In William McAndrew, "Public School Teaching," *The World's Work*, Vol. 5 (March 1903), pp. 3188, 3189. As a consequence of teachers' social isolation, the rules against their marrying, and their ability to move from city to city, they commonly formed a sisterhood. They lived together, often in a "teacherage," vacationed together, and often moved to new schools in pairs.

32. Helen Horvath, "Plea of an Immigrant—Abstract," *National Education Association Addresses and Proceedings* (San Francisco, 1923), pp. 680–82, quoted in Tyack, *The One Best System*, p. 233.

33. Anzia Yezierska, *Children of Loneliness* (New York: Funk & Wagnalls, 1923), p. 122.

34. *National Education Association Addresses and Proceedings* (St. Louis, 1904), p. 148. Haley was the first woman (and the first grade school teacher) to speak from the floor of the NEA. Previously, women's papers were read aloud by men.

35. Grace Strachan, *Equal Pay for Equal Work* (New York: B.F. Buck, 1910), pp. 41, 298.

36. Strachan, p. 118.

37. Strachan, p. 11.

Bibliography

Ames, Mary. *From a New England Woman's Diary in Dixie in 1865.* Springfield, Massachusetts: Plimpton Press, 1906.

Antin, Mary. The Promised Land. Boston: Houghton Mifflin, 1912.

Barnard, Henry. "Graduation of Public Schools, with Special Reference to Cities and Large Villages." *American Journal of Education,* December, 1856.

Beecher, Catherine. *The Evils Suffered by American Women and American Children: The Causes and the Remedy.* New York: Harper and Row, 1846.

Berrol, Selma Cantor. "Immigrants at School: New York City, 1898–1914." Unpublished Ph.D dissertation, City University of New York, 1967.

Bidwell, Percy Wells. "Population Growth in Southern New England, 1810–1960," *Quarterly Publications of the American Statistical Association,* December, 1917.

Botume, Elizabeth Hyde. *First Days Amongst the Contrabands,* 1893. Reprinted New York: Arno Press and the New York Times, 1968.

Brody, Catherine. "A New York Childhood." *The American Mercury,* May, 1928.

Bureau of Refugees, Freedmen, and Abandoned Lands, Manuscripts of the Educational Division. The National Archives, Washington, D.C.

Burstall, Sara A. *Impressions of American Education in 1908.* London: Longmans, Green, 1909.

Butler, Nicholas Murray. *Across the Busy Years.* 2 volumes. New York: Charles Scribner's Sons, 1939.

Cahan, Abraham. *The Rise of David Levinsky.* 1917. Reprinted New York: Harper and Brothers, 1960.

Carney, Mabel. *Country Life and the Country School.* Chicago: Row, Peterson, 1912.

Chadwick, John White. *A Life for Liberty.* New York: G.P. Putnam's Sons, 1899.

Chase, Lucy and Sarah (ed. Henry L. Swint). *Dear Ones at Home.* Nashville, Tennessee: Vanderbilt University Press, 1966.

Cheney, Edna Dow. Unpublished correspondence in Cheney Papers. Boston Public Library.

Chesnutt, Charles W. "The March of Progress." *Century Illustrated Monthly Magazine,* Volume 39, 1900–1901.

Child, Lydia Maria. *The Freedmen's Book.* Boston: Ticknor and Fields, 1865.

Clifford, Geraldine Joncich. "Home and School in 19th Century America: Some Personal-Historical Reports from the United States." *History of Education Quarterly,* Spring, 1978.

———"Saints, Sinners, and People: A Position Paper on the Historiography of American Education." *History of Education Quarterly,* Fall, 1975.

Coffman, Lotus D. "Social Composition of the Teaching Population." *Contributions to Education.* Teachers College, Columbia University, 1911.

Cohen, Judith. "Anna Gardner, 1816–1901." Unpublished senior thesis, University of Massachusetts, Boston, 1975.

"Confessions of Public School Teachers." *Atlantic Monthly.* July, 1896.

Confessions of Three School Superintendents. *Atlantic Monthly.* November, 1898.

Cremin, Lawrence A. *The American Common School: An Historic Conception.* New York: Bureau of Publications, Teachers College, Columbia University, 1951.

———*The Transformation of the School: Progressivism in American Education, 1876-1957.* New York: Knopf, 1961.

———*The Wonderful World of Ellwood Patterson Cubberley: An Essay on the Historiography of American Education.* New York: Bureau of Publications, Teachers College, Columbia University, 1965.

Dewey, John. *Democracy and Education.* New York: Macmillan, 1916.

———*The School and Society.* Chicago: University of Chicago Press, 1899.

Dogherty, Marian A. *'Scusa Me Teacher.* Francestown, N.H.: Marshall Jones, 1943.

Donovan, Frances. *The Schoolma'am.* 1938. Reprinted New York: Arno, 1969.

Downing, Lucia. "A Vermont Sketchbook." *Vermont Quarterly.* Fall, 1951.

DuBois, W.E.B. *The Quest of the Golden Fleece,* 1911. Reprinted New York: Negro Universities Press, 1969.

———*The Souls of Black Folk.* Greenwich, Connecticut: Fawcett, 1961.

Elsbree, William. *The American Teacher.* New York: American Book, 1939.

Estler, Suzanne E. "Woman Leaders in Public Education." *Signs: Journal of Women in Culture and Society.* Winter, 1975.

Finkelstein, Barbara and Agre, Gene P. "Feminism in School Reform: The Last Fifteen Years." *Teachers College Record,* Summer, 1978.

Finkelstein, Barbara. "Governing the Young: Teacher Behavior in American Primary Schools, 1820-1880; A Documentary History." Unpublished Ed.D. dissertation, Teachers College, Columbia University, 1970.

———*Regulated Children/Liberated Children: Education in Psychohistorical Perspective.* New York: Psychohistory Press, 1979.

Folger, John, and Nam, Charles, *Education of the American Populace.* Washington, D.C.: Census Monograph, 1967.

Forten, Charlotte L. (Edited Ray Billington). *The Journal of Charlotte L. Forten.* New York: Dryden Press, 1952.

Freedman's Bulletin.

Freedman's Record, 1865-1874. New England Freedmen's Aid Society.

Fuller, Anna. "The Schoolmarm." *Pratt Portraits.* New York: G.P. Putnam and Sons, 1892.

Gardner, Anna. *Harvest Gleanings.* New York: Fowler and Wells, 1881.

Gompers, Samuel. "Teachers' Right to Organize." *American Federationist,* October, 1915.

———"Teachers' Right to Organize Affirmed." *American Federationist,* December, 1914.

Gorelick, Sherry. "Social Control, Social Mobility and the Eastern European Jews: An Analysis." Unpub. Ph.D. dissertation, Columbia University, 1975.

Gove, Aaron. "Duties of City Superintendents." *National Education Association Addresses and Proceedings, 24th Annual Meeting.* 1884.

———"Limitations of the Superintendent's Authority and of the Teacher's Independence." *National Education Association Addresses and Proceedings, 43rd Annual Meeting,* 1904.

Greer, Colin. *The Great School Legend: A Revisionist Interpretation of American Public Education.* New York: Basic Books, 1972.

Gutman, Herbert G. "Work, Culture, and Society in Industrializing America, 1815-1919." *American Historical Review*, June, 1973.

Haley, Margaret. *Margaret Haley's Bulletin*, 1915-1916, 1925-1931.

———"Why Teachers Should Organize." *National Education Association Address and Proceedings*. St. Louis, 1904.

Hamilton, Gail (Mary Abigail Dodge). *Our Common School System*. Boston: Estes and Lauriat, 1880.

Hancock, Cornelia. *South After Gettysburg*. Philadelphia: University of Pennsylvania Press, 1937.

Haviland, Laura S. *A Woman's Lifework: Labors and Experiences of Laura S. Haviland*. Chicago: C.V. Waite and Company, 1887.

Historical Statistics of the United States, Colonial Times to 1970. Washington, D.C.: Bureau of the Census, 1975.

Holley, Sallie. Correspondence in Samuel May Papers, Massachusetts Historical Society and in The Dall Papers. Boston Public Library.

Horvath, Helen. "Plea of an Immigrant—Abstract." *National Education Association Addresses and Proceedings*. San Francisco, 1923.

Johnson, Clifton. *The Country School in New England*. New York: D. Appleton, 1895.

———*Old Time Schools and School Books*, 1904. Reprinted New York: Dover, 1963.

Jones, Jacqueline. "'The Great Opportunity': Northern Teachers and the Georgia Freedmen 1865-1873." Unpublished Ph.D. dissertation, University of Wisconsin, 1975.

Katz, Michael B. *The Irony of Early School Reform*. Cambridge, Massachusetts: Harvard University Press, 1968.

Kaufman, Poly Welts. "Boston Women and City School Politics: Nurturers and Protectors in Public Education, 1872-1905." Unpublished Ph.D. dissertation, Boston University, 1978.

Kazin, Alfred. *A Walker in the City*. New York: Harcourt Brace, 1951.

Kelly, Myra. *Little Citizens*. New York: McClure, 1904.

Lazerson, Marvin. *Origins of the Urban School: Public Education in Massachusetts, 1870-1915*. Cambridge, Massachusetts: Harvard University Press, 1971.

Leland, Minerva. Minerva Leland Papers. Schlesinger Library, Cambridge, Massachusetts.

Lortie, Dan C. *School Teacher*. Chicago: University of Chicago Press, 1975.

Mattingly, Paul. *The Classless Profession*. New York: New York University Press, 1975.

Maxwell, William. "The Personal Power of the Teacher in Public School Work." *National Education Association Addresses and Proceedings*. Asbury Park, New Jersey, 1905.

Mayo, Reverend A.D. "The Kitchen and the School-room." *The National Teacher*, May, 1872.

McAndrew, William. "Public School Teaching." *The World's Work*, March, 1903.

McCaul, Robert L. "Dewey's Chicago." *School Review*, Autumn, 1959.

McPherson, James. *The Abolitionist Legacy*. Princeton, New Jersey: Oxford University Press, 1975.

———*The Struggle for Equality*. Princeton: Oxford University Press, 1964.

Muraskin, Lana D. "The Teachers Union of the City of New York from Inception to Schism, 1912-1935." Unpublished doctoral dissertation, University of California, Berkeley, 1979.

———"The Teachers Union of the City of New York." Diane Ravitch and Ronald Goodenow, eds. *Educating an Urban People: The*

New York Experience. New York: Teachers College Press, forthcoming 1981.

Nelson, Margaret K. "Vermont Female School Teachers in the Nineteenth Century: The Social Meaning of Work." Unpublished paper, Middlebury College, Vermont, 1978.

Norton, Arthur O., ed. *The First State Normal School in America: The Journals of Cyrus Peirce and Mary Swift.* Cambridge, Massachusetts: Harvard University Press, 1926.

Pearson, Elizabeth Ware, ed. *Letters from Port Royal.* 1906. Reprinted New York: Arno Press and the New York Times, 1969.

Pennsylvania Freedmen's Bulletin.

Pierson, Helen W. "Tom's Education." *Harper's New Monthly Magazine,* January, 1865.

Port Royal Correspondence. The National Archives, Washington, D.C.

Prentice, Alison. "The Feminization of Teaching in British North America and Canada, 1845-1875. *Historie Sociale/Social History,* May 1975.

Preston, JoAnne. "Pacification and Pedagogy: Teaching Becomes Women's Work." Unpublished manuscript, Boston, Massachusetts. 1977.

Ravitch, Diane. *The Great School Wars.* New York: Basic Books, 1974.

Reid, Robert L. "The Professionalization of Public School Teachers: The Chicago Experience, 1895–1920." Unpublished Ph.D. dissertation, Northwestern University, 1968.

"Report of the Committee on Salaries, Tenure, and Pensions of Public School Teachers in the United States to the National Council of Education." *National Education Association,* July, 1905.

Rice, Elizabeth. "A Yankee Teacher in the South." *Century Magazine,* Volume 40, 1901.

Rice, Joseph Mayer. *The Public School System of the United States.* New York: Century, 1893.

Richman, Julia. "The Immigrant Child." *National Education Association Addresses and Proceedings,* Asbury Park, N.J., 1905.

Ricker, David Swing. "The School Teacher Unionized." *Educational Review,* November, 1905.

Riis, Jacob. *The Children of the Poor.* New York: Charles Scribner's Sons, 1892.

Rose, Willie Lee. *Rehearsal for Reconstruction.* New York: Oxford University Press, 1964.

Ryan, Mary P. *Womanhood in America.* New York: Franklin Watts, 1975.

"The School Mistress." *Harper's New Monthly Magazine,* September, 1878.

Shaw, Adele Marie. "Common Sense Country Schools." *The World's Work,* June, 1904.

———"The Public Schools of a Boss-Ridden City." *The World's Work,* February, 1904.

———"The Spread of Vacation Schools." *The World's Work,* October, 1904.

———"The True Character of the New York Public Schools." *The World's Work,* December, 1903.

Sklar, Kathryn. *Catherine Beecher.* New Haven, Connecticut: Yale University Press, 1973.

Slaughter, Linda Warfel (Hazel Eastman, ed.). *Fortress to Farm.* New York: Exposition Press, 1972.

———*The Freedmen of the South.* Cincinnatti: Elm Street Printing Company, 1869.

Smith, Mary Gove. "Raphael in the Background: A Picture for Teachers of Aliens." *Education,* January, 1919.

Smith, Timothy L. "Immigrant School Aspirations and American Education, 1880–1930." *American Quarterly*, Fall, 1969.

Stanton, Elizabeth Cady. *Elizabeth Cady Stanton Papers*. Library of Congress, Washington, D.C.

Sterling, Dorothy. *Black Foremothers: Three Lives*. Old Westbury, New York: The Feminist Press, 1979.

Sterling, Phillip. *The Real Teachers*. New York: Random House, 1972.

Strachan, Grace. *Equal Pay for Equal Work*. New York: B.F. Buck, 1910.

Strober, Myra H. and Tyack, David B. "Sexual Assymetry in Educational Employment: Male Managers and Female Teachers." Draft Report, Institute for Research on Educational Finance and Governance, Stanford University, February, 1979.

Sumner, Arthur. Unpublished Correspondence. Penn School Papers, Southern Historical Collection, University of North Carolina.

Swint, Henry. *The Northern Teacher in the South, 1862–1868*. 1941. Reprinted New York: Octagon Press, 1967.

Terrell, Mary Church. "History of the High School for Negroes in Washington." *Journal of Negro History*, July, 1917.

Tourgee, Albion. *Bricks Without Straw*. 1880. Reprinted Boston, Mass.: Gregg Press, 1967.

Towne, Laura M. (Rupert Sargent Holland, ed.). *Letters and Diary of Laura M. Towne*. 1912. Reprinted New York: Negro Universities Press, 1969.

Towne, Laura M. Penn School Papers. Southern Historical Collection, University of North Carolina.

Tyack, David. *The One Best System*. Cambridge, Massachusetts: Harvard University Press, 1975.

U.S. Immigration Commision. *The Children of Immigrants in Schools*. Washington, D.C.: Government Printing Office, 1967.

Urban, Wayne. "Organized Teachers and Educational Reform during the Progressive Era: 1890–1920." *History of Education Quarterly*, Spring, 1976.

Viggers, Christine. "The Importance of the Women Teachers' Organization in the Equal Pay for Teachers Controversy." Unpublished M.A. thesis, University of Oregon, 1972.

Walker, Susan (H.N. Sherwood, ed.). "Journal of Miss Susan Walker, March 3–June 6, 1882. *Quarterly Publication of the Historical and Philosophical Society of Ohio*, January–March, 1912.

Waterbury, Maria S. *Seven Years Among the Freedmen*. Chicago: T.B. Arnold, 1891.

Willard, Emma Hart. *Educational Biographies, Memoirs of Teachers, Educators, and Promoters and Benefactors of Education, Literature and Science. Part I. Teachers and Educators*. New York: F.C. Brownell, 1861.

Woman's Work for the Lowly. American Missionary Society.

Woody, Thomas. *A History of Women's Education in the United States*, 1929. Reprinted New York: Octagon Books, 1959.

Yezierska, Anzia. *The Bread Givers*, 1925. Reprinted New York: Persea, 1975.

——*Children of Loneliness*. New York: Funk and Wagnalls, 1923.

Young, Ella Flagg. *Isolation in the School*. Chicago: University of Chicago Press, 1901.

Index

The numbers in italics indicate pages with illustrations.

1508-10
5-33

Photograph Acknowledgments

Photo Research by Nancy Hoffman.

Cover: courtesy of the Samuel May Papers, Massachusetts Historical Society. **Frontispiece:** George G. Bain Collection, Library of Congress. **Pages 2–3:** photo by Frances Benjamin Johnston, Library of Congress. **Pages 46–47:** 1—photo by John R. Willis, courtesy of the Emma Willard School, Troy, New York. 2,3—Library of Congress. 4—courtesy of the St. Louis Art Museum. **Pages 90–91:** courtesy of the Samuel May Papers, Massachusetts Historical Society. **Pages 118–119:** 1,2,5—courtesy of the Southern Historical Collection, Penn School Papers #3615, Library of the University of North Carolina at Chapel Hill, and Penn Community Services, Inc. 3,4—courtesy of the Samuel May Papers, Massachusetts, Historical Society. **Pages 146–147:** 1,2,3—courtesy of the Samuel May Papers, Massachusetts Historical Society. **Pages 172–173:** 1,2—courtesy of the Samuel May Papers, Massachusetts Historical Society. 3—photo by Frances Benjamin Johnston, Library of Congress. **Pages 200–201:** photo by Jacob Riis, Library of Congress. **Pages 236–237:** 1,3—George G. Bain Collection, Library of Congress. 2—photo by Lewis W. Hine, National Child Labor Committee, Library of Congress. 4—photo by Jacob Riis, Library of Congress. **Pages 268–269:** 1—Chicago Historical Society. 2—Chicago Historical Society, DN #7581. 3,4—courtesy of Malvina Hoffman.

This book was composed in Trump and Olive Antique by Weinglas Typography Company, Port Washington, New York. It was printed and bound by R.R. Donnelley & Sons Company, Chicago, Illinois. The covers were printed by Algen Press, Queens, New York.